8/81

S0-ATM-560

STANLEY VESTAL
Champion of the Old West

STANLEY VESTAL

Champion of the Old West

by

RAY TASSIN

THE ARTHUR H. CLARK COMPANY
Glendale, California
1973

Copyright ©, 1973, by
THE ARTHUR H. CLARK COMPANY

All rights reserved including the rights to
translate or reproduce this work or parts
thereof in any form or by any media.

LIBRARY OF CONGRESS CATALOG CARD NUMBER 72-97805
ISBN 0-87062–105-x

Dedicated to my wife
MARTHAGRACE
For all the usual reasons
and many more

Contents

Illustrations

(All illustrations are courtesy of the
Western History Collections, University of Oklahoma Library)

Introduction

Writers of books about the Old West – both fact and fiction – are almost as numerous as the white and red warriors who lived that colorful chapter of American history. However, a few of these authors stand out above all the rest as literary giants. Such a man was Walter Stanley Campbell (Stanley Vestal), novelist, biographer, historian, master teacher of writers, a plainsman who loved the Indian way of life and was twice adopted by Sioux chiefs, artillery captain, Rhodes Scholar, and above all, an exhaustive researcher who sought out first-hand information about plains Indians and frontiersmen whose experiences he recorded for future generations.

Born on the Kansas frontier, Vestal grew to manhood in Oklahoma territory among the southern plains tribes, particularly the Cheyenne and Arapaho. He spent more time in Indian camps than at home, learning the lore of the hunting trail and warpath from the lips of the old chieftans. He shared in their old-time life, eating their food, taking shelter in their tents, learning their languages, and joining in their social dances.

This early association with old Indians gave Vestal a set of values quite different from the attitudes of other persons who grew to manhood in the same environment. It was purely his love and respect for the Indians that made him want to tell their history from their viewpoint, and thereby provide a permanent contribution to American literature and history. Too many false portraits had been drawn by others.

It is significant that all of Vestal's biographies were about Indians, or white men who shared his preference for the Indian way of life, particularly the Indian's freedom and independence. Throughout his life Vestal continued his close association with Indians as he wrote about them.

As the first Rhodes Scholar from the new state of Oklahoma, Vestal was educated at Oxford University. During World War i he served as a captain of field artillery in France. For forty-three years he taught first literature and later professional writing at the University of Oklahoma. From this base he roamed the great plains and the Rocky Mountains in search of material for his writings, spending weeks and months at a time among various Indian tribes, gradually growing in stature and fame.

Just as his career had two distinct categories – writer and teacher of writers – so did Vestal's philosophy, personality and character. To many he was the scholarly, intellectual university professor, Walter S. Campbell, of rather austere countenance. To others, he displayed himself as the rugged, gruff outdoorsman, Stanley Vestal, with a hearty sense of humor and a love for the Indian way of life. This dual personality is reflected in his correspondence. It is possible to read part of the way through many of his letters and determine from the general tone and language which name – W. S. Campbell or Stanley Vestal – will be signed at the bottom.

Vestal published twenty-four books, about 150 magazine pieces, five radio scripts, and countless book reviews and newspaper articles. Perhaps his greatest single achievement – certainly his proudest and best known– was a biography, *Sitting Bull: Champion of the Sioux*, in which Vestal included much previously unpublished material about the massacre of General George A. Custer's famed Seventh Cavalry in the Battle of Little Big Horn

River, June 25, 1876. More speculation, hearsay, and half-truths – as well as outstanding work – have been published and filmed about the final hours in the lives of Custer and his men than any other incident in Western Americana. Vestal learned the details of the battle from more than a hundred old warriors who fought it. In the second edition of *Sitting Bull* he included a first person account of Custer's final moments as narrated by the Sioux warrior who killed the general in hand-to-hand combat. Though the second edition was published eighty years after the death of Custer, it received prominent publicity on the Associated Press and United Press wire services for the account of Custer's death.

Vestal's seven biographies are his best work, depicting a way of life, everything from how to kill and skin a buffalo to the moral code of this or that tribe. He had as complete a knowledge of the old-time Indian way of life as any white man is ever likely to have. And the white men included in Vestal's biographies were as much Indian under the skin as were the redmen.

The seven histories were about as good as the biographies, contributing as much to the accurate picture of the Old West. In fact, Vestal was a better historian than writer, although he was highly skilled in the latter category also. *The Missouri* topped the historicals financially, in quality, and public acceptance.

Vestal's four textbooks are still used by those trying to learn to write. They provided the basis of instruction in his highly successful school of professional writing.

As a novelist, Vestal was not outstanding. Three of his four novels achieved only moderate success. Only *Happy Hunting Grounds* remained in print over the years, and this because it was only a thinly disguised history of the Cheyennes. *'Dobe Walls* was by far the best written of the four.

Six of the seven biographies, all seven histories, a book

Early Days on the Kansas Plains

As a champion of the Old West, Walter Stanley Vestal could not have picked a much better time or place for birth and early boyhood than the twilight years of that era on the Kansas frontier and in Oklahoma Territory. The time of birth, August 15, 1887, was just eleven years after the annihilation of General Custer's troops on the Little Big Horn River, three years before the murder of Sitting Bull, and four years before the final battle of the Indian Wars at Wounded Knee. By the time Vestal began championing the Old West, the era was far enough removed in the past to permit a proper perspective but still fresh enough for him to know many of the survivors. The place was a one-room wooden shack on a homestead four miles from Severy, Kansas, and about sixty miles from the Old West cow town of Wichita.

Circumstances responsible for the place of birth began about a decade after the Civil War. Mrs. Sara Wood, widow of a Civil War Union officer, gave up her home in Ohio and took her five young daughters to the frontier town of Fredonia, in the southeast corner of Kansas. A woman of remarkable independence for those days, and unusually strong character, the widow bought a large house and took in boarders for several years, until the daughters all became school teachers.

In 1885 a young lawyer from Mississippi, Walter Malory Vestal, moved into the boarding house. A romance developed between him and one of the widow's daughters, Isabella Louise, whom the family called Daisy. Mrs. Wood objected quite strongly to their marriage plans, allegedly because of Daisy's age, nineteen. Vestal was twenty-seven at the time. Likely Vestal's Southern background influenced Mrs. Wood's decision also, since she had little regard for the Confederates who had killed her brother in battle and imprisoned her husband.

The couple eloped across the nearby state border and was married September 24, 1886, at Cassville, Missouri. Returning to Kansas, they bought a relinquishment on a homestead claim about thirty miles west of Fredonia and four miles from Severy, Kansas. A single-room wooden shanty became their home, with Vestal practicing law in Severy.

A few months after Walter was born, the young father died of typhoid fever, on January 3, 1888. Daisy took her infant back to her mother's home in Fredonia, where she suffered a collapse from brain fever. During the months it took for Daisy to recover from her illness, her mother took care of little Walter. When well again, Daisy resumed school teaching, leaving the daytime care of her son to her mother. [1]

Walter's earliest recollection in Fredonia was of being on a runaway horse at the age of four, when he and his mother visited the farm of a family friend. Daisy put him up on an old dobbin bareback and led him along a grassy lane. A bunch of horses in the pasture next to the lane came tearing down along the fence to see what Dobbin was up to. The old horse broke into a run, away from Daisy, who went chasing after him. "I was on my own. I suppose I was excited, and so remembered it, but did not fall off." From this experience came his first major interest in life – a love of riding horses. [2]

---

[1] Autobiographical data, Campbell Collection, Division of Manuscripts, University of Oklahoma Library. All subsequent citations herein to "autobiographical data" are to this Campbell Collection.

[2] Letter, W. S. Campbell to H. P. Willis, Nov. 3, 1953, Campbell Collection, *loc. cit.* All letters cited herein, from and to Campbell, are in this Collection unless otherwise indicated.

Grandmother was Walter's chief mentor and playmate during the day while his mother and aunts were gone. "Kind and gentle, but firm and emphatic," she filled him with stories about the Civil War – from a Yankee viewpoint, of course. She "made me familiar with death and battle." Walter played with buttons on the floor by her sewing machine, pretending they were brave soldiers, arranging them in ranks for imagined battles. Later toy soldiers replaced the buttons. When someone sent him a rubber doll for Christmas, he talked grandmother into making a uniform for it. Grandmother also instilled in him "passionate admiration for Kit Carson and his men." Even the songs she sang to him were ballads about Kit Carson or the Union Army. [3]

Walter's mother, trying to take the place of his father, often took him out on the prairie. From these early buggy trips he developed a life-long love of the vast open plains. [4]

Thus the young mind was shaped, developing its enthusiasm for war and for fighting men, for the plains, for history, rugged individualism and other things connected with the Old West. But this was only the beginning of the events which led him to champion that era.

One night in 1894, Martin Abernathy, employed in the Indian service in the Oklahoma Territory, spent the night in grandmother's home. After dinner he opened his valise and brought out a gorgeous display of plains Indian beadwork, weapons, war bonnets with brightly colored eagle feathers, some shiny black buffalo horns and other items of Indian manufacture. The color, sheen and romance of these strange but beautiful objects were imprinted permanently on Walter's mind, along with the visitor's kindness in explaining them to a wondering boy. Walter "had never seen such colorful things and immediately acquired

---

[3] Autobiographical data.   [4] *Ibid.*

a lasting interest in the Indians." He dated his "first interest in the redskins from that evening."

Before he was eight years of age, Walter had mastered the art of horseback riding, taught him by "Uncle" George Brown, the same family friend on whose ranch he had taken his first ride four years earlier. The boy learned to gallop across country, and shoot and fish from the saddle. Few fences or other barriers existed in the Kansas of that era to impede his jaunts.

Of all the influences on young Walter, none surpassed the effect James Robert Campbell had on him. Campbell came to Fredonia in 1895 as superintendent of schools. He was then forty-six years of age, a widower with three daughters about the same age as Walter's mother, Daisy, then twenty-seven. Before long Campbell developed a romantic interest in Daisy, and became a frequent visitor in the Wood home. Walter was greatly impressed with the "strongly-built, red-mustached, boisterous and fun-loving Scotch-Irishman." Throughout his lifetime Walter met only one other man he considered "so magnetic and full-blooded" and "so vital, so full of life." That was the Sioux chief who killed Custer. [5]

During the whirlwind courtship, Daisy often played the piano while J. R. sang in his deep bass voice. Walter was a fascinated spectator. Once he asked his mother, "Are *we* going to marry Mr. Campbell?" [6]

We did, on August 25, 1896, in grandmother's house. The new family moved into a second floor apartment over a store building on the north side of the downtown public square. A strong friendship quickly developed between the very masculine J. R. and Walter. An "overdose of femininity" had plagued Walter the first ten years of his life, and he was ready for the new masculine influence. He "rejoiced in being where two men outnumbered

---

[5] *Ibid.*; also Stanley Vestal, "Fuss and Feathers," in *Westerners Brand Book* (Chicago), May 1956, p. 17; letter, Campbell to Martin Abernathy, Nov. 18, 1929.   [6] Autobiographical data.

JAMES ROBERT CAMPBELL

Vestal's step-father was at one time a researcher for historian
H. H. Bancroft. He later became a leading educator in Oklahoma.

one woman," especially with J. R.'s "very masculine ways." [7]

In earlier years J. R. had served on the historical research staff of H. H. Bancroft, whose papers are generally ranked as "one of the greatest sources of Western Americana ever assembled." The research team toured the West in those frontier times, securing – among other things – information on the plains Indians and pioneers. Among his other projects, J. R. was assigned to study the Sand Creek Massacre of 1864 in Colorado when the Cheyenne Indians were so roughly mistreated by Colorado troopers. [8] His stories about the Old West, particularly the Cheyenne Indians and such frontiersmen as Kit Carson, stirred the boyish imagination of his stepson. This drew the two "men" even closer together despite the four decades which separated them in age.

More importantly, J. R.'s sympathy with the Cheyenne as a result of the Sand Creek massacre helped form the sympathies of Walter for his later work. The first evidence of this came during the fall school term following the marriage of J. R. and Daisy. Walter's first original composition was in the fifth grade that year. The teacher assigned a narrative about a fight between whites and Indians. Walter was the only one in the class who took the Indian side. [9]

The stories told by J. R. had intrigued Walter during their first two years together. But Walter began to get similar stories first hand in 1898. J. R. was appointed superintendent of schools at Guthrie, capital of the Oklahoma Territory, last of the Old West frontiers. He left for his new post in July. Walter and Daisy followed a month later. This proved to be still another major influence that shaped the champion of the Old West.

---

[7] *Ibid.*   [8] *Dallas Morning News,* Dec. 25, 1932.
[9] Autobiographical data.

Boomer-Sooner

For a boy with a keen love of his western heritage, the ideal place to celebrate his eleventh birthday was the robust territorial capital of the last frontier, Guthrie, Oklahoma Territory, in August of 1898. Only nine years earlier the territory had been opened to white settlement. The raw newness, the excitement and lusty liveliness of the town and surrounding area appealed to Walter even more than most boys his age. [1]

Just walking along the streets meant close contact with the last of the famous Old West characters. Learning their stories became a passion for Walter, who was not backward about approaching them with questions about their exploits. Among his favorites were three of the best known marshals of the Old West. Known as "The Three Guardsmen," Marshals Bill Tilghman, Chris Madsen and Heck Thomas patrolled the streets around the clock. [2]

Walter soon discovered the Cimarron River four miles north of town. Here he passed much of his spare time swimming and playing on the sand bars and bluffs. More important, both to his present and future, here he found bands of Cheyenne Indians camped when they passed through the area. Where other youths might have fled homeward at the sight of teepees, Walter headed straight

---

[1] Diary of W. S. Campbell, Aug. 11, 1902, Campbell Collection, *loc. cit.* All citations herein to the diary are to be found in this Collection.

[2] *Ibid.,* Nov. 10, 1902: and letter, Campbell to Sidney Ohmart, Mar. 18, 1953.

for the camps. He formed his first friendships with plains Indians here, without knowing he was developing a lifetime habit. These early friendships were somewhat casual, but Walter took them seriously and set out to learn what he could. [3]

Something else Walter acquired soon after his arrival in the territory was a new name. Everyone at Guthrie assumed he was the son of J. R. Campbell, and referred to him as the Campbell kid. He gave little thought to the matter and used the name until it was no longer convenient to change back.

Walter's best friend was George Guss, the banker's son who lived next door. Part of their friendship rested on a common interest in animals, judging from the menagerie each possessed. Walter set the pace with eleven opossums, a raccoon, a cat, a flying squirrel, jackrabbit, thirteen dogs, an old yellow horse, and later a coyote, much to the envy of George and the dismay of the neighbors. And his parents never protested! [4]

In their first year together, the boys roamed the Cimarron Valley when not in school. Once they found a dead horse and decided the skin would be useful for making rawhide items. They attempted to skin the animal with pocket knives but made little headway. Since it was winter, the body had not decomposed. But it had been dead for some time and the skin was glued to the carcass. They finally abandoned the undertaking, although that rawhide would have been mighty useful. [5]

The next major step in the development of Stanley

---

[3] *Ibid.,* Jan. 22, 1922. Vestal considered the words "plains," "great plains," and "short grass country" special titles rather than merely areas, and capitalized them. When not used in direct quotations in this volume, they are not capitalized. For the Indian home, Vestal used all three spellings: teepee, tepee, and tipi. When not in direct quotations, the preferred spelling — teepee — is used in this volume.

[4] Diary of Campbell, May 1925; Vestal, "Fuss and Feathers," *loc. cit.*   [5] Letter, Campbell to Don Rickey, Nov. 30, 1956.

Vestal came in 1899 when he spent the summer months in the Cheyenne-Arapaho country that is now western Oklahoma. J. R. and Daisy taught a summer institute for teachers at Watonga, a small community of 500 persons in the primitive region. The three of them lived a few miles from town, on the ranch of J. R.'s brother, John Campbell. Of tremendous consequence to Walter were two things. First, his Uncle John had "adopted" an Arapaho boy whom he had named Warpath, and who became the bosom companion of Walter. The adoption was Indian fashion in that the boy continued to live with his parents in an Indian encampment. Secondly, this big Indian camp lay just across the river from John Campbell's ranch. Every day Walter saddled up, forded the stream and spent his time racing ponies, hunting, spearing fish, or swimming with Warpath and other Indians. In those days much of western Oklahoma was still unfenced. The Indians lived in teepees, wore moccasins and blankets and followed ancient customs. This aroused Walter's interest and he made their ways his life-time hobby. Whenever a grown white man showed up, the redskins became shy, silent and poker-faced, but nobody minded a twelve-year-old boy. There was no privacy in an Indian camp. All doors were open at all hours. And so Walter saw most things that happened there. It was an education, but it was not at all what he had expected. [6]

The first afternoon in the camp Walter got a surprise. The warriors wearing buckskin and fine feathers gathered for a dance. Just as Walter rode up, a mother came carrying her baby boy to see his father dance. Her smiling husband went to meet her, speaking fondly to his little son. But the boy, terrified by that fiercely painted face and tall war bonnet, strained back in his mother's arms, yelled lustily and burst into tears.

---

[6] Typewritten manuscript, "Indian Summer," in Campbell Collection, *loc. cit.*

Quickly the father, eager to soothe the son, took off
the war bonnet. But the child went on screaming at the
top of his voice. Walter had always supposed that Indian
babies never cried! Later, he learned that it was the
crying of a Cheyenne baby in the night which told
General Custer that he had reached the hostile camp at
the battle of the Washita.

The beating of drums, rhythmic clashing of the sleigh
bells worn by the dancers, and the wild music of the
singers fascinated Walter. Dismounting, he watched for
a while, then began to try the dance steps himself. Some
of the Indian boys watched his antics and spoke to each
other in their own language but he paid no attention.
Suddenly someone behind him jerked his shirt tail out
and knocked off his hat. Turning, Walter saw a big,
sneering Indian boy dressed in the ill-fitting blue uniform
and clumsy shoes of a government school. His hair was
cut short, but he was hatless. He said, grinning, "Now
you look more like an Indian."

Indignantly, Walter picked up his hat, clapped it on
the Indian's head, and answered, "Now you look more
like a white man." At that, all the camp boys with their
long braids, leggins and moccasins, broke into a chorus
of laughter at the schoolboy's expense. Caught by surprise, he could not bear their ridicule. Angrily, he jerked
off the hat and – anything but poker-faced – slunk away
into the crowd. Walter hung his hat on his saddle horn.
After that the camp boys accepted him. Of course, his
uncle's brand on the pony he rode was known to them.
They had guessed he was a relative of their friend and
neighbor.

Every day there was something new to see, something
to learn, something to do. Hunters shot their government
beef with arrows, butchered it handily on the grass, and
hung out the meat to dry on lines, like so much washing.
Women packed firewood and water from the river, tanned

hides, made lodge covers, moccasins or clothes. The camp crier shouted the news and orders of the day. Children played, mourners wailed, sick people took steam baths, medicine men thumped their tom-toms and chanted, gamblers tossed dice in a basket, warriors danced, chiefs sat smoking the long pipe in a circle. Lovers, wrapped for privacy in the same borrowed blanket, stood in the midst of the camp, ignoring and ignored. Sometimes at a dance, an old couple notoriously happy would stand up, hug and kiss each other, as an example to the young folks. Young people would link arms in a ring and play Indian football, keeping the ball moving round the ring, never letting it touch the earth.

Walter had a fine chance to see and share in their old-time life, eating their food, taking shelter in their tents, learning their language, sometimes joining in their social dances. His parents encouraged him. Whenever his mother saw him restless or depressed, she would put up a lunch and say, "Why don't you ride over to the camp? It will do you good to be with people who laugh all the time."

Walter soon discovered that the Indians were fun-loving, humorous, and great jesters who delighted in practical jokes. Among themselves they laughed ten times to the white man's once, and were forever twitting each other about some embarrassment that had happened twenty years before.

One afternoon the river rose suddenly and by sundown was bank full. Not knowing whether his pony could swim the flood, Walter decided to spend the night in camp with Warpath. He unsaddled at the lodge door, turned his horse loose, and put his bridle and saddle inside. When he entered the lodge, Warpath's mother had already served her family with all that was in the kettle, but made him welcome, took a little from each plate and put it on his.

After they had eaten, the boys went outside in the clear starlight night carrying their blankets. Not to be out of fashion, Walter took his saddle blanket along. The noise in the camp died down, the fires turned to ashes, but the boys made no move to go into the teepees. In good weather young men slept in the grass around the lodge where they could hear anyone coming. A prowler who stumbled over one of those silent sentries would beat a hasty retreat. With their ears to the ground they could hear the footsteps of anyone before he reached the tent.

Walter had been told that Indians were lazy. But before it was even light all the males were up, and with lariats coiled over their shoulders, took out afoot in all directions to round their ponies and drive them to water at the river. One man owned three hundred head. He was so rich he could ride a different horse nearly every day in the year.

When the horses had been watered and turned back to grass, everybody sat down to breakfast. By that time it was sun-up. But the young men and boys did not linger in camp. If one did, his grandfather was sure to chide, "What are you doing in the lodge? Get out there on the prairie with your pony." [7]

In this manner Walter spent the major part of his summer months. He found it "a colorful and interesting life" which "caught his fancy" and seemed to suit him "better than that of the small towns and ranches of the white settlers." [8]

The small town of Watonga held some appeal for him, however. The Campbells became good friends with the Thomas E. Ferguson family, publishers of the *Watonga Republican*, and visited them often. This friendship was to play an important role in the future of all three Campbells. While J. R. and Tom, staunch Republicans, discussed politics, and Daisy and Mrs. Ferguson engaged

[7] *Ibid.*   [8] Autobiographical data.

in female talk, Walter romped with the Ferguson boys, Walter and Thad, especially the latter. Walter Campbell and Thad often raced their horses down main street, sometimes clad only in breechclouts, circling around a hanging tree where a horse thief had died a short time before. The community was filled with Indians, the store windows with their handiwork.

The most important result of the summer was Walter's "falling in love with Indian life." Before he left for Guthrie, he bought a wild coyote which was to prove such a tribulation to him later. Back home, he put a collar and chain on the animal, which he named Tito, and tied it to a picket pen in the back yard. Complications came quickly. First, Tito howled whenever he took a notion, especially when the church bells rang at seven o'clock in the morning and night. "The poor beast's protest is considered a desecration by one pious brother who lives nearby and nurses most unchristian thoughts against me," Walter wrote.

Also, the Campbell's Negro lived "in fear of her life" and complained "volubly on all occasions about Mr. Walter's wolf." Each time someone came out of the kitchen door, Tito jerked "at his chain frantically in expectation of something to eat." The cook expected to be the meal rather than the feeder.

One day the cook went out to get a pitcher of water from the well, and Tito lunged against his chain as usual. This time, however, the chain broke and the coyote kept on running toward the cook. She "dropped the pitcher and fled screaming into the house." Her cries attracted the rest of the household. Tito thrust his head into the pitcher which fitted snugly on his neck so that he could not get out of it. He "went staggering about in such a ludicrous way" that everyone laughed until he cried watching it, all but the cook "who sullenly upbraided" them and "vowed she would leave at once if Mr. Walter kept that thing any moah." She refused to be placated and Walter had to get rid of Tito. But for a time Tito was an interesting and lively addition to Walter's menagerie. [9]

That winter Walter tried to put into use at least one thing he had learned from the Cheyennes – how to build a teepee. He set up a small teepee in the woods near Guthrie, and was seldom without one for the rest of his life, although later versions were considerably nearer the authentic thing. Cheyennes passing through camped in a grassy space near the creek, and found considerable amusement in inspecting Walter's handiwork. [10]

The following three summers Walter returned to his Uncle John's ranch near Watonga for additional three-month periods of riding across the prairie, especially to the Cheyenne camp. Once again he raced his pony with the Indians, swam with them in the chocolate-colored river, prowled among the teepees and learned a great deal about them. He went home each autumn even more of a confirmed lover of the Indian way of life and the Indian character and personality.

The Campbell family friendship with the Thomas B. Ferguson family received a boost in the autumn of 1901 when Ferguson was appointed the sixth governor of Oklahoma Territory. The Fergusons moved to Guthrie and the two families were together often. In fact, Daisy began to write many political speeches for Ferguson and his friends. One night at a political banquet, six politicians delivered speeches, all written by Daisy. This provided considerable amusement for the inner circle of friends who knew about it. [11]

---

[9] Campbell diary, undated entries about 1900, and May 1925; letter, Campbell to F. G. Walling, Apr. 24, 1939.

[10] Letter, Campbell to Julie Watson, Oct. 16, 1957; and Campbell diary, undated entry in May 1925.

[11] *Ibid.*, to his daughter, Malory, Feb. 4, 1948.

Walter's first interest in writing came from the Fergusons, especially Mrs. Ferguson who was a reporter for the *Kansas City Star* in addition to helping publish the *Watonga Republican*. She saw great promise in Walter as a writer, even at that early age. Her encouragement led him to his first serious attempts at writing a few years later.

Guthrie continued to provide no end of thrills for the wide-eyed boy. Its streets were packed in those days with pioneer settlers, Indians, bad men, United States marshals, and more than its share of famous and notorious personalities. He got to know the seamier side of the town's life when he bought a *State Capital* newspaper route for three dollars and used it to earn two dollars a week delivering 134 newspapers. He rode his old yellow horse around the six-mile route, and caught his first glimpse of saloon interiors by delivering papers to several. Now fifteen years of age, he enjoyed his "education" greatly. A few months later, he switched over to a *Guthrie Leader* route, increasing his daily ride to ten miles. [12]

Early-day wild west shows came to Guthrie each summer. In one of these Walter saw the first bull-dogging ever attempted. It really was bull-dogging in those days because the performer's method was to leap from a galloping horse at the bull's lips, seize the lips in his teeth and hang on for dear life. Walter went to Oklahoma City for one rodeo and divided his attention between one of the spectators, Teddy Roosevelt, and the butchering of cattle. [13]

In October 1902, Buffalo Bill Cody brought his famous wild west show to the city. Walter went to the depot in the morning when the train arrived, and met the old hunter and army scout. "He was a pallid, white-haired old gentleman, nearsighted, helplessly at the mercy of

---

[12] *Ibid.*   [13] Campbell diary, Aug. 13, and Dec. 15, 1902.

alcohol and over his ears in debt, but still gallantly riding
and shooting twenty years after he should have retired,"
Walter wrote. [14]

Another member of the show who fascinated Walter
was Johnny Baker, then billed as the "Boy Wonder" but
older than the advertisements claimed. Baker entered
the arena with his rifle and shot a few targets, then
concluded his act by standing on his head while sharp-
shooting. The first time he assumed this position, he rose
to his feet, scanned the ground, picked up a pebble and
shook his head to let the crowd know he had been standing on his head on the pebble. Then he tossed the pebble
away and stood on his head for a final round of shooting
at targets.

A few years earlier Baker had escorted the old Sioux
chief, Sitting Bull, around cities where the same wild
west show stopped. He got to know Sitting Bull inti-
mately. After the show in Guthrie, Walter questioned
Baker at great length about Sitting Bull, getting his first
information for what turned out to be his finest piece
of literature decades later. [15]

That same October, Carrie Nation descended on
Guthrie and staged some of her anti-saloon rallies. Walter
attended one of the lectures. "She is a pretty good talker,"
he admitted. "I went to be amused and stayed to admire
(as the bills say)." [16]

Bandits were numerous in the territory then, and the
source of considerable interest for Walter. The streets
of Guthrie were the scene of several gunfights between
the marshals and the bad men. In one gunfight Marshal
Bill Tilghman killed an outlaw named Bert Casey. The
body was put on public display in the window of the
undertaker's parlor, with the chest left naked to show

[14] Letter, Campbell to Joseph Balmer, Feb. 10, 1947.
[15] *Ibid.,* to Don Russell, Jan. 10, 1956.
[16] Campbell diary, Oct. 1902.

the viewers standing on the sidewalk outside the buck-
shot holes which killed him. [17]

Walter was quite an accomplished horseman by 1902,
a skill he continually improved by long daily rides across
the prairie around Guthrie, and the Cheyenne camps
both there and in the area around Watonga. But one
night he left the door to the stable unlocked and his
saddle was stolen along with all the family harness. This
was one of the few times J. R. became angry with him.
As punishment, J. R. refused to buy him another saddle.
Walter turned the misfortune into something of an advantage, however, by becoming quite skilled at bareback
riding. About the same time his Cheyenne friends taught
him to ride Indian style, using his knees to guide the
horse so he no longer needed even a bridle. He soon
had his old yellow horse trained to respond to knee pres-
sure. Before leaving Guthrie he also learned to ride
cowboy style, using the heavy stock saddle necessary
for working cattle.

The writer exercising the greatest influence on Walter
at that time was Ernest Thompson Seton, who wrote a
regular column about Indians in *The Ladies Home
Journal* as well as many books about the same subject.
Through his articles, Seton organized a nation of "Seton
Indians," small groups of "boys" from six to sixty
in various parts of the nation. Seton called himself
Black Wolf, the big medicine man of the nation. The
idea caught fire, and soon "hundreds of tribes were
organized all over the United States, each with a chief,
councilor, medicine man, and so forth. The tribes camped
out in teepees in true Indian fashion," used bows and
arrows in place of firearms for hunting, and practiced
various Indian woodcraft customs. Naturally Walter was
one of the first to organize such a tribe, calling himself

---

[17] *Ibid.*, Nov. 10, 1902; letter, Campbell to Sidney Ohmart, Mar.
18, 1953; and Vestal, "Fuss and Feathers," *loc. cit.*

Timber Wolf. He named his friend, George Guss, Big Fox. He corresponded with Seton for many years, becoming a close friend. Each always signed his letter with his "tribal name" long after Walter gave up his tribe. [18]

In his final year at Guthrie, 1903, Walter took his tribe – himself and two braves – on camping trips with their teepee along the Cimarron River and Skeleton Creek. He realized that at the age of fifteen he was "a mighty big kid to be playing Indian but it is in my system and will stay in, I suppose, until at some date in the dim future the interest in girls will supplant it." [19] As fond as he eventually became of girls, one in particular, his interest in playing Indian died only when he did many decades later.

By now Walter was quite a student of the Indian sign language, teepees, camping techniques, and so forth. He even compiled a list of all the Indian tribes in the United States and showed their relationship to each other. [20]

Usually Walter loved the expeditions of the tribe, but on one occasion the three warriors ran out of food, Walter got his feet wet and caught cold, and when they returned to camp they found their beds on fire. Walter said:

> I suppose Indian life is all right but what with the sparks and smoke, bugs and flies, heat all day and cold all night, stomach aches and cramps and all the hard work, I would rather go home and help mama. [21]

Walter's first magazine article was published the following year, 1904, summarizing rather well his tribal expeditions of 1903. He wrote the article on his tribe and sent it to *Holiday Magazine for Children*, offering to trade it for a one-year subscription. The editor of the magazine

---

[18] Letter, Campbell to his grandmother, Mrs. Sara Wood, July 8, 1902; Campbell diary, Nov. 2, 1902, and June 18, 1904; various letters exchanged between Campbell and Ernest Thompson Seton.

[19] Campbell diary, June 3, 10, 15, 18, and 26, and July 27, 1903.

[20] *Ibid.*, July 17, 1903.   [21] *Ibid.*, June 10, 1903.

promptly accepted the offer, and printed the article in the first issue Walter received.

Entitled "Our Oklahoma Tribe," it said:

Commencing early last summer scarcely a day passed that some of us were not in the woods. We were there when the sun was very warm, when the wind was blowing strong, when the ice would hold a horse and the snow was deep. We were drenched time after time by the rain. In fact, nearly all our spare time was spent in the square mile of "blackjack" (scrub oak) which we claimed as our hunting ground. We knew those woods by heart. You could not lose us in them even at night.

Our tribe was composed of two members at first, named Big Fox [George Guss] and Timber Wolf [Walter]. Later we admitted Red Buffalo on condition that he would be squaw for one week so that we, being braves, might have more time, also to let him get used to minding the chief. We got some old muslin and made an eight-foot teepee, which leaked and smoked, but of which we were very proud.

We decided that if we were to play Indian we would do so as nearly right as possible. We knew that Indians in the old days had no kettles, pots or pans, but only wooden bowls, pottery and horn spoons. We were used to cooking frog legs and meat on a green stick cleaned of its bark, so we only took a couple of small buckets, a large spoon and our scalping knives.

One day some real Indians appeared and set up three teepees a little south of us. They were Cheyennes, tall, fine looking men and fat, stunted women. The men dressed like whites but the women still wore the blanket, squaw dress, moccasins and leggins of the old times, only they were of cloth instead of buckskin. They were greatly amused at our teepee and tried to trade us a pair of moccasins for it. We soon got acquainted so well that once, when it rained, we were let into one of the teepees by a brave. . . We stayed until the rain ceased and then went home proud to say we had been inside a real Indian teepee.

At length the Indians went away and we returned to our regular Indian life. Once we were chased by the father of a boy whom we had captured and tied up. [22]

Life in Guthrie ended for the Campbells in 1903 soon after a law was passed establishing a new college at Weatherford, Oklahoma Territory. Governor Ferguson appointed J. R. the first president of the new school. Actually it was a school in name only at that time, without a single building constructed. Since Weatherford was in far western Oklahoma Territory in the middle of Cheyenne-Arapaho country, events of the next five years contributed greatly to Walter's development as a biographer and historian.

---

[22] Walter Campbell, "Our Oklahoma Tribe," in *Holiday Magazine for Children,* 1904 (exact date and page unknown).

Cheyenne-Arapaho Country

Walter made the trek deep into Cheyenne-Arapaho country in the boxcar loaded with the family household goods, his favorite dog, a pet raccoon, and his old yellow horse. Arriving in the windswept prairie town of Weatherford, he took an immediate liking to "its far-away buttes and lofty sky-line and the green-clad creek twisting through the rolling plains." [1]

Main Street Walter found "typical of later-day western movie settings. Cow ponies stood tied to the hitching racks, booted and armed cowmen wandered in and out of the pleasure palaces, and Indians in blankets and feathers squatted on the board walks." He could see rows of teepees at the edge of town and Indian ponies ranging the hills beyond. What more could he ask for?

Even before the Campbells could get settled in their new home Walter learned of a huge, permanent Indian encampment and agency called Colony fifteen miles south of Weatherford. Promptly he saddled up and rode south.

Approaching the settlement, Walter rode through a sprawling Indian village, mostly teepees, to a small collection of buildings – a bank, post office, two stores, church, a few houses, the Indian agency and the Indian industrial school. He wasted no time getting acquainted with the Indian agent, John Homer Seger, who had founded the town and school at a time when Cheyenne and Arapaho Indians regarded the killing of whites as an honorable pastime. [2]

[1] Campbell diary, Jan. 22, 1922. [2] Autobiographical data.

In the few weeks remaining before the beginning of the first school term at the college, Walter made almost daily trips to Colony. He developed a strong and permanent friendship for the old agent. A born story-teller, Seger was full of information about the Cheyenne and Arapaho. To Seger's yarns were added the experiences of two others who became Walter's close friends, John Washee, one-time Indian scout for General Custer, and George Bent, half-breed son of Colonel William Bent, founder of Bent's forts on the Arkansas River in Colorado and the Canadian River in west Texas.[3] Development of these friendships came slowly, as did the benefits from them.

When school opened on the first of September, it was about as strange a "campus" as likely will ever exist. A lone building under construction on a hilltop overlooking the town lacked many weeks of completion. Undismayed, thirteen faculty members and 114 students assembled the first day in buildings downtown, including an opera house, a church and three saloons which had been abandoned when the railroad advanced westward. The saloon buildings, with saloon signs on the front windows and complete fixtures inside, were wedged in between saloons still in "full blast." This was not the only way in which saloons figured in the founding of the college, however. It seems one of the "leading citizens" who had signed the petition requesting the territorial legislature to establish a college in Weatherford was a "banker" just as he claimed on the petition – but a faro banker in one of the gambling halls.[4]

[3] Letter, Campbell to Mrs. Sara Wood, Aug. 21, 1903; and to Miss Dorothy Gardiner, Dec. 5, 1939.

[4] Autobiographical data; and copy of a memorial address in honor of J. R. Campbell, delivered Dec. 4, 1929, in the chapel of Southwestern State College, Weatherford, Okla., by R. N. Linville; both in Campbell Collection.

Walter and a new friend, Kenneth Kaufman, both claimed to be the first student to enroll that day. More than four decades later Walter wrote: "Now that the records of those days have burned with the first building, I suppose each of us can make his claim unhampered." At any rate, Walter was at least among the first as he began, as a high school sophomore, his third five-year period of education. The college, one of those early-day "normal" schools, enrolled both high school and college students at that time.

Other students came mostly from western Oklahoma Territory, from town and farm homes of Americans, Germans, and Russians in the district. Some, who lived twenty or more miles away, rode in and hobbled their ponies to graze on the virgin prairie of the campus while they attended classes. Some walked as many as eighty miles to reach Weatherford, arriving without funds or much of anything else.

Strangest sight of all, though, was that of several students attending classes with pistols tucked in their belts. But it was not strange at the time, nor did anyone get excited about it. Carrying pistols simply was the custom of the times, especially for those who traveled long distances to attend classes. Walter carried no gun to the campus, but usually took one with him on trips elsewhere.

Ironically, chapel was among the classes held in former saloon buildings. Professor L. B. Greenfield, head of the English Department, conducted chapel using as his pulpit the bar across the end of the room. The walls of the frame structure were so thin that in the intervals between questions and answers Walter could hear the clink of glasses, the rattle of dice and the voices of gamblers in the saloons next door. [5]

---

[5] Stanley Vestal, *Short Grass Country*, p. 243.

We, who enrolled in the school that first year, felt –
perhaps more than later students – a sense of adventure.
We began at bedrock or at scratch and felt the responsibility and enjoyed the fun of organizing the activities of
the college and starting its traditions. Few, if any of
us, had been to college before, and we depended a good
deal upon certain popular professors who had come from
long established universities. College yells and songs
had to be created or adopted, teams in football, basket-
ball, tennis, and track had to be organized, and all the
activities possible in a community which did not look
with favor upon dancing, smoking, or playing cards. [6]

After a few weeks the new building on the hill was
ready for occupancy. President Campbell organized a
parade of students and faculty to march up Main Street
and on up the hill. But the procession was delayed
momentarily by a faculty member – an eastern lady –
who obstinately refused to march through the streets.
The mere idea shocked her. J. R. politely informed her
that she could either march up the hill to the college or
down the street to the depot. Up the hill she went, with
the flag-waving, triumphant column, a brass band leading
the way. [7] This was the first "gesture of effeminacy.
But nemesis was hot on our trail," Walter wrote. First,
"the saloons were cleared out by a law that forbade them
to do business within miles of an institution of learning."
Next went the pool halls, "leaving several young men
homeless." Dancing was banned later, "and there was a
growing opinion that the streets of the city were not
the best places for horse races and rodeos."

Walter majored in Latin and Greek, and with his pals
read far more of both than was required. Perhaps that
was why in later years he had so little patience with students who did not even do the minimum required work

---

[6] *The Southwestern* (newspaper, Weatherford, Okla.), May 17,
1944.   [7] *Ibid.*

in his classes. Since his step-father was president, he felt it was necessary to take part in all school activities and join everything. He played on most of the athletic teams, debated, headed the YMCA, and became – unnaturally – a mixer. His refuge from all this civilized time-wasting was the Cheyenne encampment at Colony. He abandoned the college for Colony every time he got the chance. [8]

But the trips to Colony were considerably more than just diversion. "George Bent and John Seger filled my eager ears with tales of the buffalo days," he wrote. Bit by bit he learned of Captain Silas Bent who commanded the Boston Tea Party; of Silas' grandson, William, who went west and established his famous forts on the Arkansas River in eastern Colorado and on the Canadian River in Texas. George told Walter how the fort in Colorado became the central trading post for the plains Indian tribes, particularly the Cheyenne, Arapaho and Sioux. William Bent married Owl Woman, daughter of the keeper of the Cheyenne medicine arrows. George was their son, growing up in eastern Colorado among such pioneer greats as Kit Carson, James Bridger and Joe Meek. He still lived there when J. R. Campbell met him. J. R. was researching as one of Bancroft's men at the time. [9]

Night after night Walter listened to George relate incidents of the scouts and fur traders he had known. The accuracy of what he said was attested by later western Americana historians who ranked him as the best Indian historian of the southern plains tribes. And Walter received the benefit of this knowledge first hand. Walter's hero worship of Kit Carson grew with each new bit of information he learned about him. George knew Kit well during the many years Kit was a close friend and employee of his father. Most important, though, George fought in almost all major battles between the Cheyennes

[8] Autobiographical data.　　　[9] *Ibid.*

and the whites, usually – but not always – on the Cheyenne side. He even fought on both sides during the Civil War.

As great as was Walter's fascination with Seger and Bent, he did not spend all his time with them. Every old warrior who would talk to him was sought out by the eager youth. From them he learned more than most whites about the Cheyenne ways. They treated him with kindness and friendliness, but would not tell him about their warfare. Walter thought at first they were afraid they would be punished if they talked about killing whites. But he soon learned they were equally reticent toward the Cheyenne boys. The reason was as simple as most Indian logic. Since neither Walter nor the Cheyenne boys had been to war, they were not qualified to discuss warfare. The thing Walter wanted most to learn about remained "a closed book" in spite of all his persuasive efforts.

Because of his youth, however, Walter was able to see many tribal ceremonies closed to older white men. Sometimes it was the efforts of Seger that opened these to him. Sometimes it was simply a case of the Indians paying little attention to one of his age. In those first years at Colony, however, two sacred things remained closed to him. One was the secret part of the Cheyenne sun dance, the other a chance to see the medicine arrows.

Not all Walter's interests in Cheyennes were so serious. He found plenty of time to race horses, swim and play various Indian games with the Cheyenne boys. Sometimes he just loafed around in the congenial atmosphere of the encampment and Colony. [10]

Walter practiced for football by using a half-grown calf as his opponent. He put on his football suit and "bucked

---

[10] Undated application for a Guggenheim Fellowship filed by W. S. Campbell; letter, Campbell to Miss Dorothy Gardiner, Dec. 5, 1939; various autobiographical notes, all in the Campbell Collection.

the line" against "the startled critter," blocking against its shoulders. "At first, the calf was taken by surprise, then grew wary and finally learned to charge back." They "butted heads together and blocked each other" quite like football players. As the calf grew, so did its advantage until finally Walter did not stand a chance against it. The calf seemed to enjoy it as much as Walter.

Walter represented the college for three years on the Oklahoma Inter-Collegiate Athletic Association. In this capacity he picked one of the judges for a state track meet.

> I chose a senior Rhodes Scholar from Oklahoma [Territory] feeling sure that he, understanding sport, would be able to act perfectly and so he did. In those days the athletic meets of Oklahoma colleges were rather primitive affairs and many of the contestants wore only shorts and running shoes – not even a skivy to conceal the hair on their chests. Having invited my graduate from Oxford, I was somewhat taken aback to find that when he arrived, he was wearing a gray top hat, the appropriate English costume for the Ascot Races, and binoculars in a leather case hung over his shoulders by a strap, not to mention a chrysanthemum in his buttonhole. But I will say for him that he had plenty of savoir-faire and carried off the occasion in the grand manner judging from his decisions absolutely according to the best sporting tradition. I am quite positive that nobody in the stands had ever seen such a figure before or . . . any procedures such as he followed. But I was not embarrassed. I was proud of the son-of-a-bitch. He did his stuff beautifully.[11]

Just how much Walter knew about Oxford customs at that time is not known, but likely he was just as wide-eyed as the others.

One of the extra-curricular activities exercised great

---

[11] **Autobiographical data.**

influence on Walter's future. He established and edited
the first college newspaper at Southwestern, naming it
the *Mukwisto*, a Cheyenne word meaning paper. This
helped him to develop a little as a writer. More importantly, it led him to become campus news correspondent
for *The Oklahoman* of Oklahoma City. Primarily he
wrote campus news but he squeezed in some stories about
Indian life as well.

Many activities occurred to occupy Walter's time and
keep him from going to Colony as much as he would
have liked. Once he went on a wolf hunt that ended on
the campus. He also helped establish an annual Indian
fair, with pony races and mock buffalo hunts. At one of
these fairs, two braves, He Dog and Two Crows, raced
their ponies after a steer serving as a buffalo. They
dropped the running steer with arrows which went all the
way through the animal's body.

In athletic events, the Indians sometimes provided the
sternest competition to the college. This was particularly
true in baseball, for the Indians had an especially strong
love for the sport and played it all year. Once the Colony
team came to the college for a game, and soon held a commanding lead, due primarily to the efforts of their pitcher,
a lithe young Indian named Stone-Hammer.

> A hammer he was that day. Nothing we could do
> seemed able to stop the Indians' triumphant march to
> overwhelming victory, and as the score piled up, they
> played better and better. With an Indian, nothing
> succeeds like success. Finally the word was passed
> round that the bleachers must razz the pitcher. It was
> the only hope. This was done, and Stone-Hammer,
> assailed from all sides, soon lost his assurance and con-
> trol, and with them the game. The Indians left for home
> rather crest-fallen.
>
> A return match was to be played on our field next
> week, and when we turned out to see it we found the

bleachers completely filled by Indians – male and female, of all ages and conditions from chiefs to papooses – it seemed the entire personnel of the allied tribes were present. Their wagons blocked the streets leading to the field, and overflowed into all the vacant lots round about. When the game began, all those bronze rooters began their deadly work. Throats trained in whooping the war-cry were strained to the utmost; pandemonium! Our rooters could not get together, and outnumbered, outclassed, and drowned out by the unceasing roar from the bleachers, soon gave it up and quit. Not so the redskins. They never stopped their infernal racket until the game was over and won.

Stone-Hammer smiled drily as he climbed into his father's wagon and set out for Colony, trailed by an endless caravan of covered wagons that would have filled James Cruze with hopeless envy. [12]

On one occasion a student talked an Arapaho youth named John Buffalo into attending the college. A renowned sprinter, the Indian signed the enrollment papers, then said he must return to camp for his clothing. He promised to come back next Monday and begin training. But while in camp John Buffalo found an Indian maiden to his liking, got married and thought no more of college.

On Sundays the students would bring in wild horses for the more hardy students to ride. Some of the riders could actually stick to the saddle, "at least as long as the bronc remained in sight." If Walter ever tried his luck on the wild beasts, he did not admit it.

Weatherford was named for Old Bill Weatherford, the local lawman. With handlebar mustache and pearl handled pistols holstered on his belt, he looked the old-time peace officer he was. Many bullet holes could be found in the buildings and telegraph poles where he had shot it out with bandits. One day two of Walter's friends

---

[12] *Ibid.*

got into an argument downtown and "took to fisticuffs." Old Bill came out to settle the scrap and promptly arrested one of them, asserting that he had begun the fight. "As this was contrary to fact," Walter, eager to defend his friend, protested a little too strongly when he said: "That's a lie."

"Old Bill turned his cold blue eyes" on Walter and said: "Young man, don't you give me the lie." Walter immediately "took a more moderate tone and declared more quietly, 'Well, it's not true anyhow.' "

Old Bill apparently did not forget the incident, for a little later he took occasion to confide not too quietly to a group on Main Street that Walter had certain qualities that he did not admire. When J. R. heard about it, he was furious and was actually going downtown to have it out with Old Bill. It took Walter the better part of an hour to talk him out of it. [13]

Walter still continued his regular correspondence with Ernest Thompson Seton, and his readership of the Seton column in *The Ladies' Home Journal.* In 1904 he organized another tribe of the Seton Nation of Indians, enrolling it as the Bear Band with three braves, himself as Timber Wolf, chief of the band; Hugh Webster as Arrowhead; and John Boles as Laughs-All-the-Time. [14]

The band needed a teepee, and tried making one by following the directions in one of Seton's columns. However, they soon found Seton's methods "were not Indian" and therefore not workable. So Walter and Hugh saddled their horses and rode down to Colony looking for a real Indian teepee. They found a squaw willing to sell them a set of ten teepee poles for a dollar and a half. Quickly they closed the deal, which included instructions on how to pitch it. Teepee poles come anywhere from thirty to forty feet long, and these were average Cheyenne poles.

[13] *Ibid.*   [14] Campbell diary, June 1904.

Walter and Hugh could not figure out a way to get them home except to tie one end to their saddles and drag the other end. In this manner they set out for home with their prize. But once in a while the long and heavy poles would catch in a deep rut and flip over one of the surprised horses. Likely Walter practiced his growing vocabulary of profane words during the trip. They finally reached the Webster home in Weatherford and set up their poles.

Two days later the boys bought twenty-four yards of eight-ounce canvas ducking and made the sides for their teepee. Next they painted a totem on each side, a wolf for Timber Wolf [Walter] and an arrowhead for the "brave" by that name [Hugh]. Apparently Laughs-All-the-Time did not rate a totem at that time.

The Bear Band added moccasins and "real Indian peace pipes" for all three members. They often camped out overnight on the plains, spent a lot of time playing Indian games and learning such crafts as arrow making. For ceremonials, they followed the Indian tradition as closely as possible. For smoking the peace pipe, they used one pipe, taking turns. Walter insisted on coffee for the pipe, however, because it was not "so strong as cornsilk" and because he "had enough" of tobacco four years previously.

By now Walter read regularly the publications of the Bureau of American Ethnology and "other reliable accounts of the old-time life." He continued to attend the Cheyenne sun dances and other ceremonies, and began to see more clearly the basis for Indian life and culture. He watched the Indians tan hides, build small-game traps, make bows and arrows, bead work, and even learned how to cook over the campfire. He also began to master the sign language used by all the plains tribes. He did it a little at a time, but steadily. One day he "hired Hubbell

Big Horse for 2 bits (25¢) to teach me Cheyenne for one hour. He took me in his teepee. We sat on the bed and I learned quite a bit." [15]

As a trusted visitor in the encampment, Walter gradually got acquainted with the survivors of the Sand Creek massacre, the infamous butchery of peaceful and mostly unarmed Cheyennes of Chief Black Kettle by Colonel Chivington's Colorado Volunteers in 1864. He also talked to many survivors of the Battle of the Washita in 1868, where George Custer's Seventh Cavalry attacked Black Kettle's peaceful Cheyenne Village and killed a large portion of the band, including Black Kettle. Perhaps the Indians were willing to tell him about these events because they were defensive fights rather than warpath battles. Other information Walter secured from Seger, Bent, and Ben Clark, the latter a scout and post interpreter to the commanding officer at Fort Reno for fifty years. Though only sixteen now, Walter had acquired a fantastic knowledge of the plains Indians and western history. Still, the old warriors would not tell him of their personal exploits in battle, only general information about them. As an untried warrior, he was not worthy of their comradeship in this respect, regardless of how much they respected him in other ways. [16]

Walter's account of a Fourth of July celebration at Colony in 1904 shows how carefully he studied every detail of camp life. He and a friend left home about 4:40 in the morning and rode down to Colony, arriving about eight.

> We unhitched, tied up the dog, not because I was afraid the Indian dogs would eat him as they will that, but because I was afraid the Indians themselves might eat him; and set out with my kodak to 'snap' the Redmen. We had our gun trained on the camp when a squaw came running, shouting to us 'two bits.' Then I

---

[15] Campbell diary, Nov. 14, 1903.   [16] Autobiographical data.

turned it [the Kodak] on a procession of squaws coming up the path. One of them held an umbrella, however, and put it in front of her while the others got in behind in single file. This would have made an amusing picture but I did not take it. Then some other Indians drove in . . . and put up their teepees. I watched very closely and took several pictures. At least I have learned how to tie the three poles [which are first put up] together so they will not slip. The old squaw laid two side by side, then another almost at right angles to the first two. [Here Walter added many pages of description of the teepee and how to pitch it.]

A ring of squaws had collected around a pile of freshly killed beef a short distance off on the prairie. It was already skinned and cleaned and lay on the grass in a pile with a circle of perhaps 50 Indians about it, one-sixth of whom were men. . . The able-bodied men now prepared to dole out the victuals provided by whites. The beef was already cut up so the men simply carried the pieces around and gave one or two to each squaw who squatted on the ground with their blankets and sheets over their heads, awaiting their turn. . . As each one received her share she wrapped it in a blanket or cloth and carried it off, or perhaps in her bare hands. . . Each squaw got about thirty pounds. Curs of all sizes prowled about the throng, snatching scraps whenever they could. Many flies settled on the meat as it lay in the dirt and on the whole the sight was not pleasant except when regarded as a repetition of a savage custom when a buffalo was killed. . . We took snaps of all these affairs in spite of an old red-painted rascal who wanted '2 bits' (25¢). I took his picture while he argued about it. All were issued flour, sugar and coffee. Much joking and laughter was going on all the while for Indians are always on the verge of humor when something to eat is in sight. One squaw picked up her blanket and the meat dropped out causing a general laugh in which she heartily joined. [17]

[17] Campbell diary, July 4, 1904.

Walter and his friend hurried from one event to another, intrigued especially by the parade which featured the Seger Indian school band and a clown band. Many carnival-type stands were scattered about. A highlight of the day was the speaking. Indian chiefs from various tribes "spoke softly in their own language with many signs and gesticulations. Captain Seger translated." Walter, of course, needed no translator for the sign language. In fact, he used it frequently that day talking to many Indians.

Soon after J. R. founded the new college, he became a member of the Oklahoma committee for selection of Rhodes Scholars who were picked for the first time that year. [18] Walter immediately developed a strong desire to win one of the scholarships, and mentioned his ambition many times in his diaries. "I think of little else but Oxford and a Cecil Rhodes Scholarship," he wrote in 1904. "Think of it; three years in Europe, travel in the summer and attendance at the big 'varsity' in England." [19]

The following month he added:

> I am just as sure of going to Oxford as I can be. I positively know it for in the Bible in Mark 11:22 Jesus says 'What things soever ye desire, when ye pray, believe that ye receive them and ye shall have them.' As I pray every night and sometimes in concert at chapel and always give my scholarship a prominent place in the prayer, I am certain I will get it. This does not keep me from working, however, for faith without works is vain. [20]

And work he did, especially in Greek, Latin and math, with the prospects of the scholarship dangling in front of him and spurring him to greater effort. But he could not even apply for it for another two years.

Dreams of Oxford were pushed into the background

---

[18] Letter, J. R. Campbell to F. J. Wylie, Mar. 17, 1908.
[19] Campbell diary, Apr. 24, 1904.   [20] *Ibid.*

temporarily in the spring of 1904 when the Campbell family attended the World's Fair in St. Louis. For several weeks Walter concentrated on earning money for the trip. As it turned out, he might just as well have spent the money at home, considering what he bought with it. As soon as he, J. R., Daisy and her sister, Harvie, arrived in St. Louis, Walter heard about an Indian village with Indians from various parts of the world. He immediately dragged the family to the village and began jabbering away at the unresponsive faces. Dismayed, he tried again but none of the Indians would talk. When the spectators began leaving, the oldest man of the Indian group motioned for Walter to come into the teepee. Inside, Walter found all the Indians willing to visit with him in private. Naturally Walter spent all but one of his days at the fair with the Indians. Each day he questioned the Indians by the hour, recording in his diary every detail he could learn of custom, dress and crafts of the various tribes. When not questioning and writing, he sketched pictures of the same things. [21]

Most fascinating to Walter was the Apache, Geronimo, who "sat at a desk in an alcove from a narrow rail catwalk through which tourists filed to buy his autograph." The old warrior "scribbled his autograph on a card and offered it for a dollar." While Walter stood there wide-eyed, "thousands of people passed by, and hundreds bought his autograph and shook his hand." [22]

Walter did not record in his various diaries and papers whether he bought one of Geronimo's autographs. But he bought many other items close to his Indian-loving heart, particularly an Indian drum and some eagle feathers. He could have secured most of the items at home, but this did not lessen his pride in his new possessions.

---

[21] *Ibid.*, numerous entries between Feb. and July, 1904; letter, Mrs. J. D. McCoid to Ray Tassin, Apr. 18, 1962, in the author's possession.

[22] Letter, Campbell to John Fischer, May 6, 1957.

After the fair, the adults went on to Chicago but Walter headed for home and an extended camping trip in Cheyenne-Arapaho country. In Weatherford he collected his band of "Seton Indians" and provisions enough for several weeks. Then he hired a Negro with a wagon to haul them, their teepee, equipment and supplies fifteen miles south. Here they set up camp on a rather level stretch of prairie about fifty yards from Cobb Creek. The water was clear, swift and shallow, and just right for their camping, fishing and games.

First off, the boys disposed of their civilized clothing and donned leggings and breechclouts, rather appropriate dress for southwestern Oklahoma in August. Next they settled down to a few weeks of "perfect life" on the prairie, without the worries and cares of civilized society. One night, however,

> We had just spread a blanket outside the door and were eating our supper . . . when up came a storm and we had much ado to get everything into the teepee and peg it down before it caught us. It was a bad one. The wind shook the teepee to and fro like a reed until we hung on the anchor rope to keep it from blowing over. Also, the seams leaked in places as did the door. We had no ditch around the teepee to carry off the water and the floor was soon flooded. [23]

Many Indians were in the area. Frequently small bands rode up to the camp on their ponies. All of them wanted to know what the boys were doing there, where they lived, where they got their teepee and where was their wagon. Some of them seemed to think the boys had some kind of medicine show and asked if they intended to put on their show in Colony. They just could not understand that anyone would camp out purely for pleasure. Several of the younger groups played the Indian wheel game with the imitation Indians, "slightly to the

---

[23] Campbell diary, various dates during Aug. 1904.

detriment of the wheel." The Indians displayed a keen interest in the drum Walter bought in St. Louis, and all of them wanted to buy the eagle feathers. Apparently the latter was a scarce item on the southern plains this late in the Old West era.

On one occasion three Arapaho boys took quite an interest in Walter's peace pipe. They asked to smoke it, so the three Arapaho and three "Seton" Indians "made medicine" in the teepee. The records do not show whether the "Setons" were still using coffee instead of tobacco.

The weeks slipped by in much this manner, with the boys fishing, swimming and playing Indian games, sometimes alone, sometimes with visiting Indians. Walter passed his eighteenth birthday at the camp. But the fall school term eventually sent them back to Weatherford.

Walter wrote a great deal about Indian life now. His success at trading an article about his "tribe" for a subscription to *Holiday Magazine for Children* led him to write more articles for publication. He sold two others to the magazine, one on how to build an Indian-type willow bed and another on how to play the Indian hoop game. A little later one of the sons of Governor Ferguson became editor of the newspaper at Cherokee, Oklahoma Territory, and bought Walter's first published short story. Naturally it was an Indian yarn, entitled "The Glories of Youth." [24]

Walter was something of a character about the campus and town, due to his "going native" at every opportunity. He wrote: "Nowadays when I go by people say 'How, John'," and jabber unmeaning lingo at me in imitation of Indian talk. Then there are hints about me marrying a squaw and so on. But I don't care." [25]

The famous novelist, Hamlin Garland, once stayed with

---

[24] Letter, Campbell to F. G. Walling, Apr. 24, 1939; and autobiographical data.   [25] Campbell diary, Apr. 25, 1905.

the Campbells while researching two historical novels. Walter took Garland to Colony where the writer gathered materials. During Garland's stay with the Campbells, J. R. arranged for him to address the college assembly. Garland read a paper

> boasting of his pioneer ancestry – and left his audience
> stone cold. Then . . . Seger, . . . who had
> driven Garland up [from Colony], was invited to speak.
> Seger got up and entranced us by the hour with true
> stories of Indian life and his own pioneer endeavor set
> in our own plains country. [26]

This early contact with one of the top literary figures of the day doubtless had some influence on Walter's later ambitions to become a writer.

In 1906, Captain Seger took Walter to a Cheyenne sun dance at Big Jake's Crossing on the Washita River. Here he got his first look at the secret part of the sun dance, a religious event so carefully guarded from white eyes. He later learned that the only way to understand Indians was by first comprehending their religion. From this sun dance he acquired a much greater insight into warrior ways.

One part of the ceremony featured the telling of war stories around a fire in the dance lodge. Once the fire was started, it was replenished periodically by warriors. In turn, each approached the small fire carrying an armful of small sticks. He held one stick up high in his right hand while he told in a few words how he had killed an enemy or counted coup (touch an enemy in battle). The stick represented the conquered enemy. Then the warrior hurled the stick into the fire while musicians thumped loud applause on a big drum. He kept repeating the performance, each time for a different enemy he had struck or killed, until his sticks were all in the fire. In

---

[26] Stanley Vestal, *The Book Lover's Southwest,* p. 243.

this manner the valor of the Cheyenne kept the fire burning for three days and nights of dancing. A fire burned in Walter also, fed by his desire for knowledge about Cheyenne warfare.

Instead of satisfying the long-time hunger of Walter for accounts of Cheyenne battles, these brief tales merely whetted his appetite for greater details. But he still found his lack of war experience an insurmountable handicap. He tried every means of persuasion to get the old warriors to talk to him, but all remained adament. Except for Seger, he would not even have been able to learn what he did. And he still could not get close to the medicine arrows.

That same spring Walter "had a severe attack of 'girlitis' which promised to prove fatal for a time." Cause of the attack was one Elsie Brewer, a student from Oklahoma City. Somehow he survived until summer when he and Ray Larimer went on an extended walking trip through the Wichita Mountains to Fort Sill. Here, while watching the Apaches dance, he suffered a relapse and "was enamored of an Indian girl." [27]

Statehood for Oklahoma, November 16, 1907, brought disaster to the Campbells. J. R. had been appointed president of the college by Governor Ferguson, himself a Republican appointee. The first elected officials of the new state were Democrats, who made the educational institutions political spoils. Nearly the entire faculty was discharged within a few weeks in the middle of the school year. In fact, no official notice was sent to J. R. that he was fired. He first heard about it when a friend telephoned him and said he had read the notice in a newspaper. Walter described it as a "scurvy trick!" The influence of Grandmother Wood and J. R. had long since made Walter a confirmed Republican. This incident made him a bitter and unforgiving one.

[27] Autobiographical data.

The "political dictator," as Walter called the governor, sent a new staff to Southwestern. "Whenever a stranger was seen climbing the hill" to the college, "the students laid wagers as to what chair he was to fill. Some of these may have been able men. Others were not."

The Democratic administration also took away from the college the right to confer degrees, which caused strong resentment among Walter and his classmates who were nearing graduation.

> The new president made a tour of inspection of the college plant as soon as he arrived. All went well until he reached the rooms of the Department of Fine Arts. There he found a number of plaster casts of classical statues, some of them in an altogether shocking state of nudity. Horrified, and perhaps fearing that such a scandal might abruptly terminate his new authority, he ordered the janitor to run and get his tools and chisel off the offending members. Thus he prevented his charges from the contamination of culture, and reaped a harvest of inextinguishable laughter. [28]

Rather than leave the short grass country where he had been so useful and made so many friends, J. R. preferred to become superintendent of schools at nearby Arapaho, Oklahoma, a few miles west of Weatherford. The family continued to live in Weatherford for the balance of Walter's final year in school there.

The calamity was softened somewhat in January when Walter was selected to take the examination for a Rhodes Scholarship. The first step toward his long-awaited goal filled him with excitement. He took the examination on January 22-23, and passed handily. Next step was to go before the committee on selections. J. R. was still on this committee, but took no part judging Walter's appli-

---

[28] Biography of J. R. Campbell written by W. S. Campbell, Campbell Coll., *loc. cit.*

cation. Walter still won the appointment, however, as he had long "known" he would. Much of the recent gloom vanished from the big house on Custer Street that day. The three-year scholarship was to start in September 1908.

Ten of the first students at Southwestern composed the first graduating class that spring, without degrees, among them Walter and his close friend, Kenneth Kaufman. [29]

Walter spent the summer preparing for his Oxford trip, and running down to Colony as often as he could. The prospect of going half a world away from his Cheyenne friends and from the short grass country was not a happy one for him, but his enthusiasm for Oxford made it bearable. It was an inner struggle between outdoorsman Stanley Vestal's desire to live like an Indian and the intellectual Walter S. Campbell's hunger for knowledge and foreign travel. He did not hesitate about going, however.

In August, Walter helped Daisy and J. R. move to a new home in Arapaho. Then he left for New York and on to England, leaving his beloved prairie for the land of little sunshine.

---

[29] Graduation program in the diary of W. S. Campbell.

An American at Oxford

Due to a summer bout with typhoid, young Campbell did not feel too well on his arrival in New York. The other Rhodes Scholars took tours of the city and wound up their stay there with a farewell party. But Walter spent most of his time in his hotel room. One show was all he managed. He joined the others only when sailing time arrived. The large group boarded a small liner and started overseas.

During the leisurely voyage the boys got acquainted and were old friends when they reached Liverpool. Walter had a little trouble getting past customs. Since it was common in those days for Western Oklahomans to carry guns for protection while traveling, Walter packed a pistol. He had no use for the weapon, and for the next three years had trouble with customs each time he returned to England with it. Another Rhodes Scholar from the Old West country also took a pistol to England with him, but soon found a use for the weapon. At Oxford his servant drank the westerner's liquor on the sly, so he left his gun alongside his brandy bottle, "thereby frightening the college 'scout' into unwanted sobriety." Walter said neither he nor his friend were "more blood-thirsty than other young men. We had simply never questioned the custom of taking a gun along." [1]

Traveling by train, the scholars arrived at Oxford on their third day in the country. The quiet city had but one motor taxicab and a single horse-drawn tram car

---

[1] Vestal, *Short Grass Country,* p. 242.

which rocked and lurched along at a snail's pace past an occasional car, flock of sheep, and depressing gray buildings. The new arrivals were met by Sir Francis Wiley, secretary for the Rhodes Trust at Oxford.

Rhodes Scholarships were established by Cecil Rhodes to bring together young men of different countries to improve international relations by forming friendships among fellows who were likely to be leaders at home. The first Rhodes Scholars went to Oxford in 1903, numbering only a few. Next year the first large group arrived and was "made over by the ruling class in England and treated to social experiences" denied later groups. Walter was the first Rhodes Scholar from the new state of Oklahoma, although some came from Oklahoma Territory prior to statehood. By the time Walter arrived the aristocracy had tired of the novelty and no longer paid much attention to the scholars.

The first order of business of their arrival at Oxford was to get in one of the twenty-one colleges. A new student made application for the college of his choice, much as American students sought memberships in fraternities. Walter put

> Christ's Church [one of the colleges] first and others after and finally Merton College. I had nothing to go on but a guide book about the school which a friend of mine had given me, but I was fortunate. Merton College accepted me. Merton College was small, but select, a college with an excellent reputation though somewhat expensive fees, a beautiful architecture and altogether just such a college that I would choose now if I had a choice to make. Confidence or fate or good luck was with me and I have never had cause to regret having been admitted to that college. [2]

Walter moved into his quarters in Merton College

---

[2] *Stanley Vestal,* "How to Win a Rhodes Scholarship," in *American Oxonian*, July 1926, p. 99.

and found that each student had his own sitting room, bedroom and pantry. Since he still had a little time left before the term opened, he and another Rhodes Scholar went to London to get supplies. They bought dishes, brooms, even silver, because part of their meals were brought to their rooms. They also needed the silver for entertaining each other as guests at tea or meal time. Walter made one little mistake in these purchases. He wanted his initials "w. s. c." engraved on his possessions. But in his innocence of English customs permitted the salesman to talk him into getting only the letters "w. c." on the grounds that it would be cheaper. Walter did not know it but in England "w. c." was an often used polite term for water closet, or toilet. During the next three years he found himself the frequent target of jokes by guests who came to have breakfast, lunch or dinner with him and found his silver so inscribed. Walter later took some comfort in the fact that Sir Winston Churchill had the same initials and had been subjected to the same humiliation. But that helped him none at the time.

Walter felt some anxiety about "getting off on the right foot academically." He knew that at the end of the first term he had to pass two preliminary examinations. Also, he had been warned that English methods of instruction were different from those to which he was accustomed. Since he wished to make no mistake at the beginning of his university career, and since no one made any suggestions as to what he should do, he set out to get advice on how to prepare for the exams.

Having been the son of a college president in America, Walter felt no awe of academic dignitaries. He therefore informed the chief servant who kept the gate of the college that he wished to see the warden of Merton. This was arranged and Walter crossed the cobbled streets to knock on the door of a gloomy mansion. In his ignorance of English custom Walter had no idea what pre-

cedent-shattering action he was taking. The warden of
Merton had almost no contact with undergraduates,
except in extreme cases where disciplinary action was
needed.

Walter was ushered into the gloomy cavern known as
the warden's lodging. Two rather frightened-looking
young women were in the sitting room, apparently sup-
posing that Walter had come to receive sentence for some
dire crime. Some awkward moments of silence followed
before the warden loomed in the door of the next room
and inquired Walter's purpose. The warden was a big,
stolid-looking person, and "deaf as a post," Walter wrote.
Walter's object was "to find out what in hell I was supposed to do." But the warden "was quite unable to
understand what the hell I wanted there." It was some
time before Walter could overcome the handicaps of
the warden's deafness, his own American accent, and his
unparalleled request. Finally the warden got the idea
and "blurted out that I should see the dean."

Walter thanked him and headed straight for the dean,
a tall, affable and well-tailored gentleman who greeted
him warmly and chatted with him for a few minutes.
After Walter explained his desire to prepare for the
exams, the dean sent him to the senior tutor. He headed
for the tutor's home, walking with an Englishman named
Gibb. Enroute they met the tutor, without Walter knowing it. "Being a respectful American and meeting an
older man I kept to the right." Unfortunately, this placed
Walter closest to the wall as he passed the tutor. Gibbs
expressed his amazement. "You have a lot of cheek
to take the wall of a senior tutor," Gibbs said. Up to
that moment Walter did not realize that in the old days
the sewers of England ran down the middle of the streets
and superiors "always took the wall," and the inferiors
walked on the side nearest the center of the street.

They reached the home of the tutor and waited while

other undergraduates talked to him. Walter found the
tutor a "jolly sporting type" whom he liked first off.
When it was his turn, he approached the tutor and gave
his name.

"Ah, yes, Mr. Campbell," the tutor said. "You're up
for divvers [one of the exams]. Can you tell me what
this examination covers?"

"Yes sir," Walter returned unhesitatingly. "I'm to
read Matthew, Mark, and the Acts of the Apostles in
Greek and be prepared on the subject matter of these
books."

The tutor looked at him "quite like a bird" and said:
"You are an American, Mr. Campbell?"

"Yes sir, I am."

"Ah, yes, I quite understand. In England we say
St. Matthew and *St.* Mark. But I suppose as an American you object to all titles."

At that most of the undergraduates waiting their turns
broke into laughter. Walter smiled as best he could,
realizing this was part of his initiation into Merton. The
tutor tried hard to conceal his amusement at an undergraduate who would go to all the trouble to get to work.
Finally he advised Walter to see another tutor, one
further down the faculty scale, who in turn sent him
further down the line to another who repeated the
process. Finally Walter wound up in the common room
in the presence of a little mouse of a chaplain. Even then
Walter scarcely suspected that he was getting the run-
around as part of his education in the Oxford system.
He was getting desperate and explained to the chaplain
the trouble he was having. "But what am I going to
do?" Walter inquired.

The chaplain smiled brightly and answered, "Why don't
you take up golf?" Then the chaplain explained the
English plan of training an undergraduate. In English
public schools boys were subjected to harsh discipline.

The British realized, however, that such discipline would not train a man for independent thought. The first step at Oxford, therefore, was to teach the youth to stand on his own feet and do his own thinking. In their first eight weeks at the university, the Michaelmas term, all rules were suspended and all freshmen turned loose. They were not expected to do any work or to prepare for any examinations, but were encouraged to become independent souls, and get the hang of intellectual society.

This freedom lasted only until Christmas vacation began. During this time both the teachers and the senior men did everything to break down the student's reliance on the opinion of others. If a freshman parroted an opinion of his father or some schoolmaster, the entire senior college jumped on him. It did not matter what he thought or what he said, but he must have some opinion of his own or lose face. The English students "poured a barrage of questions" about America at Walter, questions he could not answer. He was never so embarrassed and ashamed. [3]

Despite his leisurely first term, Walter had some work to do. One morning the porter of the college handed him a note telling him to report to one of the teaching fellows, Mr. Goddard, for further instruction. It was a showery morning and Walter mounted the stairs to Goddard's quarters wearing his new gown and cap, feeling that at last he would find out what was expected of him. He thumped on the oak door and heard a faint invitation to enter. Closing the door behind him, Walter found himself in a long, comfortably furnished room with windows looking out on the quad. Opposite the windows, a stooped, youngish man sat cross-legged like an Indian on a pillow with his back to the coal fire in the grate. Walter handed him the note and identified himself. While

---

[3] Autobiographical data.

Goddard read the note, Walter looked around the large room, noticing stacks of manuscript papers in a row on the floor, about one foot apart. Goddard grunted and got up, lighted his pipe and mumbled something to Walter. Then he began to pace the floor, stepping neatly from one stack of paper to the next and muttering something to himself. The spectacle of a renowned scholar parading up and down on stacks of manuscripts so fascinated Walter that he was unable to pay attention to the mutterings. It was some minutes before Walter realized Goddard was mumbling instructions to him on his future studies. Then Walter scrambled to get as much of the instructions as he could before Goddard dismissed him.

These early difficulties soon passed, and Walter got what he regarded as two lucky breaks. One was his tutor, George Gordon. The other was his English teacher, Sir Walter Raleigh. Certainly the two influenced him greatly, not only by teaching him, but because both were writers and encouraged him to write. "These two men . . . were the king-pins of the School of English Language and Literature in my date and they both performed great services for me and opened my eyes to a great many things which I would not have known otherwise," Walter wrote. Sir Walter "was the most inspiring lecturer . . . at Oxford, and I did seminar work with him." All the department heads were nationally prominent persons who taught seminars and lectured.

The first time Walter went to his tutor he took a strong liking to him. Gordon was a dapper little man with a large head, and one of the most indolent persons Walter ever knew. "But he was just the man for me, calm and cool and clever, and able to arouse emulation and at the same time balance and discussion among his pupils." [4]

---

[4] *Ibid.*

Walter soon became a convert to the Oxford tutoral system. He said of it:

The tutor at Oxford was interested solely in the success of his pupils in the final examinations and was in conspiracy with the pupil to defeat the examiners by turning out papers which they could not refuse. Thus the relationship of the teacher and pupil was close, intimate and friendly. Such an association is one of the chief treasures that a man carries away from a place like Oxford. In America, on the contrary, the teacher who examines the student and gives him his grade is not regarded as a rule in such a friendly spirit, but rather as someone to be outwitted or an enemy. This is a most unfortunate arrangement. It would be far better to let anybody picked up in the streets set the examination than to have the teacher who gives the course set it, in my opinion. We can never have real scholars or have the feeling that we are all learners from the freshmen up to the PhD until we have that friendly and helpful relationship. If I were a millionaire and wanted to found a college, I would certainly abolish the American plan of having the teacher give the examination and the grades. These things should be given by outsiders. At Oxford at any rate the examinations were set by the board of examiners expressly chosen for the purpose, none of whom were teachers of the men taking the exam. Most examiners came from other universities than Oxford. Of course, in order to get leading scholars they paid the examiners very well with the result that every teacher in an English university was eager to become an examiner and thus add a bonus to his usual pay. In this way the exams were set and conducted by the ablest scholars in the country. George Gordon was a good lecturer, an excellent tutor and an agreeable companion, one whom I am happy to have known. I was lucky in my tutor who afterwards became president of Merton College and so vice-chancelor of the University of Oxford, served as an offi-

cer in the first World War and published some notable
books. I was also fortunate in knowing Professor Walter
Raleigh. [5]

Sports at Oxford were not compulsory but obligatory.
Each student was expected to play on some college or
university team, because hard exercise was considered
necessary to maintain good health. But Walter found
most British sports somewhat beyond his Yankee talents.
Early during his first year he tried out for the Rugby
team, without benefit of instruction. The "uninformed
American was continually doing the wrong thing," he
wrote. At the end of the match the team captain told
him: "You know, Campbell, I don't think I can use you
again." So Walter tried lacrosse, which suited him better
because it was an American Indian game imported by
England. He played tennis and soccer with moderate
success, did some rowing in boat races, and in his free
time went boating, hiking and cycling over much of
England. But he could not do the one thing he loved
above all else – ride horseback. His one regret at Oxford
was that he "could not afford to ride to the hounds."

The traditional British tea time brought only scorn
from Walter at first. He had "never had tea before. Men
didn't drink tea in my country," he wrote. But eventually
he became completely British in this respect. The thing
that converted him to a tea sipper was the realization
that an Oxford tea party was "just like a Cheyenne feast."
Everyone sat on the floor, shoved his plate under the
sofa, smoked and talked. The various English traits he
learned to admire the most were those most similar to
American Indian traits.

But Cheyenne camps had more women than men in
them. Oxford had only men. "This rotten system of not
having co-education makes one long for feminine com-

---

[5] *Ibid.*

pany, and desirable feminine company is not to be had here except in the summer time," he wrote. He liked "a community of men" but "with women to break the monotony." [6] But "proper maidens" were seldom seen by Oxford students, and "the other type" was all too easily met. Walter viewed the situation a bit scornfully because "there are more rescue homes for unwed pregnant females here than in any city in the kingdom in proportion to its population." He preferred co-education and "its accompanying morality." [7]

At the end of his beginning term at Oxford, Walter made his first trip to the continent, arriving in France early in December 1908. A snowstorm hampered but did not prevent his touring the country. He arrived in Paris December 18 and spent Christmas there.

Only a small portion of the vacation was play. Oxford had three eight-week terms to a school year, each of the first two followed by six-week vacations at Christmas and Easter, and the third one followed by a sixteen weeks' summer vacation. Students started vacations by going to London for a week, then to some remote country spot, some village where there was swimming or tennis or something to keep them fit. They spent four weeks at hard reading in preparation for examinations when they returned to the University. The quizzes were given at the end of the vacation and did not come at the end of the term. During the term at Oxford they did not have enough time for study, so had to do much of it during the vacation. Groups of four or five vacationed together, often taking a tutor along to direct their studies. This was called a reading party. The final week of vacation they spent in London also, going to theaters, museums, concerts or what-not. Walter usually had to wire the Rhodes Trust for an advance before the vacation was over

[6] Letter, Campbell to his mother, Nov. 8, 1908.
[7] Campbell diary, Oct. 27, 1908.

because he found "the stipend hardly adequate for the sort of life that Oxonians live." [8]

Actually, Walter's money troubles – which became a routine part of his life – went considerably deeper than inadequate funds from the Rhodes trust. From Oxford he acquired the notion that gentlemen spent most of their lives in debt. It was the proper and gentlemanly thing to do. This notion was to cause him considerable heartbreak in later years. Even while at Oxford he piled up debts, borrowing heavily from his parents.

Once the next term began, Walter soon settled into a routine of study, social gatherings and travel. Study he found rather easy. "My tutor is such a slacker that I almost entirely set my own pace, which . . . is apt to be a very leisurely one." [9] Later he learned the leisurely pace accomplished more than he had thought earlier. His tutor, George Gordon,

> was a genial soul. . . . On fine days he would take me out into the deer park and we would sit on a log or bench while the dappled deer grazed around us. There I would read my essay and he would criticize it and tell me where I had muffed the subject and tell me what to read to correct it, advising me that so and so would be on the examining board and he was a fanatic about Robert Burns just in case, and all that sort of practical advice which was so very helpful. On other occasions he would bring out two or three fellows together. We would have a discussion and an argument in which he always took the weaker side against the strong so as to give everybody a chance to say what we had to say and to present his argument to his best advantage. . . . And then on cloudy days he would take me down to the senior common room under the dining room and the tower of a sort of gloomy basement. [10]

[8] Autobiographical data.

[9] Letters, Campbell to his parents, Feb. 28, 1909.

[10] Autobiographical data.

Walter made his first appearance before the chief dons of Merton on March 15, 1909, in the senior common room. The dons faced him across a table and discussed his progress. A report from his tutor was read, showing he "continued to do good work." They also gave him advice for continued progress.

Like most Britishers of that day, Walter traveled by bicycle. A young chap named Morris owned the shop which serviced his bicycle. Occasionally, when his assistants were busy, Morris pumped up the tires for him. Later Morris invented the Morris car and became the Henry Ford of England.

Much as Walter liked England, he hated the damp and often sunless climate, and longed for his plains country. "I can't see how one who knows what sunshine is could fall fearfully in love with England," he wrote. [11]

The final term of the year ended June 19 and he sailed for home ten days later. But his visit to Oklahoma was short. He and J. R. soon went to Chicago where J. R. enrolled for graduate study at the University of Chicago and Walter prepared for the exams due on his return to Oxford in October. They found some time for relaxation, however. When Buffalo Bill Cody brought his wild west show to town Walter renewed his acquaintance with the old hunter and scout. This was something of a mistake, however, for it made him homesick.

Later in the summer a Rhodes Scholar friend of Walter's from an eastern city came to Chicago and stopped to visit him. During one of their bull sessions Walter found out the dude had never heard a coyote howl, so they went to the Chicago zoo. "I took him to the wolf cage and started my falsetto whine [which he had learned from his pet coyote a few years earlier]. Sure enough the wolves began to howl." Walter was not quite pre-

---

[11] Letter, Campbell to his mother, May 29, 1909.

pared for what followed, however. "The crowds and the police came running and we got out of there as quickly as we could without running." [12]

In September, Walter sailed again for England, this time not quite so eagerly, and not without some homesickness. Aboard ship "the salt spray drizzles on me . . . until my face tastes salty. I prefer dust." [13]

The fall term started October 9. Soon afterward Walter made another discovery of later importance to Stanley Vestal. With no short grass country to roam across, no Indians to visit and interview, he turned to books and manuscripts for vicarious adventures. The world famous Bodleian Library of Oxford contained just about everything of this nature he might want. Back in one dusty corner he found an unpublished diary of Pierre Esprit Radisson. Walter read and re-read, just about memorizing, the personal experiences of the French explorer and fur trader who discovered the Mississippi River and Lake Superior. Through the long hours of that second Oxford winter he read how Radisson founded Hudson's Bay Company and of his other exploits as a hunter, trapper, trader, diplomat and officer in the French navy. This reading strengthened his growing ambition to write about the exploits of such men. To his mother he confided: "I am becoming interested in prose and prose-writing. This is obviously the art which appeals most to the present age." [14]

All of the Oxford influence obviously had a part in this drift toward writing, particularly Sir Walter Raleigh and George Gordon. Perhaps he also was influenced by another Rhodes Scholar of that time who shared his writing interests, one Elmer Davis, also destined to achieve considerable fame as a writer.

---

[12] *Ibid.*, to his daughter, Dorothy, May 6, 1950.
[13] *Ibid.*, to J. R. Campbell, Sept. 28, 1909.
[14] *Ibid.*, to his mother, Feb. 10, 1910.

At the end of his second year Walter attended a luncheon honoring Kermit Roosevelt, then left for Germany and Holland. Despite his longing for the plains country, he spent the entire summer vacation traveling and studying in Europe and England, more of it in Switzerland than anywhere else. Enroute back to Oxford that autumn he stopped off in Paris.

Any remaining doubt about Walter's future evaporated during his final year at Oxford. He begun work on several "pieces of literature" and wrote home about his plans for research among the Indians in western Oklahoma. He decided that it was "high time someone gave the Indians a decent character and a portrait of something more than the crude caricature or romantic impression which at present make up the general share of literature on this subject." [15]

Walter's first book length work appears to have been *Sallow Moon*, which he had privately printed twenty-seven years later after he had become a successful writer. Why he paid to have it published is not known, for his prestige by then was considerable. No known copies are still in existence, but excerpts from it printed in one of his textbooks indicate it included instructions on how to write. It was published under the pen name of Walter D. Merton, of obvious derivation. He did not rate the book highly, and never listed it among his published work.

Walter's early philosophy of writing was that of the intellectual. He wrote:

> The average magazine writer does not write literature. He writes for money. It is doubtful whether such a writer pulls any weight at all. He draws a big cheque perhaps but he produces no lasting work, nothing therefore that appeals to the lasting qualities of human feel-

---

[15] *Ibid.*, to his parents, Oct. 8, 1910.

ing. Except in so far as such a person encourages the reading habit he is a parasite, as much as any other parasite. [16]

How greatly this concept was to change in succeeding decades. But many notions about writing acquired while at Oxford were to stay with him permanently. A particular one was

not to write from notes, but to digest my notes and write without them the next day. This is the way to write well, because the reader is asking you to speak your piece, and not just to repeat what other people have said before, as you will do if you have notes under your nose when you write. [17]

Walter realized he would have to support himself in some profession while devoting his efforts toward writing, so he reluctantly began preparation for a temporary teaching career.

I do not look forward with any degree of pleasure to my work as a teacher. I regard it, I fear, as a temporary bore, as a means to a living merely. Whether I have the ability or not, I have some confidence and a great determination to write if I have to starve for it. [18]

During his final spring semester he was offered a scholarship to Harvard for graduate study but turned it down. "I cannot see that any college will help me much now. . . . What I need for writing is time (and practice) and therefore money." [19]

This final year also saw the development of a strong friendship between Walter and a freshman at Oxford, one Christopher Morley, who also was possessed with ambition to conquer the literary world. As he had done

[16] *Ibid.*, to his grandmother, Jan. 31, 1911.
[17] *Ibid.*, to Sidney Ohmart, Mar. 18, 1953.
[18] *Ibid.*, to his grandmother, Feb. 11, 1911.
[19] *Ibid.*, to his parents, Apr. 16, 1911.

with another who had ambitions to write – Elmer Davis – Walter found a kindred soul in Morley. They renewed this friendship in later years after Morley became one of England's most famous writers.

The long awaited graduation day arrived in June of 1911. J. R., Daisy, and Hazel Brockway, a family friend from Arapaho, Oklahoma, made the long trip to England to see Walter read for honors and receive his bachelor's degree in English language and literature. Then Walter showed them the sights in England and part of Europe during the remainder of the summer months. The family sailed from Liverpool for New York on August 18, 1911, closing the Oxford chapter of Walter's development. He arrived home owing his parents $2,000 he had spent above the $4,500 scholarship.

The Lean Years

Walter had little time for renewing old friendships in Colony before he left for Oklahoma Agricultural and Mechanical College, Stillwater, to be interviewed for a teaching job there. Once he learned the duties of the job, he lost all enthusiasm for it so he felt no disappointment when someone else was selected. Instead, he accepted a $1,200-a-year job at Mechanical High School in Louisville, Kentucky, teaching English, Latin and algebra. He arrived in Louisville on September 24, 1911, with no real enthusiasm for this job either. The superintendent greeted him cordially and explained his duties. Then he told Walter the school had four hundred boys, "none of whom goes to school to learn." [1]

Walter settled down to the rather sedate life of a high school teacher, nine hundred miles northeast of the prairie country where his spirit roamed. He often attended theater productions, went hiking and generally tried to adjust to his sedate life, but never quite made it. Living alone, far from home, left him plenty of time for writing, but nothing to write about. He soon developed a strong urge to go among the Cheyenne for research material to use in his writing. He also chafed at the restraint of life as a school teacher. By mid-term he was near the point of rebellion. He decided:

> I like boys – as boys – not as pupils. I am not enthusiastic over my work, or my pupils. I do not believe (1) in

[1] Letter, Campbell to his parents, Sept. 23, 1911; and to Mrs. Lucille Houston, Oct. 1, 1954.

indoor education   (2) in the hodge-podge book learning
that goes with it.   . .

But I will starve to death with only fresh air in my
belly out on the plains before I will teach longer than
that in any dusty hole that goes by the name of a house
of education.   . . [he longed] to get the soot out of
my lungs where folks are not so plentiful and there is
room to think. [2]

The one saving grace for Walter that first year in
Louisville came to him by accident. He attended a lecture
at the University of Louisville on "The Art of the Plains
Indian" as told by Frederick Weygold. The lecture filled
Walter with new ambition to write. After it was over
he went up to the speaker's platform, introduced himself,
and soon had acquired a valuable new friend. Weygold
told him about his ten years of collecting Indian objects
for German museums, and of his work as a painter of
Indian subjects. Weygold spoke Sioux and the plains
Indian sign language, and was a personal friend of most
principal men in the Teton (Ogalala) Sioux tribe. Most
important, "He was the man who gave me the key to
the understanding of the Indian – which is to understand
his religion." [3]

Walter invited his new friend to his home, and the
two spent a lot of time together that spring. They exchanged knowledge, with Walter learning new techniques
for research. In addition to his art, Weygold was the
author of numerous papers published in German publications about the Indians. "His friendship was especially
valuable inasmuch as he was an artist, so that his point
of view was parallel to my own," Walter wrote. [4]

Despite his time with Weygold, Walter still experienced
long periods of despondency. In despair he turned to play

---

[2] *Ibid.,* to his parents, Nov. 11, 1911.

[3] Campbell diary, Jan. 22, 1922.   [4] Autobiographical data.

writing as a means of overcoming his depression. This helped for a while. Still, he wrote, "I am tired of my job. I won't live in this barbarous way another year." He thought he might be able to earn a living by writing, but at contract signing he agreed to return to Louisville for another year. He simply had no other way to earn a living.

A summer at Colony among the Indians gave Walter enough vigor to return to Louisville in the autumn for another try at high school teaching. He transferred to Male High School, however, which he thought might be better. He also took on a part-time job teaching English and medical Latin several hours weekly at the Louisville Dental College. He was more interested in writing plays and scenarios, the latter of which he turned out two each week. None sold, however.

This second year turned out worse than the first for the rebellious Walter. Louisville simply was too far from the short grass country and Cheyenne camps, other high school teachers disgusted him with their attitudes and incompetency, and high school boys in that eastern city did not measure up to his outdoorsman notions. The boys gave him the firebug treatment the second year, building fires in his desk. [5] One day a basket of paper was set on fire in the toilet. Walter was the first to arrive at the source of the smoke, and soon had it extinguished. Another fire started in a teacher's desk the same day. A fire engine, hosecart and hook-and-ladder rig rushed there, but the fire went out of itself, much to the disappointment of most of the students.

Walter struggled through the school year with ever increasing dissatisfaction, and with the growing determination "to stop teaching now and forever. . . I set out to be a writer and a writer I will be." He felt

---

[5] Personal interview with Dwight V. Swain.

a "strong distaste . . . for teaching, and condemnation of the methods, matter and men in education." [6]

Despite his attitude, Walter could find no better way to earn a living and was forced to agree to return for another year in the Louisville school system.

Walter encountered his first really hostile treatment from the Cheyennes in the summer of 1913 at a sundance camp in western Oklahoma. The camp lasted several weeks before the three-day dance, and at first Walter roamed about freely without trouble. But he found few old friends from Colony there. Most of the five thousand Cheyenne present either came from other parts of the Cheyenne-Arapaho country or did not know him very well.

Shortly before the sun dance started, Walter accidentally witnessed the medicine arrow ceremony from a distance. The four sacred arrows, two with power over animals and two with power over humans, were in the custody of the tribe's most trusted warrior. In time of battle, the keeper of the arrows would point them at the enemy to make him easier to defeat. Always carefully guarded, the arrows were never shown to white men. Although the Cheyennes were no longer at war, they preserved the sacred arrows as a symbol of the spiritual soul of the tribe. Walter's glimpse of the arrows was one of his most satisfying moments among the Cheyennes that summer. [7]

But with the sun dance drawing closer, Vestal found himself the target of hostile glances wherever he went, especially from the young men who did not know him. Part of the reason became apparent to him when an old warrior began riding through the camp announcing that Woo-cha-ih, Man-in-White-Hat, was there to spy on them

---

[6] Letter, Campbell to his parents, May 11, 1913.

[7] Stan Hoig, "Medicine Arrows," in *Oklahoma Today,* Spring, 1962, pp. 26-38.

and interfere with their religious rites. Walter was wearing a white Panama hat. [8]

The sun dance, which Walter had witnessed twice before, was frowned on by the federal government. In fact, many attempts had been made to suppress it, due to the self-inflicted pain to the dancers and the illicit sex act which came at the end of the dance. Those who knew Walter laughed at the notion that he was a government spy, but others remained unconvinced. After all, they pointed out, he had been gone from that area for many years and could have taken such employment. At any rate, he remained very much under the watchful eyes of five thousand Cheyennes. An Indian policeman named Big Man began following him everywhere. Big Man was so fat he could not sit on the ground, and had to carry a three-legged stool with him, but he did not let Walter get out of his sight.

One wizened old warrior approached Walter and asked him in sign language if he were not afraid that a herd of horses would run over him and kill him. Not aware that such a plan for killing him was under consideration, Walter was rather nonchalant about the question and the old warrior went away. The adage that the best way to commit suicide was to interfere with a man's religion was as true with the Cheyennes as with other races.

The self-torture part of the sun dance came when participants stuck skewers through the muscles of their chests and attached these by thongs to the end of a rope hanging down from a pole around which they danced. During the dance, each participant lunged back until he broke loose, tearing the chest muscles. Objections were expected from the "government spy" over such antics, but Walter watched in silence and ignored his watchers.

On the final day of the dance, Big Man stuck closely to Walter, as usual. When it came time for the sex act,

[8] *Ibid.*; and letter, Campbell to Dr. R. T. House, Sept. 30, 1946.

Big Man approached him and assured him there was
nothing more to see that night. This amused Walter.
Having seen the dance twice before, he knew it was time
for the chief to take one of the leading women of the
tribe into a teepee for sexual intercourse as a symbol
of tribal fertility. But, having no desire to watch the
act, Walter willingly went away with Big Man.

It was some months later when a Cheyenne friend,
Paul Goose, told Walter the reason for the hostility
toward him. For some reason the Indian agent at Can-
tonment had taken a dislike to Walter and spread the
word that he had come there as a government spy. Walter
suffered no ill effects, and even received his first Indian
name – Man-in-White-Hat – although there was no particular honor attached to the name. [9]

Despite his pleasure-filled summer, Walter felt no better
about his job that fall. The day the new term began he
wrote: "It seems I am to have six classes filled with the
usual allowance of rough-necks and half-witted." He
simply was bored with the lack of anything to do except
teach, and frustrated by the lack of money to do what
he really wanted most – travel and research among the
plains tribes, and write about what he learned.

Actually, Walter did do a little more than teach. He
engaged in considerable research of a second hand variety,
reading all sorts of printed material about Indians. But
he longed for first hand research, the basis for all good
fact writing. He began a book about Indian teepees, and
wrote numerous magazine articles and short stories about
Indians and the Old West, with little success at publishing them. As the rejection slips mounted, he became more
determined to find out why he could not succeed.

Finally Walter decided to accept the offer of his parents
and live at home in Arapaho while doing research among
the Indians there. "After all," he wrote mother, "the

---

[9] *Ibid.,* and to Malory Campbell, Sept. 25, 1957.

plains is the only habitat for me. . . I want to produce the book on the tent of the plains, and make it the final word on that subject." [10] He had other books in mind also, but wanted to start with one about the teepee.

Naturally, one last incident had to occur to sour him on Louisville even more, although neither the city nor the school was responsible. A smallpox epidemic broke out there, resulting in a city-wide vaccination program. Walter's arm became infected from the vaccination and his doctor told him it would have to be amputated immediately. But a friend rushed him to a Jewish hospital where a Jewish surgeon of greater skill saved his arm. Thirty years later Walter still felt grateful to that Jewish doctor, and bitter toward the county health officer who vaccinated him and the physician who had nearly amputated his arm. The hospital bill cleaned out the savings Walter had planned to use for research, but this did not lessen his determination to return to the plains.

The prospect of getting back to the short grass country perked up Walter in the spring of 1914. In his final weeks at Louisville he wrote several caustic statements about his job there. "I give up in disgust, trying to teach a lot of young devils their lines in the farce called high school education." He referred to his stay at the boys' school as being

> in jail. I thank God daily for my soon deliverance from this place, and would pray for the destruction of the inhabitants as well, if they were not sufficiently cursed in abiding here. . . I desire only to escape from this accursed home and this damnable trade. . . The whole nation might die with its head in my lap before I would teach another day's school. . . I wish I had disposed of myself in some other way before I descended to be the keeper of swine, and a companion to owls. [11]

---

[10] Letter, Campbell to his parents, Feb. 9, 1914.
[11] *Ibid.*, Apr. 5, 1914.

With this attitude, it was no surprise that Walter rejected an offer from a family friend, University of Oklahoma President S. D. Brooks, to teach there that fall. This would have put him within easy distance of the Cheyenne, but at a salary of only $900 a year compared to the $1,200 he received at Louisville. More importantly, the job meant teaching and Walter wanted no more of that.

Although anxious to get back to the plains, Walter went from Louisville to Chicago for research in the plains Indian section of a museum there, living with two Oxford friends. Finally, he went west, determined to succeed at writing or starve. [12]

From Arapaho, Walter chased Cheyennes all over Western Oklahoma, only to run up against the same silence he had always encountered concerning their battles. He found plenty of other areas they would discuss, however, for he was well-known to many of those he interviewed. George Bent, the half-breed, and Ben Clark, the old scout, helped him more than anyone else, since neither was reluctant to tell what they knew of the warpath days. Walter also measured the teepees of different tribes and learned to make and set up each type. For long periods of time he camped out with various tribes, making hundreds of sketches and acquired a trunk load of notes.

The generosity of the plains Indians made it possible for Walter to remain among them for extended periods, because

No plains Indian ever went hungry while another man of his tribe had meat in his tipi. The Indian required no invitation to the feast; it was his *right* to share with all men of his own blood, and he walked right in, sat down, and expected to be served. Moreover, he *was* served; the Indian was nothing if not hospitable. . .

[12] Campbell diary, Jan. 22, 1922.

Only once have I seen this custom violated – under
provocation. I once invited myself to dinner in a strange
camp of Indians, when I was miles from home. The
old warrior – who had evidently been so used by some
stingy white man – led me out, handed me the ax, and
pointed to the woodpile. I knew Indians well enough
to realize what caused him to act so, and I began to
make the chips fly. Before I could split a second stick,
he took the ax from me, led me in, and told his wife
to serve me.

Some weeks later, when passing that way, I made it
a point to repay his hospitality by carrying a big water-
melon into his tent and placing it before him. The old
man sat there speechless, hanging his head in shame.
I had had no intention of embarrassing him, and hurried
out, as ill-at-ease as he was. [13]

After a year of this research, Walter found himself
unable to make a living at it. For the year's work he
sold only two articles to the *American Anthropologist*,
one describing the Cheyenne three-pole foundation-type
teepee, the other the four-pole teepee of the Crows. He
received only fifteen dollars for the first, and nothing
for the second until twelve years later.

Depressed beyond anything he had ever known, Walter
realized by the summer of 1915 he was beaten. The
experiment had added to his understanding of Indians,
and to his debts. This left him in a receptive mood when
President Brooks once again offered him a teaching job
at Oklahoma University. That fall he became the youngest faculty member at the university, ranked as an instructor at $900 a year salary. At least he could tramp
over the plains country and continue his research whenever the notion struck him.

Norman and the university combined were hardly more
than a few buildings huddled on the prairie when Walter
arrived there in September of 1915. The only cab was

---

[13] Vestal, *Short Grass Country*, p. 262.

a black horse-drawn affair also used for funerals. Walter
rode out to the campus on the south side of town in a
horse-drawn bus with steps and entrance in the rear.
The campus was spotted with buffalo wallows. Buildings
included only an old wooden gymnasium, the administration building, a science hall, law building, and library.
The student body and faculty were modest in size, and
Walter soon knew them all by their first names. At that
time it was required that student dances have one married couple and one single man as chaperones. Walter
often served as the bachelor chaperone, and got to know
the students socially. In fact, one of the deans referred
to him as just a member of the student body.

> When a dance was being given for the three fraterni-
> ties and three sororities in the city, the men of one
> fraternity would charter a bus, visit the three sororities
> and pick up their dates. And the second fraternity, in
> order of seniority, would do the same, the third follow-
> ing. Thus everybody got to the dance on wheels. [14]

Walter soon decided he had made a wise choice in
going to Oklahoma University. Here students were more
interested in learning what he tried to teach, quite a
contrast to the attitude of high school boys toward literature. This brought out the best in Walter who soon
achieved the reputation of being a "brilliant young teacher." He was "filled with interesting details about literature and writers." His special field at that time was
literary criticism, especially Browning. [15]

Demands on Walter's time were not so great at Oklahoma University, leaving him more time for writing and
research. Administrative policies pleased him also, especially the liberal and progressive attitude of President
Brooks toward education, and his sense of frontier humor.

----

[14] Len White, "The Triumph of Stanley Vestal," in *Sooner Magazine,* Oct. 1957, pp. 5, 7.

[15] Interview with Dr. Fayette Copeland.

Walter loved to quote the president's comparison of the Oklahoma University campus on the south side of town with the state mental hospital on the east side of town, the "east campus." According to Walter, the president said, "The only difference is that to graduate from one of these, you must show signs of mental improvement." [16]

Walter soon began to publish articles in newspapers, in the University magazine, and in a syndicated magazine supplement, *Oklahoma Monthly*, which was inserted in "leading country papers" of the state. The editor of the supplement was his old friend, Walter Ferguson of Watonga.

As he achieved this quite modest success at writing, Walter became a little worried because so many people by the name of Campbell were publishing articles and books at that time. He decided he needed a pen name that would be more distinctive. When he mentioned it to his mother, she said: "Why don't you write under your own name?" She meant, of course, the name with which he was born. The idea appealed to him, so Stanley Vestal was born again. At the university he remained the scholarly Walter S. Campbell, but to his growing number of readers he became the Indian expert and outdoorsman Stanley Vestal. [17]

Money troubles which had plagued Walter since his early days at Oxford had multiplied with his fifteen months unemployment prior to going to Oklahoma University. His university salary of $100 a month for nine months did not make it possible for him to reduce his debts any. Fees from writing were hardly worth the trouble at that time. Still, Walter remained the optimist, always hoping to catch up soon by writing and selling something big.

In March of 1916 Walter was admitted to the degree

---

[16] Autobiographical data.
[17] Letter, Campbell to Paul Flowers, May 5, 1947.

of master of arts at Oxford University. He acquired this
degree by keeping his name on the college books and
paying a nominal annual fee. It was "to all intents and
purposes an honorary degree." [18]

The president notified Walter in April 1916, that his
salary for the next school year would be raised to $1,000.
But this failed to arouse much joy in him, for what he
needed was a big literary jackpot. He decided "that
money is the inevitable answer to every question I ask
of life – the one end of every quest." Seeking it, he spent
the summer among the Cheyennes again, trying to break
through the barrier of the old warriors who still refused
to talk about their wars. That was the sort of information needed for a literary jackpot, but it eluded Walter
still.

The autumn term of 1916 found Walter twenty-nine
years old and "quite taken" with one of his freshman
students, Isabel Jones of Oklahoma City. Professors dat-
ing coeds was not frowned on in those days as much as
later years. Walter found it

> hard to dwell effectively on the merits of love lyrics –
> of which our text is largely composed – with everyone
> in the room thoroughly aware that your best girl is in
> the front row of the class. Believe me, I need all the
> dignity and control Oxford and Cheyennedom ever gave
> me. [19]

Unfortunately for Walter, Isabel was engaged to another professor in the English Department, L. N. Morgan.
And a third man, apparently another professor named
John, made it a quadrangle affair of the heart. Isabel
shared the interest of Walter and his best friend, Paul
Carpenter, in writing, which gave Walter an opportunity
to be with her often. In fact, he and Paul brought Isabel

---

[18] *Ibid.,* to Leonard B. Beach, Sept. 29, 1947.
[19] *Ibid.,* to his mother, Oct. 29, 1916.

into their "firm" and collaborated on writing a movie script. Morgan became

> rather worried by the frequent conferences we have. He is so far gone that he regards all men with suspicion. If my hopes were as great as his suspicions he would have cause. She is a good scout and restores my faith in human nature – which I had almost lost. Her very presence is healing. And she is witty and clever – else we wouldn't have taken her into the firm. And for looks – zowie! [20]

Walter must have had Morgan more worried than he thought, for Morgan told him of a job in Boston in an effort to get him away from Norman and Isabel.

Despite Isabel's betrothal, Walter managed some dates with her that winter while the "firm" knocked out three movie scripts. None of the scripts sold, however. The rejections merely strengthened their determination to find more time for writing. "Jonesy and I both need the money, and I am bound to have it," Walter wrote. [21]

When he took Isabel to a Kappa Alpha dance in January 1917, he was hopelessly lost to her charms. The next day he poured out his feelings in a letter home:

> She is certainly some queen – beautiful, brainy, witty, and a good scout. . . Good Lord, why wasn't that girl twins? What does a man do to deserve a girl like that? I had rather have the left over dates with Jonesy than be married to most of them . . . or have all they have to give. She has restored my faith in human nature, and has made life seem more worth living. [22]

Even when he could not take Isabel to dances, Walter went stag and danced with her often. No college freshman could have had a worse case of what he called "girlitis." By late February Walter could stand it no

[20]*Ibid.*, Dec. 6, 1916. [21] *Ibid.*, Jan. 6 and 14, 1917.
[22] *Ibid.*, Jan. 6, 1917.

longer. Walking across the campus with Isabel, he told her he loved her. "Isabel was rather startled. . . I had to tell her. I had kept my secret until I was bursting with it." She did not return his love, but that did not discourage him. "Winning Isabel will be no easy task. . . Nobody could love her more than I do." [23]

Walter tried a little too hard to win Isabel's affections, however. Three weeks after he declared his love, Isabel told him rather firmly not to ask for more dates. This rejection, accompanied by another on their latest movie script, filled him with a hopeless frustration. In despair he wrote "mama" for advice. "Am I to take her at her word and never ask for a date again?" [24]

For nearly a month Walter did take her at her word, until she asked him to get her a cartridge belt and gun to wear to a costume dance she was attending with her fiance. Typically, he spent the day rounding up an entire western costume for her, which made quite an impression. "I was very pleased that I did all this for her," he wrote home. [25]

Five days later the United States entered World War I. Walter immediately volunteered for the first Reserve Officer Training Corps unit – in the cavalry, of course. He was not called into active service until mid-May, which was long enough for him to finally lose all hope of winning Isabel. He gave up the fight, and wrote home that he really did not love her. Perhaps he even convinced himself, momentarily.

[23] *Ibid.*, Jan. 15 and Feb. 21, 1917.
[24] *Ibid.*, Mar. 16, 1917.   [25] *Ibid.*, Apr. 1, 1917.

Boots and Saddles

Like many doughboys of the first World War, Walter Campbell went off to what he called "the glorious adventure" only to have it turn sour on him rather quickly. He was one of ninety cadets to arrive at Little Rock, Arkansas, May 15, 1917. They boarded trucks and headed for nearby Fort Logan H. Roots, climbing up a long winding road to the fort on a high rocky bluff overlooking the Arkansas River and Little Rock. Here they found themselves part of two thousand cadets in the nation's first Reserve Officer Training Corps, "knee-deep in dust and deprived of individual rights." [1]

With his fellow cadets, Campbell was issued two blankets and a canvas bed sack, then told to fill the latter with hay. Next they were assigned quarters in a barracks twenty by two hundred feet long, with rows of cots three feet apart. Then came the well-known army medical processing. They were marched through a chute onto a screened porch for physicals and vaccinations. Campbell pointed to a smallpox vaccination scar, one that nearly cost him his arm, and said it was not yet eighteen months old. The medic vaccinated him anyway, replying, "This one is not eighteen seconds old."

Two days after his arrival Campbell lined up with the other cadets in close order by companies on the drill ground, facing a barracks. A group of dignitaries sat on the second-story gallery, watching the formation. The governor of Arkansas made a speech, followed by a Jewish

---

[1] Letters, Campbell to his parents, May 20, 1917, and one undated.

rabbi, while a military band provided the sound effects. Campbell wrote:

> All the speakers complimented us, advised us, and ended up by laying wreaths on our graves! Then we put our hats on our left breasts and raised our hands while the oath was read and the men said "I do," listening to the ticking of their wrist watches. It was a solemn occasion and a handsome one. [2]

Campbell's oath was for three months' service as a private. He "swore away life, liberty and the pursuit of happiness." Actually, he and the others remained technically civilians for the duration of their officer training program. His service record dates his enlistment as starting three months later.

The cadet captain of Campbell's company was a "major in the reserves and an old ass . . . a Spanish war veteran who can't give an intelligent order and who inspires neither liking nor respect." But Campbell rated his instructor very highly. His daily routine was the usual drilling, manual-at-arms and so forth, along with yard bird, kitchen police, and "gunnery at a glance."

On his fifth day in camp Campbell indicated a complete lack of sympathy for military life and became "heartily in favor of exterminating the people who do like it, and who have forced it on the rest of us." [3] The camp, which had only a bank, post office, one barber shop and four showers for two thousand men, did not make him feel any more kindly toward military life.

Campbell did develop a strong liking for his battery commander, Captain Phillip Booker, a profane and fiery little man. "He was the idol of us all," and his battery looked forward to the day when he would become regimental commander in place of the colonel they disliked so heartily – and profanely.

---

[2] *Ibid.*, to his mother, May 20, 1917.   [3] *Ibid.*

Like most soldiers early in their training periods, Campbell missed home and social life. He even gave some thought to marriage after getting his commission. "I don't know who the lucky girl will be, though I think some one I know already would do. But she hasn't written me even a card since I came here." [4]

The one he already knew who would do, came to the camp several weekends to see her fiance, who also was there for training. This proved both a joy and a thorn to Campbell. He did not care to serve with his rival, but it gave him an opportunity to see Isabel occasionally, and even talk to her. In early June she and a friend drove over from Oklahoma University for the weekend. Campbell saw her at dinner and talked with her briefly. "I half suspect she is already married to her fiance," he wrote home. [5]

During his first thirty days of training, Campbell was in the cavalry although he did not get near a horse or wear a uniform. Then he was transferred to the Field Artillery, which pleased him more because horses were used more in the artillery than elsewhere, including the cavalry. His knowledge of horses soon proved to be a valuable asset. To his many other methods of horseback riding he now added army style, and how to play polo. It was almost enough to make him like the army.

Instruction in artillery began three days after the transfer. Just training the cadets to function as a battery had both exasperating and humorous moments. Campbell wrote:

> The first day out one team turned too short and upset a caisson at a walk! Naturally the canoneers tumbled off their seats at once. It is hard enough to stay there when the caisson is right side up. . . Such incidents occur almost everyday in the regulars when the man or horses feel good. You see, Field Artillery is not a lady-

[4] *Ibid.,* to his parents, May 27, 1917.   [5] *Ibid.,* June 8, 1917.

like branch of the service. It is all sweat and roughness and dirty work with horses and heavy guns and dirty harness. . . The gun drills involve six horses to a team with 17-yard intervals between. This makes it hard to drill them as a voice won't carry. So arm signals and whistles are used. . . This is Field Artillery. I wouldn't belong to anything else except aviation for anything. In aviation you are responsible for yourself alone. I am, I fear, incurably an individualist and a spectator of life. But with all of my interest and love of outdoor life and realizing the equal danger, dirt and roughness of the two existences, I would much prefer the old Cheyenne way of life to the soldier way. I do not take kindly to discipline or orders. It takes all of my spirit of patriotism and pride in folks, my battery and my country to make me swallow it. [6]

Isabel began to write letters to Campbell after some of her visits to camp. They were rather impersonal, at first, addressing him as Mr. Campbell. By July she was calling him w. s. On one of her visits he invited her to a dance on her next trip. She delayed a decision until she returned to Norman, then had to decline because she had decided not to make the trip on the day of the dance. [7]

Near the end of training Campbell became discouraged about his chances of getting a commission. He had been hoping to get a first lieutenant's rank. Now he decided he would be better off transferring to aviation, so he went to the quarters of his battery commander, Captain Booker. It was the lunch hour, but the first sergeant told Campbell to go on in to Booker's room. Campbell found the captain lying on the bed. In a formal manner, Campbell requested a transfer to the new Air Corps. Booker said nothing, but just lay on the bed laughing. Campbell stood at attention, getting red in the face, until the situation became intolerable. Then he saluted and

[6] *Ibid.*, July 12, 1917.

[7] *Ibid.*, from Isabel Jones to Campbell, July 6, 1917.

went out, leaving Captain Booker chuckling on the bed.

A few days later Campbell learned the reason for Booker's reaction to his transfer request. Recommendations for commissions had already been made, and Campbell had been recommended for the rank of captain, but Booker could not tell him about it before the official announcement was made.

Campbell's liking for the battery commander increased accordingly. Later he wrote: "I have sometimes suspected that I was commissioned because I could cuss nearly as well as he [Booker] could." Actually, Campbell's talent for handling horses played the biggest role in his selection, for horses were the key to artillery during World War I.

The commission as a captain in the Field Artillery came on Campbell's thirtieth birthday, August 15, 1917. However, many of his friends, including Paul Carpenter, flunked out. This distressed Campbell, but he wrote home happily that Isabel's fiance had failed to make the grade in the first camp and had been placed in the second group for additional training. [8]

The successful candidates were assigned to the 335th Field Artillery, 87th Division, and would be stationed at the newly constructed Camp Pike a few miles away upon their return from their first furloughs home. Campbell would command Battery F. Commissioned with him as a second lieutenant and placed in the next battery was Robert Samuel Kerr, later to become governor of and United States senator from Oklahoma. The two became good friends, for they shared a common admiration for rugged individualism. Kerr later described Campbell as "a gentleman and natural leader of men. His outfit competed very well every time it was put to the test." [9]

---

[8] *Ibid.,* to his parents, Aug. 9, 1917.

[9] *Ibid.,* to his parents, Aug. 9, 1917; to Hal Muldrow, Jr., Apr. 10, 1944; and from Robert S. Kerr to Ray Tassin, June 18, 1962, in the author's possession.

Just before leaving on his furlough Campbell wrote his parents that he wanted to see Isabel in Norman while enroute home. Norman was not far out of the way to Thomas, Oklahoma, where J. R. was then superintendent of schools. "You've no idea how one's absence makes the heart grow fonder," Campbell wrote. "That woman has got to love me." But he held little hope that Isabel would ever have him, and he was unable to visit her as planned. [10]

When the newly commissioned officers of the 335th Field Artillery returned from furlough early in September 1917, they were ordered to pack up for the move to nearby Camp Pike still under construction. [11]

> We piled all of our effects into motor-trucks, mounted on top of them and rode away amid a cloud of dust and a cracking cut-out over the ruttiest of roads to Camp Pike. Just as we reached the entrance to the camp it began to rain and what with the oiled roads and the mud and the traffic we stalled and skidded and got hung up during the remaining mile and a half of our journey. . . There isn't enough level ground to form a company. And what there is is filled with logs and lumber and cut up with ditches and foundation cuttings. The whole camp is a mess of frame buildings spread over rolling timbered country and populated by soldiers, laborers and vehicles of every sort. Some ten thousand laborers are here. [12]

The officers found themselves without any men to command, at first. Campbell was assigned an empty barracks and was told his men would arrive soon. The empty building was all the army supplied him – through regular channels. It did not even have interior walls. He found it impossible to get even the simplest items, such as cots

---

[10] *Ibid.*   [11] *Arkansas Democrat* (Little Rock), July 25, 1954.
[12] Letters, Campbell to his parents, Sept. 8 and 9, 1917.

VESTAL IN UNIFORM, WORLD WAR I
Commissioned a Captain in the Field Artillery, Vestal
spent his last six-months' service in Europe,
being released from duty March 19, 1919.

and tables, through routine channels, due to short supplies. But Campbell was the sort of officer who place the welfare of his men above such handicaps. First he started fixing up the barracks by "scrounging for lumber and carpenters." He even partitioned off a room for his first sergeant. Other battery commanders soon copied his ideas.

With the building ready, Campbell started "rustling for what I lack for my outfit – cots, straw, tables for the mess, and the like. . . Today I set out to gather in all the supplies I could." He did this "rustling" by securing from divisional headquarters

an order for transportation for my hypothetical cots. Thence I was sent to the office of the Construction QM at the far end of the camp. There I got no satisfaction, but a verbal order to take all the cots in a certain area that were not in use. You see, the cots go with the building, and as it was at first intended to fill all the buildings in a certain area first, the cots are there. So I hiked back again to the other end of camp (Here we beg a ride from everyone under the rank of general, and generally board a car instead of asking). The Transportation Officer had no wagons or trucks available, but said the QM aforesaid had some detailed to him. The CQM said he had never received same. So the TO sent a sergeant with him (via motorcycle and a cloud of dust) to the CQM and got his written order for two wagons for my cots. Then the sergeant and I made a search for the wagons and their boss, in vain, but found some others. So the sergeant at my suggestion commandeered two of them and I drove off with them, taking the order as protection. I got a detail of rookies for the work and two lieutenants, and drove off after cots. A drive over to the doughboy quarters (1 mile) brought us to a shack used as a police dept. There we found cots to spare and filled our wagons with 90 of them. We got loaded in spite of the protests of a doughboy lieutenant who said

they were his cots. We got started off, but the said
lieutenant had consulted his lieutenant colonel and came
rushing down to say that we could not have the cots, as
they were in his regimental area. So I talked to him,
getting off the second wagon – until the first wagon had
gone on out of sight. Then I went on up to see the
colonel. He said no, no, no. He wanted my order. I
referred him to the cQM, so he called up the boss of
the said cQM and was sagely advised to hang on to any
cots he might have. So it was all off. And by that time
the first wagon was a half-mile off. I asked to use the
phone and talk to the cQM and get permission. Said
Lt-Col left (I thot he had) and as the phone was busy
I confided to the said Lt (who was so uppish) that in
my opinion, and with all due respect, I thought his col.
didn't have a damn word to say about the cots. This
was overheard by said lt-col, who was some peeved.
White with Rage. But as he didn't wish to be taken
for an eavesdropper he didn't speak of it. He came in
storming and said I must unload at once. Just then
the col. came in and inquired. Carl and I explained
again, oiling the waters. The Col. wished to avoid a
tangle of order, he said, and after fifteen minutes palaver
– having explained vividly the sufferings of the rookies
in FA – he said, "Take the cots along, but don't come
back to my regimental area." So we went. Capt. Booker
would have been proud of us. . . And you should
have seen the supply officer when I turned up with the
cots that he had been trying to get for a week. [13]

Campbell did not get to keep the cots, however, because
some of the men had arrived for one of the other batteries
of the 335th. "But it was fun," he wrote home. "This
afternoon I got 120 more cots." The following day he
"rustled 1,185 cots before they stopped us. . . Stealing
cots (with an order, of course) is fun." [14] He used the
same unofficial means to secure mess tables, pay vouchers

[13] *Ibid.*, Sept. 22, 1917.   [14] *Ibid.*, Sept. 23, 1917.

and other items, becoming a sort of unofficial regimental supply officer. Whenever anyone needed something, he came to Campbell instead of trying to get it through the long and often unsuccessful regular channels. This earned Campbell the reputation as champion "moonlight requisitioner" of the 335th. He managed better rations, better billets and more equipment for his men than any other officer could get. His men soon recognized that he was genuinely interested in their welfare, and tried doubly hard to be a good outfit. [15]

Campbell hardly became acquainted with his men before he was ordered to Fort Sill in southwestern Oklahoma for the first War Class School of Fire. Enroute there, he stopped off in Norman and attended a dance between trains. "She was very nice to me," he wrote. [16] In fact, Isabel's attitude encouraged him so much he returned to Norman every week-end while at Fort Sill.

Fort Sill was not new country to Campbell. The sprawling military reservation in the Wichita Mountains was only about sixty miles south of Weatherford. But going there as a newly commissioned captain was a little different than his trips there as a youthful sightseer.

Campbell arrived at Fort Sill on September 30, 1917. The old part of the post had undergone little change since it was constructed in 1869, at the peak of the Indian wars. Campbell described it as "a little pioneer post on a hilltop, with a square parade ground and old stone barracks, stables, and officers' quarters. On one side was a second and newer post with its own parade ground, and beyond that a firing range." [17]

When he reported in, Campbell found himself one of fourteen captains in the class, outranked by fifteen majors, seventeen lieutenant colonels and five colonels. As one of the junior officers, he could not even get quarters that

[15] *Ibid.*; and interview with Fayette Copeland, 1960.
[16] Letter, Campbell to his parents, Oct. 1, 1917.   [17] *Ibid.*

first night. Headquarters of the "school of fire" was an old building once used as an Indian store. Campbell slept on the porch of the building that night. But he did not mind as much as others might have, because the old post played a major role in the saga of the Old West. Across the porch where Campbell lay had walked Quanah Parker of the Quohada Comanches, Satank and Satanta of the Kiowas, and many other famous chiefs. On the porch of a stone building facing the parade ground General Sherman had almost been killed by Comanches and Kiowas. Across the parade ground had ridden many of the horse soldiers Campbell knew so well from research – men like General Ranald Mackenzie and General George Custer. In one of the nearby buildings Apache Chief Geronimo had spent the last years of his life. Campbell must have yearned to forget about the war long enough to write what he felt that night and many other times during the next three months. But military service came first and his only writing was in his diaries and letters home.

The second day

> We were put in wool tents, unheated, lighted by lanterns, with canvas cots and straw on the floor. The weather . . . was severe. . . But if the tent was cold, our firing problems on the bleak hills were colder, and when we could we hovered around bonfires built for such comfort as the wind allowed. [18]

During the training Campbell suffered a slight illness and was confined to the base hospital. While there he saw a notice posted on the bulletin board forbidding patients to shoot buffalo from the windows. It was yellowed with age, even then. But nearly forty years later he returned to the fort for a visit and it was still posted.

After several week-end trips back to Norman, Campbell grew bold enough to propose to Isabel once more. This

---

[18] *Ibid.,* to Malory Campbell, Nov. 4, 1957.

time she accepted. They made plans for their marriage to be held during his Christmas leave which was to follow his graduation from the school of fire.

Campbell completed school December 20, 1917, and left immediately for Dallas, where he and Isabel were married the day after Christmas in the home of her sister. A few days later he returned to Camp Pike more interested in his new bride than in artillery training. [19]

Campbell soon settled into a routine of instructing his own men in what he had learned at Fort Sill, conducting classes two hours each morning and each afternoon. His battery consisted of 187 men, 147 horses and four mules.

Within a month of his return to Arkansas, Campbell really turned sour on military life. He reported the regiment had changed in spirit from "eagerness to determined plugging on in spite of utter dislike of the commander . . . a petty tyrant," and "the meanest man in the army, a coastal artilleryman who knew nothing of field artillery and had absorbed too much sun and liquor in the Philippines." [20]

Campbell continually sought ways to outwit the headquarters officers who took the best men and horses for themselves. He became a good friend of the regimental remount officer who notified him a day ahead of time when new horses were to be issued. This enabled him to select his mounts before the headquarters group picked them over. "Of course, the colonels and majors soon ranked me out of the best horses, but at that I was always well mounted in the army." [21]

Campbell also developed a subterfuge for keeping his best men. One day headquarters company officers notified him they were coming to inspect his battery. He told his men they were to be looked over for transfer, and that their transfer depended on the impression they made on

[19] *Ibid.,* to his parents, Dec. 27, 1917, and Jan. 8, 1918.
[20] *Ibid.,* Feb. 14, 1918.   [21] Autobiographical data.

the inspecting officers. "You never saw such slovenly soldiers in your life as these were when inspected. I raved and swore at them for their awkwardness. Only one man was taken. It was as good as a play." [22]

The adjutant for the regiment, M. J. "Pup" Harrison, was one headquarters officer Campbell respected. Although "cooped up all day in the same office with the c.o.," he was cool, patient and good humored, Campbell wrote. [23]

Campbell's independent spirit also rebelled at many other incidents. One of his lieutenants failed to sign a sick report one day and the colonel confined all officers of the battery to the camp for two weeks. This meant Campbell could not be with his bride for that period, which was a little too much for him. He immediately arranged for Isabel to stay overnight in the hostess house of the camp. He often found himself detained in camp for several nights in a row for petty duty or some minor infraction by those under his command. In March all the regiment was restricted to camp except from noon Saturday to 10 p.m. Sunday.

Campbell fared no better with the medical corps, which on one occasion forced him to personally measure the feet of all his men, for health records. But his most unpleasant experience with the medics came in March.

I had an attack of tonsillitis and finally went to the regimental surgeon, who was rather an incompetent, small town doctor who had jumped at the chance to get into a uniform and earn a decent living. He looked at me and gave me a cc pill and told me to get into the truck waiting outside, that I was going to the hospital. I got into the truck, but after it started I realized that it was not heading for the Base Hospital, but in another direction. It drew up at an ordinary barracks and I was

[22] Letter, Campbell to his parents, Jan. 20, 1918.
[23] *Ibid.*, to M. J. Harrison, Sept. 9, 1954.

told to climb down. I went in and found that this was sort of an isolation ward or detention house for officers with the mumps. As I had never had the mumps, and we were all kept in one large room, I was considerably disturbed. I chose a cot over in the corner and hung up a blanket between me and the other fellows and stayed behind it all the time. Food was brought in three times a day, but I would not eat with the others. I protested to the officer in charge that I did not have the mumps. But he had his orders, I suppose.

There was no examination at this place. We were just captives. The officer in charge spent most of his time playing poker with the convalescents, and seemed to derive much satisfaction and considerable money from this occupation. He was very much annoyed with me because I did not come out of my corner to play. After a day or two of protesting and demanding an examination by a competent physician, I realized that I was a prisoner and would have to get outside help to escape. It was impossible to leave the building by the door. And the officer had stationed a guard about it consisting of two enlisted men armed with rifles and – believe it or not – fixed bayonets. When I saw the fixed bayonets, I realized that the officer was no soldier and soon discovered that he did not know how to post a guard. For at a certain time, as the guards marched around the building, neither of them could see my window. I soon figured out a way to fool them. I put on my uniform and belt and as soon as the first guard had rounded the corner out of sight, I jumped down, closed the window, ran a few yards from the building and turned and came walking back towards it just as the second guard appeared. He, seeing an officer approaching, halted and presented arms. I saluted. He turned and went on. And I walked over to the Jitney stand, boarded a cab, drove to Little Rock and spent the night with Isabel. Through her efforts, after several attempts, I was able to contact a medical man from the Base Hospital who looked at me and pulled wires to have me released. I escaped without getting infected and went to the Base Hospital to have my tonsils out.

The surgeon sat me down in the chair, put a bucket between my feet, told me to open my mouth, put in his little wire clippers and clipped out my tonsils just like that. They fell in a bucket and the operation was over. There was no anesthetic.

They put me in a ward with a number of other officers. But the tonsils did not heal quickly. And when [Isabel] called, I had to write what I wished to say to her while she would answer orally. In this way we carried on animated conversations for some days. The nurse, I suppose seeing that we were lovebirds, ransacked the wastebasket to see what I had been writing to [Isabel]. There she found something I had facetiously written. There was a glass door between the ward and the corridor which led to the operating room and every little while someone was wheeled past, going to or returning from the operating room, not only soldiers but their wives and children. Isabel commented on the number of people being wheeled by and I scribbled "The stiffs go by all day long." This is what the nurse found and brought to the attention of the officer in charge of the hospital.

He took this as an insult to him and his hospital and demanded an explanation in writing. I explained the circumstances. But he was not satisfied, and kept me in the hospital for forty days all told – or thought he did.

The nurse had carelessly left my uniform hanging behind the screen by the bed. And after I was perfectly well again, I discovered that I could get up and dress after the night nurse had gone, walk out the door and take a cab to town, returning in time to meet the day nurse in the morning. So my punishment was not so bad as it might have been. But before he let me go, he had me examined by every specialist on the Base, including the psychiatrist, if you can call a doctor of that time by such a title. [24]

24 *Ibid.*, to Dorothy Campbell, Jan. 19, 1956.

And so the irritants multiplied, making Campbell more and more discontented with army life remote from the battlefields of France. Inevitably, overseas orders arrived and the 87th Division moved out for Camp Dix, New Jersey, in June 1918. En route Campbell wrote: "The flies are legion on this train. At first I thought all the people who flapped their hands as we went by were waving at us. But I believe now that they were just brushing off the flies." [25]

Although Camp Dix was supposed to be a temporary duty station, nearly two months passed before the regiment moved again. Campbell chafed at the delay. Even after Isabel joined him there he wanted to head for France.

The money troubles which had plagued Campbell since his early days at Oxford multiplied with his marriage. Isabel was apparently a better manager of their financial affairs, but both wrote numerous letters to Campbell's parents thanking them for loans and gifts, usually mentioning their continued shortage of funds. Just how much Campbell owed is not known, but his debt to his parents was a large one, and growing.

Boredom over inaction at Camp Dix ended September 1, 1918, when the regiment sailed for Europe. One night at sea Campbell strolled along the deck of the transport and noticed his hated commanding officer leaning over the railing. For just a moment Vestal thought how easy it would be, and how much good it would do the regiment, if he were to push the colonel over the side of the ship into the sea. He did not seriously consider doing so, but the opportunity was there, and he recognized it. But he passed up the opportunity and in later years was fond of telling his friends that he saved the colonel's life by resisting the temptation when he had the chance.

---

[25] *Ibid.,* to his wife, June 19, 1918.

Some of Campbell's men were too seasick to eat the regular food provided for enlisted mess. True to his custom of looking after his own, Campbell stole soup from the officers' mess and gave it to his men who could not eat anything else. This sort of thing endeared him as a battery commander.

The regiment landed in southern France and headed inland. Along the route children welcomed them with cheers and requests for money and food. "Everyone is glad to see us for obvious reasons," Campbell wrote. They were billeted in Camp Montiersharme near Chateauroux, southwest of Paris. They did not see any evidence of war except aircraft above and an occasional Red Cross or prisoner train. As had been the case at both camps in Arkansas, the regiment found its latest camp unfinished. Campbell's men slept in a big warehouse while building barracks. Once again, Campbell resumed his "moonlight requisitioning." Frequent rains resulted in mud everywhere, slippery and deep. "We skid and flounder and wallow and wander around our little orbit all day in big rubber boots," he wrote. [26]

When Campbell's battery completed its barracks, he found himself with "practically nothing to do. The battery runs itself and my sole activity is signing papers and censoring letters." [27] Campbell was no ordinary censor, however. Concerning this task, he wrote: "Wives and sweethearts must have been startled to find an occasional letter blue-pencilled, with punctuation and spelling corrected in an alien hand – the habit of an English teacher. I would find myself doing it." [28]

Having trained the 87th Division in field artillery for a year, the army now put the men to work building rail-

---

[26] *Ibid.,* one undated, another Sept. 23, 1918; one to his parents, also undated.

[27] *Ibid.,* to his wife, Oct. 19, 1918.   [28] *Ibid.,* undated.

roads in the Chateauroux vicinity. Campbell "fretted over missing at least a taste of combat," but talking to German prisoners was as close as he could get to the enemy.

When Campbell first left Isabel behind at Camp Dix, she went to Weatherford to stay with his parents for a short time. Then she went to Norman and worked at the university briefly before going to Dallas to live with her sister until her husband's return. Not long after their separation she learned she was pregnant. Campbell quickly assumed his first-born would be a boy, and began referring to the coming child as the "little captain." This led to some banter between the parents-to-be over who would arrive in Dallas first, big captain or little captain.

Near the end of October 1918, Campbell and other regimental officers received orders to attend another school of fire while their men continued to build railroads. The officers left November 1 for the school at De Sauges near Bordeaux, and began training November 5. This got them out of the mud, but into the sand dunes. Campbell said the area was as "sandy as the bed of the Canadian [a river in Oklahoma]." The officers marched from barracks to class and back "like rookies." Exasperated, Campbell longed for just one fling at combat before the show ended. Five days later the armistice came. "I was cheated of my chance in the war," he wrote. "I never got to go over the top." [29] After that, the school became a bore and army life became something to abandon as quickly as possible.

About this time Campbell was recommended for promotion to the rank of major. The division commander, General Martin, turned down the promotion because "A policy has been adopted by the War Department not to

---

[29] Campbell diary, May 16, 1925.

appoint or promote any further officers in the army of the United States for the period of the emergency." [30] Campbell's only regret in the matter was the loss of extra pay that would have come with the rank.

Later in the month the school of fire ended and Campbell resumed command of his battery, which was then moved to the small village of St. Loubes in the middle of the vineyards near Bordeaux, a small port city in southern France. The men were billeted in barns, houses and haylofts, while the officers moved into private rooms. Campbell wrote:

> I don't know whether this town was in existence when Roland fell at Por Rocesvalles or not. But I am sure it has not been cleaned since it was first built. And, as the medical inspector is after us, we are cleaning it up. [31]

The medical inspector blamed Campbell's men for all the garbage thrown out of windows into the streets by citizens of the village. Campbell's job was to inspect and keep clean the areas around the quarters of his men. "The brigade commander says dung in the streets and alleys is all right. It's the scraps of paper and tin cans that menace our health." [32]

A month or so after the Armistice, Campbell took command of the First Battalion, 335th Field Artillery, but remained a battery commander also. As a result, once again he was recommended for the rank of major. But the promotion was still pending four months later when he was discharged. [33]

Keeping his men out of trouble and occupied for the remainder of their service became more difficult with the

---

[30] Letter, Gen. Martin to Col. L. S. Ryan, Nov. 24, 1918.

[31] *Ibid.*, Campbell to his wife, Dec. 14, 1918.

[32] *Ibid.*, Dec. 30, 1918.   [33] Autobiographical data.

passing weeks. Raiding wine cellars became a favorite pastime of the men.

Some of his men from Iowa relieved their boredom by getting a goat for a mascot.

> The animal was fond of having his back scratched, and when the soldiers discovered the peculiar reaction of the goat to this scratching, they came from miles around to see him perform, with the result that somebody was scratching his back from morning to night.
> . . . Such a magnificent display of unremitting virility was the envy and delight of all beholders. [34]

Orders to move from St. Loubes to the port of Paulliac arrived February 2, 1919. The Division boarded the SS "Martha Washington" on February 21 in a rainstorm which failed to dampen the spirits of the homeward-bound doughboys. They sailed the following day and reached Newport News, Virginia, March 8. Campbell barely had time to wire Isabel before the outfit left for Camp Stewart. Just before departure, he gave the battalion guidon to a first sergeant. While the men were marching to the train that would take them to Camp Stewart, the division commander ordered the waterproof cases removed from the guidons. "It was a joy to see his face when the bare pole came to light," Campbell wrote. [35]

Campbell felt even better by March 15 when he was sent on to Camp Dix, New Jersey. An exuberance engulfed him on the day of his discharge, March 19, 1919. "I am now a citizen of the United States, free, white and 31," he wrote Isabel. "This morning I rushed through my physical exam, signed all my papers, pulled wires, turned in my blankets and got my discharge at noon exactly. . . Then I check baggage, told the officers

[34] *Ibid.*   [35] Letters, Campbell to his wife, Mar. 9 and 16, 1919.

goodbye, and drew my final pay [$287] and took the 3 p.m. [train]." [36]

As returning soldiers usually do, Campbell headed straight for home, or at least to Dallas and Isabel, arriving there about a month ahead of the "little captain." He and Isabel went on to Oklahoma City where their *daughter*, Malory, was born April 19, 1919.

---

[36] *Ibid.,* March 14 and 18, 1919.

The Mature Years

During the many years of his research and writing prior to his war service, Campbell always encountered two obstacles he could not overcome. First, although the old Indians regarded him as a good friend, they would not tell him about their fighting experiences. Second, he could not find the "secret" or "magic formula" that would convert much of his writing into salable manuscripts. He came home from France determined to overcome both obstacles, and soon learned the first one no longer existed.

Since he arrived home too late for the spring term at Oklahoma University, Campbell decided to teach summer school at Southwestern State College in Weatherford, and do research among the Cheyenne. By this time his stepfather had returned to Southwestern as a professor, so Campbell, his wife and infant daughter lived with his parents. This gave him a nearby base for his research.

Both good and bad luck greeted him in the Cheyenne camp. Now that he himself had been a soldier, the old chiefs and warriors were willing to tell him about their own war experiences. It was as simple as that. He was now one of them. Unfortunately, however, a major portion of the older men had died in an influenza epidemic which swept the country during World War I. The younger men were valueless for research purposes because they had no first hand knowledge of the plains wars and Campbell wanted nothing second hand. Even George Bent was among those who had died. Still, Campbell set about getting the war stories from those who were left. Through the summer he compiled a tremendous volume of material on Cheyenne history. Although he still had not discovered the "secret" of writing to sell, he no longer entertained any doubts about his eventual success.

Campbell turned again to writing poetry, articles and short stories, with only slight success. Some ingredient was still missing from his work. Literature about Indians had long been popular with the American public, and he believed his material and literary style superior to much of what was published in periodicals of the day. He published a few magazine articles, but the major markets indicated little interest in what he sent them. In 1920 he began organizing his vast amount of research material on Cheyennes and frontiersmen into book-length manuscripts. Just sorting it out was the work of years.

In the spring of 1920 Campbell was selected secretary for Oklahoma to the Rhodes Scholar Committee, and remained on the committee until near the end of his life. The great volume of correspondence he conducted in this respect, and several published articles, reflected his love and gratitude toward Oxford and the Rhodes Trust.

Several steps in the development of Campbell as a writer and teacher of writers occurred in 1922. One of these was his association with several young men who shared his interest in professional writing. Although he did not at that time teach regular courses in writing, he did help some of the students in his literature and English classes in that direction. From this came his first ideas about teaching writing. Most of the group also belonged to a writer's club which Campbell organized and sponsored, and as members often visited in his home. Several later achieved considerable success. Best known of the group was Lynn Riggs, whose play "Green Grow the Lilacs" became the musical "Oklahoma" which ran on Broadway in New York City longer than any other stage production up to that time. Riggs was just beginning to write when Campbell first became associated with him. The only member of the group already a successful writer was William Foster Harris. Graduating in 1925, Harris went on to a pulp magazine career before returning to Norman in 1937 to help Campbell establish the professional writing school there. [1]

Campbell's second "little captain," another daughter, Dorothy Hayden Vestal Campbell, was born April 22, 1922. After a boyhood spent in a houseful of women, he now found his adulthood much the same. He did not complain, however.

Hardly a month after the second daughter's birth, Campbell began another step in his climb toward literary success. He spent the summer writing the initial draft of his first book-length project, not counting the one he wrote while at Oxford and later had privately printed. Campbell said the summer was "beastly hot and I had a west room at home so I stripped to G-string and moccasins and sweated it out." In August he went to cool Estes Park, Colorado, to complete the manuscript. Entitled *Happy Hunting Grounds*, the book was fiction based on the history of the Cheyennes. His purpose was to present a comprehensive picture of plains Indian life based on myth, legend, history, eye-witness accounts and his own observations. Incidents he used were not only actual, but typical. [2]

Campbell's factual material for the book came from his close association with the Cheyennes since he was twelve years old. Not many white people knew as much about Cheyenne history, and Campbell crammed into this novel much of his vast knowledge about the tribe.

While teaching in Louisville a decade earlier, Campbell had formed a friendship with Frederick Weygold, an artist and collector of Indian art objects. Now Campbell

[1] Personal interview with Foster Harris, 1962.
[2] Stanley Vestal, *Happy Hunting Grounds,* p. vi.

took Weygold in as a partner on the project, getting him
to illustrate the book with numerous drawings on Indian
life. Shields, teepees with detailed symbols, battle scenes,
and other aspects of Cheyenne life were accurately por-
trayed by Weygold. Not many novels included such extensive illustration, but Campbell believed it was necessary to accomplish the purpose of the book. [3]

Whether Campbell tried to sell *Happy Hunting Grounds*
at that time or held it back for additional polishing is not
known, but he did not sell it then. Likely he tried several
publishers before withdrawing it. Certainly he worked
on it from time to time in ensuing years.

Returning to Norman in the autumn of 1922, Campbell
began work on two other closely related book-length
projects, a biography of his boyhood hero, Kit Carson,
and a book of ballads about the Old West. A majority
of the ballads dealt with the exploits of Carson and the
mountain men, so the two were related to each other.
Also, both related to *Happy Hunting Grounds* because of
the close association of Carson and the mountain men
with the Cheyennes. In all his research among Cheyennes
and frontiersmen, Campbell never passed up an opportunity to talk about Carson. But the most important
sources of information for the novel about Cheyennes,
the biography of Carson, and the book of ballads, were
the same – his stepfather, J. R. Campbell; George Bent,
who was closely associated with Carson when the latter
worked for Bent's father; John Homer Seger, the Cheyenne Indian agent; and the more important Cheyenne
chiefs. Some of the ballads, however, Campbell first heard
from his grandmother while he sat on her knee as a
pre-school boy.

Work on the biography and the ballads kept Campbell
busy for several years, but he still found time to write
some shorter material. The summer of 1923 he went to

---

[3] Autobiographical data.

Colorado and visited some of the sites important in the life of Carson and other giants of the fur-trade era, particularly Bent's Fort on the Arkansas River.

The 1923-24 school year was a rather typical one for Campbell in several ways. First, his debts spiraled upward and continued to worry his wife. This led him to another situation that typified his life – that of having too many projects going at once. Already working on three books and turning out shorter material in an effort to overcome his debts while teaching full time, he took on the additional burden of editing a book written by John Homer Seger. *Early Days Among the Cheyenne and Arapaho Indians*, published in 1924 and reissued with minor changes in 1934, was based on Seger's fifty years among the two tribes. In the foreword, Campbell claimed only to have arranged the material, which he said appeared just as it was written by Seger. [4] Campbell wanted no credit except for having helped his old friend and informant who had taught him so much about the plains Indians. But a later director of the University of Oklahoma Press said it was so heavily edited by Campbell that for all practical purposes it was his work. [5]

Campbell also added to his work load by doing additional research for other projects. When he first came back from the war and found most of the old Cheyenne warriors and chiefs dead, those still living told him the northern plains tribes had fared better than some tribes during the flu epidemic that decimated their own ranks. They said there were still plenty of old-timers alive in the Dakotas and Montana, particularly among the Sioux tribes. Campbell had not paid much attention at the time, because he was not acquainted with the Sioux.

---

[4] John Homer Seger, *Early Days Among the Cheyenne and Arapaho Indians,* ed. by Stanley Vestal, foreword page.

[5] Savoie Lottinville, "Walter Stanley Vestal," in *American Oxonian,* Oct. 1958, p. 243.

Now the idea of getting Sitting Bull's warriors to tell their story intrigued him. Accordingly, he began doing extensive library research on the Sioux.

A third typical situation was Campbell's fretting over the American education system, which he considered far inferior to the Oxford system, and the shortcomings of the white man's way of life compared to the Indian way. Campbell preferred the Oxford teaching method, with each student having a tutor and examinations administered by someone other than the tutor. As for the restraint of civilized society, Campbell chafed for the freedom of the Indian way. [6]

Campbell's thinking was identical to that of the plains Indian and the frontiersmen, who were much alike except for the natural color of their skin. Campbell even wore a breechclout around the house in the hot summer months, as much in protest of civilization as for the comfort it brought. And his ideas for rearing his children came straight from the plains Indians. In all his years among the Indians, he only once saw an adult strike a child. Once as he sat talking to a chief, a screaming child fled past the open door of the cabin pursued by an angry woman carrying a stick. Instantly the old chief jumped up, ran out, rebuked the woman, and led the weeping child into his cabin. There he sat down, took her on his lap, petted and comforted her. Soon everyone in the camp brought a gift or a tidbit of some sort or a kind word until the child became quiet. Then the chief assured Campbell that the child's mother was crazy. The other Indians slunk away, ashamed such a disgraceful thing had happened in their camp. [7]

Campbell put aside his book-length manuscripts in the summer of 1924 and went hunting for more material.

---

[6] Campbell diary, undated entry in June 1923, and Jan. 29, 1924.

[7] Autobiographical data.

Isabel took the girls to Atlanta, Georgia, for a visit with her sister. Campbell began his search with a motor trip along the old Santa Fe Trail through Kansas, Colorado, and New Mexico. From Santa Fe he went north into Wyoming and the Black Hills of the Sioux Nation, retracing other trails, visiting the sites of historic battles and forts, and interviewing old-timers wherever he found them. Crossing the plains of South Dakota, he stopped off in historic Deadwood, then followed the course of the Missouri River through Nebraska and Kansas. He returned home fired with enthusiasm for writing books about the old Santa Fe Trail and the Sioux. And he had found material for additional ballads about the Old West. But first he had to complete the writing projects already under way.

By now Campbell was only months away from the turning point, or key period, of his literary career. Since his days at Oxford he had been grinding out vast quantities of words with quite limited success at publishing them. In later years he described this as his apprenticeship period. Gradually he came to realize there was no "magic formula" or "secret" that separated success from failure, or professional from amateur. The nearest thing to a magic formula was simply to keep writing, to study carefully the specific market for which he wanted to write in order to gauge what that market would buy, to study the works of the masters in each market area in order to learn their techniques but without copying their literary style, and above all, to write only about subjects which interested him greatly.

By this time Campbell was doing all the things he felt were essential to success, and this began to pay off in 1925, slowly at first. But he published regularly for the rest of his life, and the name Stanley Vestal became better known than Walter S. Campbell. In this pivotal year he published a number of articles, stories, and ballads in such publications as *American Mercury, The Frontier, Poetry: A Magazine of Verse, Southwest Review*, and others. [8] A bit of luck started this deluge. He sold ballads about Kit Carson to *Southwest Review*. The same day he received the April 1925, copy in which the ballads were published, he also received a letter from H. L. Mencken, editor of the *American Mercury*. Mencken had seen a copy of *Southwest Review* before Vestal did, had read the ballads and liked them well enough to ask Vestal to submit others to him. Vestal mailed several and Mencken bought three. More important, this led to a strong friendship between the two and to additional *Literary Digest* reprinted some of the ballads.

The same week of Vestal's initial sale to *Southwest Review*, the Oklahoma University was visited by Harriet Monroe, editor of *Poetry: A Magazine of Verse*. She was on a tour of the southwest and had just read the ballads which caught the attention of Mencken. She called Vestal and asked to see some of his other verse. Vestal handed her some of the better ones from his book on ballads, and she selected three which she published in the July 1925 issue of her magazine.

These publications were not of great importance, but they added to Vestal's incentive and earned him some recognition among literary people. But instead of completing his present projects, he began a novel about the collapse of the fur trade in the Old West, entitled *'Dobe Walls*. This made four book-length projects under way for him, all related to his boyhood hero Kit Carson.

Isabel worked as hard as her husband to learn the writing business and began to succeed about the same

---

[8] *Ibid.*

[9] Letters exchanged between Campbell and H. L. Mencken, Apr. 18 and 24, May 6, Aug. 14, Oct. 17 and Nov. 25, 1925.

time. Her top markets were *Harper's Bazaar, Smart Set,* and *Poetry: A Magazine of Verse.* [10]

Vestal wanted to give up teaching for awhile and devote all his time to completing his book-length projects, but he was too deeply in debt. He owed a year's salary, but this worried his wife more than him. Though he, too, now had a fear of poverty, his reaction to indebtedness was more one of rebellion at having to live according to economic needs of civilized society. [11]

Despite his financial plight, Vestal went ahead with another expensive research trip in the summer of 1925. With his family, he drove out to the Texas panhandle to Adobe Walls, Colonel Bent's Fort on the Canadian River, a trapper's headquarters during the fur trade era. Then they drove on to Colorado, camping along the way, with Vestal studying the terrain and acquiring voluminous notes about historical sites and trails. During one three-day camping period in Yellowstone National Park, Vestal found a park ranger reading his recently published ballads about Kit Carson. Next Vestal interviewed some old timers in Cody, Wyoming, then drove to Montana for interviews in a Crow Indian encampment. Here he acquired additional material for the lengthy article he was writing about the Crow teepee. On the return trip Vestal took his family to Santa Fe, New Mexico, for relaxation while he did research and some writing. The thirty-three day trip covered four thousand miles. Like most of his trips, it added as much to his indebtedness as it did to his knowledge about the Old West.

Vestal's writing was interrupted for awhile in the fall of 1925. Throughout his life to this point, he had been closer to his mother than the average boy and young man. She had exercised an unusual degree of influence

---

[10] Autobiographical data.

[11] Campbell diary, entries of May 13, May 16 and June 9, 1925.

over him, encouraging him to write, and to study both academically and among the Indians. Of all the influences which led him to become a writer and to acquire his knowledge of the Old West, Daisy was one of the most important. She died that autumn after a brief illness. Her death, coming while she was still in her fifties and apparently in good health, left Vestal too despondent to work for some time. [12]

Another crucial year followed for Vestal. He started 1926 in debt $3,500 and with four book-length manuscripts in various stages of completion, all of which he felt certain were salable. He polished up the book of ballads and started it circulating among publishers. Then, in three months time, he wrote the final draft of *Kit Carson*. With two daughters, one seven and one four, he found it impossible to work at home, so he did his writing in his car. Vestal said:

> I would drive out in the morning to some lonely place and go to work. On alternate days I would go over my notes and get ready to write the next day, but I never wrote from notes. You never write well if you have notes under your nose. [13]

Vestal published some shorter material that year, three ballads and an article in *The American Mercury*, an article in *The American Oxonian*, and a few others. But mostly he worked on *Kit Carson, Fandango: Ballads of the Old West*, and *Happy Hunting Grounds*. Before the year ended he had all three circulating among publishing houses. Then he turned his attention to *'Dobe Walls*. Wanting to finish it also that year, he applied for a Guggenheim Fellowship that would permit him to work on it full time. But his application was rejected. [14]

---

[12] Autobiographical data.

[13] Letter, Campbell to Lewis Watson, Nov. 28, 1945.

[14] Autobiographical data.

CHIEF WHITE BULL AND VESTAL
White Bull was chosen by the Sioux in June 1926
to lead their delegation across the Little Big
Horn Battlefield on the fiftieth anniversary of
the fight with Custer's Seventh Cavalry.

For about seven years now Vestal had wanted to do extensive research among the northern plains tribes, particularly Sitting Bull's Sioux warriors. An incident in 1926 led him into this new research area. This was the fiftieth anniversary celebration of the Battle on the Little Big Horn River in which General Custer was killed. The Seventh Cavalry, Custer's outfit, and the leaders of the Sioux nation were to meet in friendship on the old battlefield. When the spring school term ended, Vestal loaded his family in his car and headed north. They spent the first night in Benedict, Kansas, in the home of Daisy's sister, Vestal's Aunty Harvie. Here Isabel became ill and they were unable to attend the celebration.

Later Vestal learned almost every tribe of the northern plains was represented at the gathering in Montana. Also present were several governors, eminent historians such as George Bird Grinnell, famous writers such as Mary Roberts Rinehart, famous movie stars such as Bill Hart, and a vast number of soldiers, particularly the Seventh Cavalry. From all the old Indian warriors, Chief Joseph White Bull, one of the two nephews reared by Sitting Bull, was chosen to lead the Sioux across the battlefield. In charge of the Seventh Cavalry was General E. S. Godfrey, who had exchanged shots with White Bull in the Little Big Horn battle half a century earlier.

General Godfrey, with sabre in hand, led five troops of the Seventh Cavalry across the battlefield from the south to meet the Indian column. With him were seven troopers who survived the campaign. With White Bull marching from the north were eighty Sioux and Cheyenne survivors of the battle. When the two columns met, White Bull raised his open hand in the sign of peace. Godfrey sheathed his sword and rode forward to greet the chief. They clasped hands. White Bull presented the general with a blanket, and the general gave him a large American flag.

From the description of the battle given by the Indians later in the day, one of the army officers, Major Alson Ostrander, concluded that White Bull was among those who shot down Custer and the men immediately around him. He asked White Bull, "Are you the man who killed Custer?" White Bull replied, "maybe." [15]

The mere fact that White Bull was chosen above all others to lead the Sioux across the battlefield was enough to arouse the interest of Vestal. When he later learned that White Bull admitted he might have been the one who killed Custer, Vestal made up his mind to learn White Bull's full story. But that would take time. The top chiefs and warriors of the Sioux had little to do with white men. Vestal could not just walk up and ask White Bull what he wanted to know, and get more of an answer than had Major Ostrander.

Returning to Oklahoma University that autumn, Vestal maintained his usual packed schedule, working some on *'Dobe Walls*, reading everything he could find on the Sioux, and writing several plays and shorter material. He sold a 5,000-word fact article, "The Tipis of the Crow Indians," to *The American Anthropologist*, in January 1927. But this was soon forgotten when he made his first book-length sale, *Fandango: Ballads of the Old West*, to Houghton Mifflin Company. Soon after, his wife, Isabel, matched his success by selling and publishing her first book-length work, a novel entitled *Jack Spratt*. The twin success brought considerable recognition to the couple. One review said "*Fandango* shares with John G. Neihardt's epics the honor of introducing the pioneer West into serious contemporary literature." [16] The book also received praise from other national publications, such as the *New York Times* and the *New York Herald*

---

[15] Stanley Vestal, "White Bull and One Bull," in *Westerners Brand Book* (Chicago), Oct. 1947, p. 47; Stanley Vestal, *Warpath*, p. 252-4.   [16] *New Orleans Picayune*, Apr. 17, 1927.

Tribune. [17]   At the same time Vestal was selected to "Who's Who Among North American Authors," and "Who's Who in America."

The recognition, along with Isabel's success, earned the couple an invitation to spend the summer of 1927 at Yaddo, a writer's colony near Saratoga Springs, New York. This meant an opportunity for Vestal to finish *'Dobe Walls*, and for Isabel to work on her second book. He secured sabbatical leave for the 1927-28 school year and headed for Yaddo.

---

[17] Various newspaper clippings in autobiographical data.

Yaddo and Sioux Country

Yaddo was an old mansion owned by Mr. and Mrs. Spencer Trask, a wealthy New York couple who left it for the entertainment of artists and writers. Many literary figures of the day went there, some to work and others to play. Walter and Isabel, burning with writing ambition, regarded the invitation as a grand opportunity to write full time. They arrived at Yaddo June 30, 1927, and "loved the grand old house and gardens." [1]

One of the first persons they met there was a former student of Walter's, Lynn Riggs, already an established playwright and at Yaddo working on another stage production. They also formed a close friendship with another guest there, Tennessee Anderson, former wife of the noted author, Sherwood Anderson.

The Campbells soon settled into a work-day routine both exhausting and productive. Isabel described their days in these words:

> My husband generously insisted that I take the only study, so he had to do his work on the dining room table, . . . Our schedule was rather strenuous. After breakfast our little girls attempted to do the dishes for us, I shut myself into the study and Mr. Campbell shut himself into the dining room. Only the horrible clatter of our Underwoods kept our thoughts from being distracted by the cries coming from the kitchen. "Mother, Malory is splashing dishwater on my – – " "Mother, Dorothy won't dry the forks properly." There

[1] Campbell diary, June 30, 1927.

was only one way to keep thinking about the project at hand, and that was to keep the typewriter going full tilt all morning.

After the dishes were finally washed, the children waded in a stream running through the property and visited three little friends up the hill.

At twelve o'clock, I dashed into the kitchen, threw some potatoes into the oven to bake, cooked some steak and prepared any green vegetables we could get from the huckster who drove past every day. . .

After dinner and another bout at the dishes, we went back to more writing. During the afternoon, as our daily stints neared completion, we were both anxious to get an opinion on what had been written and it often happened that we collided in the doorway, each with a sheaf of yellow, single spaced words grasped in the hand.

"Listen," I would cry at the same time Mr. Campbell would shout, "What do you think of this?" And we would both begin to read at once. Then we would straighten the tangle out and read to each other what we had written.

This would be about four o'clock in the afternoon. Then we would get in the Chevie, drive the three miles to town and buy our food for the next day's rations.

After supper we scandalously wasted an hour sitting under the big maples that lined the brook, which was a gurgling one and nine o'clock saw us sound asleep." [2]

While they were at Yaddo, Walter and Isabel made a number of trips to New York City. These they regarded as more rewarding than the opportunity for writing, due to the contacts they made with many publishers. On one trip, in September, Walter sold his biography of Kit Carson to Houghton Mifflin, receiving an advance of $400. Soon after he made a similar deal with Lyons and Carnahan of Chicago for publishing his *Happy Hunting*

---

[2] Isabel Campbell, "One Genius in a Family Is Not Enough Say the Campbells," in *Sooner Magazine*, Oct. 1929, p. 19.

Grounds as a juvenile book. In the latter case, the publisher raised two objections. First, he did not like the illustrations made by Weygold. Professional artists could do better, it was argued. But to Vestal, accuracy meant more than artistic quality, and he felt that only a person with Weygold's background among Indians could properly portray the points needing illustration. The publisher also returned the manuscript to Vestal for revision on the grounds that the literary style was too difficult for young readers. "Take that first sentence, Mr. Campbell," he said. Vestal found the first sentence was too long so he broke it up into three sentences, waited awhile and sent the manuscript back without further change. The firm then published the book and it sold well for nearly three decades. Vestal figured that the first sentence was all the publisher had read. [3]

Vestal claimed that when a publisher asked him to make changes in a manuscript, he would agree on condition that he also be allowed to make changes in the royalty checks. If he ever actually made such a suggestion to a publisher, he likely did it much later in his career, when he was a more established writer.

Both *Kit Carson* and *Happy Hunting Grounds* were published in the spring of 1928, adding to the now growing fame of Stanley Vestal. *The New York Times* praised *Kit Carson* for its "accuracy, prose style and passages of terrific, heartbreaking effect." It was also lauded for "containing no phony hero stuff, but the earthy qualities of the great scout," who "opened up an empire, not because he intended to do that, but simply because he liked the life." [4] The Good Reading Committee of America later placed the book among the 1,500 best books ever

[3] Autobiographical data, and letter from Campbell to Mr. and Mrs. Jack Zaruba, Dec. 15, 1955.

[4] *New York Times,* Mar. 25, 1928, book review section, pp. 7, 12.

published. [5] *The New Republic* review said: "This volume is a valuable addition to the studies of Western heroes, and (Vestal's) sketch of some phases of frontier work . . . is as good as any yet written." [6] The prominent Old West historian J. Frank Dobie, writing for *The Nation*, said Vestal had produced "a book of balance, perspective, and authority, free from both heroical cant and 'bad man' parading." [7] Other publications also gave the book an enthusiastic reception.

Vestal's love for frontiersmen like Kit Carson is evident throughout the book. Carson was only sixteen when he first went to Taos, New Mexico, headquarters for traders and trappers. For twelve years he trapped beaver and fought Indians with such notables as Jim Bridger and Joe Meek. He married first an Arapaho girl and later a Cheyenne squaw, and in later life a Mexican girl in Taos. After silk hats replaced beaver head gear, ruining the trapping profession, Carson spent fifteen years as a hunter for Colonel William Bent at Bent's Fort on the Arkansas River, Colorado. Then he scouted for the army for five years, including the first and second Fremont Expeditions in the Rocky Mountains and Far West. In 1853 Carson became the agent for Ute and Apache Indians. He served as a lieutenant colonel in the Civil War, commanding the troops which fought the combined southern plains tribes at Adobe Walls in the Texas Panhandle. [8]

Vestal's first novel, *Happy Hunting Grounds*, did not receive the acclaim of the book on Carson. First, it was published as a juvenile book and likely was not widely read by adults. While fiction, it was only thinly disguised

---

[5] Autobiographical data.

[6] Allen Nevins, "Kit Carson," in *New Republic*, May 16, 1928, p. 401.

[7] J. Frank Dobie, "Kit Carson and Sam Houston," in *The Nation*, June 6, 1928, pp. 650, 652.   [8] Stanley Vestal, *Kit Carson, passim.*

history. In fact, at times Vestal got so involved in cultural and historical detail he wavered from his main story line. The fiction theme involved a Mandan Indian wounded in a raid against the Crows and left behind by his companions. He took refuge in the tent of a Cheyenne chief until he recovered. The chief protected him, even to the point of leading his warriors in battle against the Sioux who wanted to slay the Mandan. But the Mandan repaid the chief by stealing his wife and killing his small son. The Cheyenne followed the betrayer to the Mandan village and killed him.

Aside from the so-so fictional story line, the book provided keen insight into the plains Indian way of life. Vestal described in great detail such things as the calumet dance, various customs, and the religion of the Cheyenne and Mandan. [9]

When Vestal finished *'Dobe Walls* later in 1928, Houghton Mifflin accepted it for publication in 1929. Vestal sold some short work to *The American Mercury* and other magazines. Such success after so many fruitless years would have caused many writers to ease off for awhile and bask in the hard earned glory. But with several months remaining on his fellowship, Vestal went on to a greater project – and greater success – in Sioux country.

For several years Vestal had been reading everything he could find about the Sioux in general, and the most famous of the Sioux – Sitting Bull – in particular. He rated Kit Carson the greatest of the white plainsmen, and Sitting Bull the greatest of the plains Indians. Having published a biography of Carson, he now wanted to do the same for Sitting Bull. [10] Accordingly, he left his family in Oklahoma in the spring of 1928 and drove north toward the Dakotas.

[9] Vestal, *Happy Hunting Grounds, passim.*
[10] *Dallas* (Texas) *Morning News,* Dec. 25, 1932.

With the Sioux, as with the other plains tribes, it was necessary to be introduced to the tribe by some old friend who knew his integrity, and who knew that he did not represent the government. Vestal later learned that in Canada it was best merely to show Indians a letter from a public official to get their full cooperation because they trusted Canadian officials. But they distrusted all public officials in the United States and would not co-operate with anyone connected with the government. They were too suspicious due to past experiences in dealing with American officials. [11]

Vestal's luck stayed with him in getting properly introduced. He stopped to see the state historian for North Dakota, who turned out to be the father of a Rhodes Scholar and anxious to help another Oxonian. He knew Sitting Bull's old cronies and relatives, and was liked and trusted by them. His introduction of Vestal to the Sioux made possible the first step of the research. The Sioux held the same respect for age (Vestal was now forty and had gray hair) and for war services, as did the Cheyenne and Arapaho in Oklahoma.

But this was only the beginning. Vestal still had to prove himself worthy of Sioux trust before they would offer him much help. He was an old hand with plains Indians, however, and knew how to prove himself. This involved always keeping his word, never breaking a promise, never misleading, always being open and frank, and absolutely honest at all times. He knew that if any part of a statement was not literally true, the Sioux would consider it a complete lie. In turn, the Sioux dealt with him the same way, once they were certain of him.

All this maneuvering took many weeks in the Sioux camps that summer, but eventually paid off. The two men he wanted most to interview were the two who had

---

[11] Stanley Vestal, *New Sources of Indian History, 1850-1891*, pp. 121-130.

been closest to Sitting Bull during the Indian wars, Sitting Bull's two nephews, Chief Joseph White Bull and Chief Oscar One Bull. But he dared not approach them directly. He contented himself with whatever Indians he met through formal introductions.

At first only the relatives of Sitting Bull talked, but gradually the friends came to him also as word of his project and integrity spread. He moved about the camps in North and South Dakota, Montana and Canada, interviewing all day every day. [12] He soon came to the conclusion that the white man's records were very incomplete and inaccurate, telling a story of the Sioux that was quite different from the one he was now learning. And the more he learned, the more enthusiastic he became with his project.

Just as the best white citizens are not commonly among those who loaf around the courthouse, so the best Indians were seldom found hanging around the agencies. Vestal often found it necessary to drive a hundred miles from the more settled areas to find the type of man who still had the spirit of the old days in his heart. One such warrior was quite bitter because the army would not let him enlist as a scout during World War I. He tossed his gray head and his eyes flashed with indignation as he said, "It is always better to die fighting, but they will not let me fight. Now I shall have to die in my bed someday because I got my feet wet. Is that any death for a warrior?"

Vestal agreed with him. [13]

Another old warrior Vestal met was wholly unreconstructed. One day he told Vestal why:

> The agent told me I must act like a white man. So I went to town, bought a bottle, got into a poker game and woke up in jail. Then the missionary scolded me

---

[12] *Dallas Morning News,* Dec. 25, 1932.

[13] Autobiographical data.

because I had imitated white men. I say, let them get
together. Let them make up their minds, if they want
me to follow the white man's road. [14]

The Standing Rock Reservation spanned the border
between North and South Dakota, with headquarters at
Fort Yates, North Dakota. When Vestal began making
the rounds of the camps on the reservation, he followed
a routine procedure of persuading a white man in whom
the Sioux had complete faith to introduce him to the
leading chief and explain his purpose. That was how he
finally met Chief Oscar One Bull, youngest of the two
nephews Sitting Bull had reared as sons. They met at
a camp on the Grand River south of McLaughlin, South
Dakota. What excitement Vestal must have felt as he
stared at the small, ancient warrior. The beadwork on
One Bull's shirt commemorated his part in the Custer
fight and other battles. The old chief was friendly, but
Vestal still had to persuade him to talk.

Whenever an old Indian made a formal request to
another, he would fill a pipe and present it along with
his request. If another Indian smoked the pipe, he
thereby pledged himself to grant the request. For burning a man's tobacco was an act of friendship and the words
of friendship floated upward with the smoke to the sun,
which witnessed the agreement. Vestal once expressed
doubt that the smoke reached the Heavens. "If it doesn't
go there, where does it go?" the Indians demanded tri-
umphantly.

So when Vestal made his request for information from
One Bull, he gave him tobacco. One Bull did not refuse
the tobacco. Neither did he smoke it. A chief must be
deliberate and make no hasty decisions. Vestal knew
better than to offer pay. The old time Indian was not for
hire, however much he liked presents and might expect

---

[14] *Ibid.*

reimbursement for his expenses and entertainment while conferring with Vestal. He cared little for money. What he craved was prestige. And unless he felt that talking to Vestal would bring him prestige among his fellows, nothing could be done. The task was to convince him that helping Vestal would bring him prestige. Vestal also knew that one of the best methods of getting a warrior to talk was to point out the danger involved. Whenever there was any danger to face, the bravest Indian was likely to declare, "*I* am a man; *I* will do it," and start off, and so dare the rest to follow.

Luckily for Vestal, considerable bitterness still existed among whites around the Sioux agencies over the destruction of Custer's command on the Little Big Horn. Many of the Sioux still feared to discuss their deeds in that battle. Vestal convinced them that talking to him was a test of courage. As a result, One Bull immediately became the first to take the risk. He agreed to tell Vestal what he knew about his Uncle Sitting Bull, and about the Sioux wars with the whites. One Bull kept his word, and other members of the band soon joined him in helping Vestal.

Thus began one of Vestal's closest friendships, and one of his most rewarding. One Bull lived among the Hunkpapa Sioux, the tribe to which his mother and his uncle, Sitting Bull, belonged. Born in 1853, he was adopted by Sitting Bull four years later when Sitting Bull's only son died. With this close association, One Bull was able to supply Vestal with the intimate details he sought about Sitting Bull. [15] Most of the remainder of the summer Vestal spent in or near One Bull's cabin on the banks of the Grand River. Often he interviewed the old warrior and his friends and relatives nine or ten hours a day.

In each camp Vestal found it necessary to begin his

---

[15] Vestal, "White Bull and One Bull," *loc cit.*, p. 47.

research by talking to the principal chief first. Otherwise the chief would feel slighted, and when Vestal went to him for information would say, "My friend, I am sorry. I will not talk. I do not like to contradict the stories of my fellow warriors."

Seniority and protocol were quite important among the old warriors. Every man's list of war honors – the horses he had stolen, the guns he had captured, the coups he had struck, the scalps he had taken – all had their definite ratings and insignia. And since the events for which these citations were given were narrated in public at frequent intervals, everyone in the camp knew the record of every warrior down to his last eagle feather. One after another, the old men in One Bull's camp told Vestal their stories. Some warriors would make a statement but would not answer questions. Others were willing to discuss their battles, while some would endure cross-examination for hours on end. But not a man would tolerate an interruption. According to Indian manners, to interrupt a man while he was speaking was regarded as the greatest of insults.

And if any man thought himself slighted, he was likely to resent it and refuse to cooperate. One day, One Bull's cabin was filled with old warriors. While the talk went on, a stranger came in, sat down, and listened for some time. Then suddenly he stood up, turned abruptly, and stalked out.

"Who was that?" Vestal whispered to his interpreter.

"Elk Nation," the interpreter whispered back.

Vestal knew that Elk Nation was one of the foremost warriors in his tribe. He guessed at once that Elk Nation was indignant because he had not personally welcomed him on his arrival. Hastily Vestal excused himself and hurried out of the cabin. The erect old man was striding along, brandishing his cane. Vestal caught up with him, made his apologies, led him by the hand back to the cabin, and seated him in the place of honor beside Chief One Bull. Thus Vestal saved his research in that camp.

Vestal allowed each informant to choose his own interpreter, both to make him feel at ease and to give him confidence in the translation. Usually the informant chose some middle-aged relative who understood old-time ways and the old-time meanings of Indian words. Sometimes such men had a very imperfect command of English. But it was easy to solve that problem, because among the plains Indians no man had to ask permission to enter a lodge or cabin. He merely came in and sat down. As a kinsman, any man was welcome. This made it easy for Vestal to hire an additional interpreter, one who understood English well, and have him drop in to listen to the talks. The extra interpreter, of course, never spoke during the conference. But after dark he would come to Vestal's campsite and tell of any mistakes made by the interpreter chosen by the chief.

As an additional check on accuracy, Vestal could keep up with the conversation pretty well himself for much of what was said also was given in sign language. Occasionally Vestal caught something in sign language that varied with the spoken version as translated by the interpreter, or at least understood it well enough to question his own interpreter later.

Time ran out for Vestal long before he completed his research, although he had gathered a great volume of material. He said good-bye to One Bull and made arrangements to return the following summer, then headed for Norman and the 1928-29 school year at the University of Oklahoma.

Returning to University life did not end Vestal's Sioux research, however. Soon after his arrival home he nailed some planks across the rafters in his garage. This "den" or "workshop" he furnished with a chair, a box for his typewriter, a fan and a shelf for a few reference books.

When he was up there working, few people knew about it or bothered him. [16]

And work he did that school year. He conducted a staggering amount of correspondence with relatives and friends of Sitting Bull, filling in the gaps of what he had already learned. He also corresponded with numerous Old West historians, federal researchers, old soldiers and settlers, Indian agents and missionaries. From all across the nation and Canada he secured various types of materials, such as old letters, photographs, diaries, and anything else that revealed something about the Sioux.

When Sinclair Lewis came to the campus later in October, Vestal took time out to get acquainted with the famous writer and to entertain him at campus dinners and gatherings. Lewis praised the work of Vestal, although it was quite different from his own work.

Having received only half salary during the previous year while on sabbatical leave, and having spent a large sum on his extended research trip, Vestal found himself in even worse financial difficulties now. The money he received from his first four books was spent long before it was received, and still his debts remained discouragingly high. Isabel continued to fret over their financial plight, and hoped that her own writing might reduce the total to a manageable figure. But added sales eluded her.

Bad health plagued the Campbell family also, at that time. Walter, Isabel, and their oldest daughter, Malory, all suffered from asthma and hay fever. Twice Malory nearly died of pneumonia. These conditions, plus his rather poor salary at the university, prompted Vestal to contact several eastern schools about possible employment. However, none of the offers received was attractive enough to lure him away from the plains. [17]

---

[16] Letter, J. D. McCoid to Ray Tassin, June 25, 1962, in possession of the author.

[17] Various letters to and from Campbell during the winter of 1928-29.

ISABEL CAMPBELL AND HER DAUGHTERS
MALORY (*left*) AND DOROTHY (*center*).

Before 1928 ended Vestal had one experience that was both amusing and a little sad for him. Since his early boyhood in Guthrie he usually had a teepee which he used from time to time. When his girls got big enough he kept one for them in his backyard. Oklahoma University, serving a state with the largest Indian population in the nation, naturally had many Indian students. Some 500 of these Indian students organized an Indian club, and Vestal gave them the teepee he owned at that time. A few days later he came home gloating because none of the club members knew how to put up the teepee, and had to call on him to show them how. He also was saddened by the incident because it was just one of the many indications that the younger generation of Indians knew little about their own culture. Vestal worked for many years to spark an interest among the campus Indians in the ways of their ancestors. [18]

On one occasion the teepee provided Vestal with a pleasant moment. One night when he had guests a sudden northern wind blew out the north windows of the Campbell home, making it icy cold inside, Vestal was unwilling to break up the party, so he invited the guests to move out into the teepee which he kept pitched in the backyard. The guests were dubious, but he talked them into putting on their coats and following him. In a few minutes he had a fire going. The guests soon backed up against the sides of the teepee, warm and comfortable, their faces glowing. The party continued for three hours while the wind howled and sleet covered the shelter. [19]

'*Dobe Walls* was published in the spring of 1929, making four book-length publications in print for Vestal and giving him additional prestige. The book did not arouse the enthusiasm among critics with which *Kit Carson* was

[18] Letters from J. D. McCoid, June 5, 1962, and from Mrs. Harvie McCoid, Apr. 18, 1962, to Ray Tassin, in possession of the author.

[19] Vestal, *Short Grass Country*, p. 76.

WALTER AND ISABEL WITH THE FAMILY TEEPEE
The teepee was a permanent fixture in the backyard.

received, but about a dozen newspapers gave it favorable
reviews. The story line followed the exploits of a man
working for Colonel William Bent at Bent's old fort on
the Arkansas River in Colorado. As fiction, it was not
outstanding. The hero rescued a girl from Indians, fought
Indians when necessary, overcame white and Mexican
villains, and won the girl's love. As happened with *Happy
Hunting Grounds,* *'Dobe Walls* was more history than
fiction, with the story line bogging down at times. Yet
the factual parts depicted life as it was at Bent's old
fort. This was the real value of the book. [20]

Publicity from this latest book helped Vestal win a
promotion to associate professor. This meant a raise of
$200, boosting his salary to $3,000 for nine months teaching. Any kind of raise was welcome, but $200 hardly
made a dent in Vestal's monumental debts. And he
planned still more expensive research for the coming
summer.

Somehow Vestal found time to write some short
material and make several talks before historical groups
in Texas, Kansas and Missouri during the school year.
In June 1929, he and Isabel drove out to the gigantic
New Mexico ranch of Waite Phillips of Tulsa, one of
the brothers who owned Phillips Petroleum Company.
Their four days on the ranch were intended as a brief
vacation, including horseback riding. But Vestal soon
learned that one of the caretakers was a direct descendant
of the Indian woman who guided the Lewis and Clark
expedition across the west. The opportunity was too great
for Vestal to pass up, so he sacrificed part of his vacation
time to interview the Indian.

From New Mexico, Vestal went to Boulder, Colorado,
where he was speaker for a conference on western history.
Then Isabel returned to Norman and Vestal drove on to

[20] Stanley Vestal, *'Dobe Walls, passim.*

the Dakotas. He went by way of Kansas to pick up his younger cousin, J. D. McCoid, son of his Aunt Harvie. Dallas McCoid went along with him to the Dakotas to help with the driving and to take notes while Vestal interviewed the Sioux. They secured a chuck box to one running board of the car and fastened bedrolls to the other running board. For the rest of the summer they would be camping out on the plains. In Nebraska they were joined by Professor M. G. Smith, Oklahoma University anthropologist, who accompanied them on part of the expedition that summer.

They Made Room for Him

By the summer of 1929 Vestal was certain that most printed material about the Sioux was faked and false, that the facts he received from the Sioux were accurate to the smallest detail. Many things convinced him of this. First, he would ask the Indians in one camp for all the details of specific battles and incidents in Sioux history. From them he would get the names of persons who participated, who was wounded or killed, the exact nature of the wounds, even the exact words spoken by Sitting Bull and other Sioux notables at treaty talks and other meetings. Then he would move a hundred or more miles away, perhaps from the Standing Bear Reservation in North Dakota to the Cherry Creek Reservation in South Dakota, and ask for the same details. Seldom did he find the slightest variation in the accounts. Although the second group questioned lived far from the first group, and seldom had contact with them, Vestal received the same details, names, even the exact wording of speeches uttered thirty, forty and fifty years earlier. [1]

Vestal would then go among the other tribes, the Cheyenne allies of the Sioux, the Crow enemies, the Blackfeet, and into Canada, and still he would get almost exactly the same answers. He would not accept any statement as accurate without verification from at least one other informant, and to many events he found as many as twenty eyewitnesses. All informants had to be eyewit-

---

[1] Letter, J. D. McCoid to Ray Tassin, June 10, 1962, in possession of the author.

nesses, and he took along a second interpreter to make certain the interpreter chosen by the informant made no mistakes. [2]

Indian informants were not the only ones sought by Vestal, however. On this trip he traveled across the Dakotas and Canada, interviewing steamboat pilots, scouts, interpreters, a settler who had been scalped by Indians, soldiers, fur traders, and others with first hand knowledge of the Indian wars. From all this research, Vestal found no significant variations in versions. There were instances where fifteen or twenty informants living in a thousand-mile area – all of them participants in a particular battle – told Vestal the names of the same twelve or fifteen Indians killed in some fight. But when Vestal examined war department records in Washington the following year, he found army officers had reported hundreds of Indians killed in the same engagement. Vestal had no doubts about army officers having grossly exaggerated their claims, and that Indian informants were just the opposite. He wrote later:

> I have generally found the Indians to be more reliable than the officers when you check upon them. They were not hampered by loyalty to West Point or worried about newspaper publicity. They were very objective, and their love of prestige depended upon what they did in a fight. . . Over and over I found War Department reports at fault when checked with Indians and the diaries of the officers and men concerned. [3]

The Sioux were just as careful with what they said to Vestal. Usually the man who had agreed to talk brought along two old friends to serve as witnesses. But these witnesses were not there to verify the statements

[2] *Ibid.*, and from Campbell to A. B. Welch, Sept. 19, 1928, and to Ralph Velick, Oct. 2, 1957.

[3] *Ibid.*, Campbell to Don Russell, Dec. 4, 1956.

made to Vestal. They were there to listen to the informant so that, if the interpreter or Vestal made any mistakes in recording his words, the old chief's reputation for veracity would not suffer in the tribe. A formal statement about the warfare of the tribe was regarded as a matter of the most serious importance, especially as they knew that their statements would be published. Most of these old warriors would not even repeat hearsay, even though they knew the truth about a given fight as well as those who had taken part in it. They would say, "No, I cannot tell you about that. I was not there that day. You must see so-and-so." Then Vestal had to drive two hundred miles to interview so-and-so. [4]

A big portion of Vestal's research in 1929 still centered around One Bull and his people. He was with them on the Fourth of July when an Indian parade was staged in a nearby town. Some of the younger Indians wearing war bonnets, buckskins, and moccasins marched up Main Street and around the square, a distance of two miles. At the end of the march one of the young Indians spotted Vestal sitting in his car looking on. He stumbled over to the car and crawled in. "For Pete's sake," the youth said, "take me to the hotel where I can get some shoes on. My feet are killing me." [5]

Since the goal of the old-time Indian was personal prestige, his worst vice was jealousy. This weakness Vestal sometimes turned to his advantage by getting a group of old warriors to play the game called "matching coups." A "coup," the greatest honor among the old warriors, was the striking of an enemy with the hand or with something held in the hand – such as a knife, tomahawk, lance or stick – during battle. The Indians awarded no honors for shooting a man from a distance, and actually refused to admit young Indian combat veterans of World

---

[4] Autobiographical data.   [5] *Ibid.*

War i to the old warrior societies because they had struck no enemy in this manner. When Vestal talked the old warriors into "matching coups," one would tell how he had earned some war honor. Then another would try to match the deed with some feat of his own. In the course of an afternoon a good many brave deeds were narrated. And always there were plenty of eyewitnesses to the deed present to make certain no one exaggerated.

Sometimes when a war story was being told, a shrill-voiced old woman standing nearby would open her mouth and let out a quavering war-whoop that chilled Vestal. Or a warrior imitating the sounds of actual hand-to-hand combat would utter the ferocious snarling roar of a wounded grizzly about to charge.

Now and then Vestal saw a dark scalp of Indian enemy hair in medicine bundles, or carried in war dances at night. And on one occasion an old blind man, who had put on all his war regalia for a ceremony, wore hanging from his own scalp-lock a long golden curl, snatched from the head of some unfortunate white woman long ago. The old man's blindness had kept him from realizing how the world had changed.

Once or twice Vestal felt himself momentarily unwelcome in some big camp when the warriors paraded and reminded some old woman of her son or brother who had ridden off to fight the soldiers and had not come back. When she stood on the prairie weeping and wailing, Vestal felt very lonely among all those dark stricken faces. But when the wailing ceased, everything went normal again and they were friends as before.

One old warrior still kept a fast horse staked out beside his tent and wore his war charm or amulet hanging around his neck, so that he would be ready for battle if troops charged his camp. He had never understood why the troops had attacked him in the old days, so now he saw no reason why they might not jump him again.

Sometimes the women saved the day for Vestal by arousing their men to interest and getting them to talk. Once when an old man had refused to help him, Vestal sat in the old man's lodge with his own interpreter. The old chief's wife sat across the lodge, busy with the tin plates on which she served dinner from the kettle with a capacious spoon of yellow mountain sheep's horn. Vestal turned to her and said, using the politest form of address, "Grandmother, where were you when Long Hair Custer attacked your camp?"

The old woman looked up and laughed. "Grandson, I remember very well. It was a hot morning, nearly noon. I was sitting under a tree near the river with my stone hammer pounding up some dried buffalo meat to make pemmican. My sister sat with me holding her baby. Then we heard the shooting up the river a long way off. A bullet smacked into a branch overhead and sent down showers of bark and leaves. I dropped everything and ran through the camp out onto the prairie. From there we could see the bluecoats across the river through the white smoke slowly rolling down the hill."

"Grandmother," Vestal said, "Show me the hammer you used that day."

She laughed again. "Grandson, I never went back for my hammer. After the fight, we moved camp. I never thought of it again until we had traveled two sleeps. I have never gone back."

They were at the Lame Deer Agency, only a short drive from the Custer battlefield.

"Then, Grandmother," Vestal said, "Let me invite you and the chief here to drive over to the battlefield this afternoon. Perhaps you can find your hammer and stone again."

There was no debate about the invitation. Of all the evils that surrender brought those nomadic Indians, none was so bitter as the frustration they felt in being confined to a reservation – though it might contain ten million acres. If there is anything an old-time Indian loved it was a trip, especially a trip to a battlefield. Within the hour the Cheyennes had pointed out the site of their camp when Custer fell. Leaving the car, they followed the old woman as she walked slowly toward the river. The cottonwood tree under which she had sat, of course, had gone long since, and she prowled about uncertainly.

Suddenly Vestal heard her cry out and saw her bend down among the weeds. When Vestal came up she held in her hand a round grooved hammer stone as big as a fist. At her feet a larger flat stone the size of a dinner plate lay half buried in the earth. The wooden handle of her hammer had long since rotted away, but the stones were just where she had left them. Half laughing, half crying, she gathered them up and carried them to the car. Her emotion broke the chief's reserve, and they all had a wonderful afternoon going over the field while the chief pointed out where he had fought and where certain other Indians and General Custer himself had been shot down.

At the foot of the bluffs the old chief stopped to laugh. "Here I tried to catch an army mule. It was packed with ammunition and came plunging down the hill. But before I could reach it, it threw up its nose, smelled the Indians and ran up again." [6]

Tribal rivalries also helped Vestal with his research. When the Crows learned that Vestal was getting information from their old enemies, the Sioux and Cheyennes, Vestal found them very willing to co-operate and give their side of the case. And whenever he could arrange a conference between warriors and enemy tribes, he had a field day. Both sides bragged and challenged, and a great deal of detail came up for checking that might

---

[6] *Ibid.*

otherwise never have been told. Such arguments were sometimes heated, but never became bitter. One day in the cabin of One Bull, Vestal brought up the subject of the Custer fight. One Bull and his wife looked at each other and began to laugh. Vestal wanted to be in on the joke, so the jolly old woman got out an ancient cavalry saddlebag. It was mended with sinew, and she said it had been used as a valise in her family for many years. She had picked it up from a dead soldier's saddle after Custer's last stand. The point of the joke was that Sitting Bull had forbidden his relatives to take any of the lot, believing that, if the Indians craved the white man's goods, it would prove disastrous to the Sioux. So his nephew One Bull never had a trophy of the fight he helped win – until he married Scarlet Whirlwind Woman, who brought the saddlebag into his cabin. One Bull made Vestal a present of the saddlebag. Through incidents like this Vestal gradually accumulated a vast amount of data about the most famous battle in Old West history, as well as Sioux history in general. [7]

Plains Indians have a strong race pride. One day while consulting some old men in an Indian town, Vestal noticed across the road a fine two-story house painted white with green shutters and a new car parked in front. An Indian woman and two children were playing in the yard. Presently a young man wearing a neat business suit, his shoes shined and his hair cut like a white man's, came over and said he wished to ask Vestal a question. In his lapel he wore the button of the American Legion. He spoke excellent English. Of course, Vestal wished to be friends with everyone and was happy to oblige, but the Indian's question put him in a quandary. He demanded, "Who is more intelligent, the white man or the Indian?"

---

[7] *Ibid.,* and letter from Campbell to E. S. Luce, Jan. 3, 1952.

In vain Vestal tried to brush off the young fellow. But the Indian insisted that Vestal answer his question. Vestal therefore decided that he would tell him the truth as he saw it. He said, "White men and Indians vary in intelligence. Some are smart and some are foolish. The Indian is smart about the things which interest him. The white man is the same. But so far as I can see, the smartest Indians are just as intelligent as the smartest white men. I see no difference in them."

The Indian was not pleased, but kept after Vestal, trying to make him say that white men were more intelligent than Indians. Finally, disappointed that Vestal could not agree, he went off. Vestal then learned that the Indian was one-sixteenth white and that the full-bloods living in hovels and tents all about him threw this up to him and told him he was not as smart as they. In self defense he had gone to college, built himself a fine house, bought a good car and dressed his family like his white neighbors. But it was all to no purpose. The full-bloods were not impressed.

In fact, Vestal never met an old-time plains warrior who did not take it for granted as perfectly obvious that Indians were superior to white men physically, mentally, and morally. They attributed their defeat not to any superiority of white people, but to the greater power of the white men's God. As Watan put it, "The only thing you brought us that was better than what we had is Christianity." [8]

Indians had a keen sense of humor and were fond of practical jokes. Often Vestal's interviews with the warriors were enlightened by comic interludes. One warm afternoon while Yellow Hawk and Vestal sat smoking between talks in Yellow Hawk's teepee, a young Indian in store clothes and with hair cut short, indicating that he had gone away to school, approached the teepee. The

---

[8] Autobiographical data.

side of the tent had been raised four or five feet from
the ground to let the breeze blow through. The visitor,
by stooping a little, could look in and see Yellow Hawk's
pretty daughter who sat demurely with both her feet to
one side doing some beadwork across the lodge. The
young man was evidently much attracted to the young
woman, but Indian etiquette did not permit him to address the girl directly in the presence of her father. He
stood looking in, displaying his fine clothes for the benefit of the girl, and talking at a great rate to her father
about himself, his horses and prospects. For all his college education, he was as good at blowing his own horn
as any old-timer in the camp.

It would have been rude to interrupt him, and all in
the teepee sat quiet. While he prated, another young man
wearing moccasins, with long braids framing a humorous
face, slipped noiselessly up behind him. There, all unknown to the braggart, he began a satirical comment in
the sign language, turning to ridicule every statement
the anxious suiter made. The girl and her father sat
poker-faced while the comedy went on, until they could
hold in no longer. Then everyone burst out laughing.
The talker looked around, saw that he had been made
a fool of, and hurried away. Of all weapons, ridicule was
the most deadly to the Indian. [9]

Old warriors liked to draw pictures of their exploits
on dressed skins, cloth, or paper. In the old days they
used water colors laid on with a marrow bone. But by
Vestal's time colored pencils were used. These drawings
show the warriors, horses, and buffalo in profile without
perspective, outlined sharply in action.

One picture shown to Vestal depicted a horse with
an arrow sticking in its left side. The artist laughed as
he explained to Vestal, "I shot that horse to keep the
enemy from getting him. My arrow struck his ribs on

[9] *Ibid.*

his right side. But here you see the arrow in his left side, because in a picture, of course, a horse always faces left."

Vestal made copies of the drawings in the Smithsonian Institution depicting Sitting Bull's exploits. When he showed them to the old warriors, each readily identified them, giving Vestal details of Sitting Bull's raids upon enemy tribes and against white men. Though few of the old men could speak English, Vestal found some who had learned to write in the Sioux langauge, and who had records of their own battles written sixty winters before. When possible, Vestal obtained these records, or true copies, whether written or pictured.

Vestal and Dallas traveled often at night, since they had sleeping bags in the car and it was fairly comfortable to drive and sleep in shifts. But Dallas eventually became afraid to let Vestal do much of the driving after dark. It seems Vestal allowed the car to wander from one side of the road to the other. He told Dallas it was the easiest way to drive, and he was thinking about his writing. Dallas woke up one night to find Vestal driving on a flat tire without noticing it. Vestal often complained of the car not working properly. Actually, according to Dallas, he kept the gas pedal in one position all the time. When climbing a hill, the car would slow almost to a stop. And Vestal gave little thought to doing anything to the car except putting gasoline in it. A few years later he burned the engine out of his car because he neglected to put in oil. That was the last car he ever owned; after that he used public transportation. The car just would not take care of itself as a horse would. [10]

On one quick trip to Ottawa, Canada, Dallas and Vestal had trouble locating a post office. Dallas stopped the car to ask a policeman for directions. Apparently his Kansas accent was too much for the officer. Dallas re-

---

[10] Letters, J. D. McCoid to Ray Tassin, June 5 and 25, 1962, in possession of the author.

called later: "I was making absolutely no headway when Vestal came out with the best English accent I have ever heard. And it was the only time I ever did hear him use it, but he did get results." [11]

As the end of the summer drew near, Vestal and Dallas stepped up their pace. They ended August in Bismarck, North Dakota, where Vestal interviewed all sorts of people, including another white man who had been scalped by Indians and an old lady to whom Sitting Bull had given a ring when she was a young girl. [12] That night they camped on a hillside near Bismarck, just north of a big valley filled with buttes and hills. A mile to their left they could see timber along the Missouri River. And three miles south were some big Sioux camps, where Vestal spent the first day of September interviewing several old warriors.

On September 2 they drove south to Fort Yates, North Dakota. Here Vestal talked to ten warriors in a single day. Vestal sat in the council tent and smoked the peace pipe with the old warriors, but Dallas was only twenty years old and was not allowed inside. He sat just outside, behind Vestal. According to Dallas,

the talk was of our friendship and our usual investigation into the deeds of Sitting Bull and his tribe. However, I remember that this meeting was dominated by one old chief who wanted to talk only of HIS exploits. . . The womenfolk were not permitted in the council tent, so they sat food outside near the door where lesser chiefs could reach it. . . The food was a stew of honest-to-goodness jerk [dried meat]. The Indian children were given pieces of jerk for a between-the-meal snack, and it literally took hours of boiling to make it tender and edible. There was salt in the stew, but no other seasoning. As the Indians smoked the peace pipe, it was passed around the circle and had to

---

[11] *Ibid.*   [12] Letter, Campbell to his wife, Aug. 31, 1929.

be held in both hands. The right hand held the bowl firmly and the left hand was placed mid-way up the stem. It was passed around the ring so that someone always had both hands on it. The pipe was never put in one's mouth, as is the white man's custom. Instead, it was pressed against the lips much as when one blows a trumpet.

The meeting lasted about three hours and was really quite an experience. [13]

The next stop on their general movement southward, three days in and near McLaughlin, South Dakota, was to be one Vestal would remember and treasure for the rest of his life. After two days of talks, Chief Oscar One Bull announced to Vestal and those present in his cabin that he wished to honor the white man who was honoring them with his work. Then, with an appropriate ritual, One Bull adopted Vestal as his son and therefore as a member of his tribe. He conferred on Vestal the name of his own father, a famous Miniconjou Sioux chief of earlier days. The name, Ki-yu-kan-pi, meant Makes Room, or They Make Room for Him. The idea behind the name was that the Sioux made room for Vestal in their hearts. [14] That evening One Bull's wife gave Vestal an eyewitness account of the murder of Sitting Bull. "She saw Sitting Bull dragged from his bed and house, and shot unresisting in cold blood," Vestal wrote home. [15]

The following and final day for Vestal with One Bull that summer included a trip to an Indian fair in McLaughlin. They camped near the fairgrounds. While Vestal and One Bull were in Vestal's tent talking, One Bull's grandson ran inside and urged the old man to enter a horse race for Indians over seventy years old. One Bull

---

[13] Letter, J. D. McCoid to Ray Tassin, June 25, 1962, in possession of the author.

[14] Letters, Campbell to his daughters, Sept. 6, 1926; to Father Augustine Edele, Feb. 17, 1947; and to Ira Rich Kent, Sept. 10, 1929.

[15] *Ibid.*, to his daughters, Sept. 6, 1929.

only laughed at the idea until he learned there was a first prize of twenty-five dollars. Then, with Vestal's urging, he hurried outside and bridled his fastest horse. Vestal helped him mount, and away One Bull raced bareback, running his mount to warm it up before the start. Then the contestants lined up for the race. At the word "go" half a dozen old-timers dashed around the mile-long track, quirting their horses to top speed. In the final stretch One Bull shared the lead with one other rider, but kicked his mount into the lead and finished first by twenty yards. When declared the winner, he let out a war-whoop, and tossing his quirt into the air, rode off without looking back to see where it fell. He and Vestal went back to the tent, where One Bull spent the rest of the afternoon telling Vestal about the fast horses he had ridden when he was a boy and serving as jockey for his uncle, Sitting Bull. That night One Bull went to the main street of town and led a big street dance in full regalia, going strong long after the young bucks were exhausted. Vestal was really proud of the old man. [16]

Next day Vestal and Dallas left for home with their prized research notes and a warm feeling for a successful summer's work. Vestal arrived in Norman September 9 after 2,500 miles of travel.

---

[16] *Ibid.,* and autobiographical data.

His Name is Everywhere

Back in Norman, Vestal continued to read everything he could find in print about the Sioux, comparing the accounts with his research notes and checking out various points of conflict. He wrote numerous letters that year, many of them to the Sioux via literate relatives and agents. The more he studied and compared, the more he believed the white man's records were incomplete and inaccurate regarding the Sioux.

One of the letters from the Cherry Creek Indian Reservation was among the most important Vestal ever received. It came from Chief Joseph White Bull, brother of One Bull and the eldest nephew reared by Sitting Bull as his son. Since the fiftieth anniversary celebration at the Custer battlefield in 1926, Vestal had wanted to gain the confidence of White Bull, not only because the old chief had led the Sioux parade across the battlefield but also because he was one of the greatest Sioux warriors. Vestal believed White Bull could provide him with data no one else could give him, for he had been in many battles with Sitting Bull and had been close to him from boyhood to Sitting Bull's death.

When Vestal first started his research among the Sioux he spread the word about his project so all Sioux would know about it. He was sure White Bull had heard of his work. But Vestal had been careful not to see White Bull or visit him on Cherry Creek, South Dakota, where his band camped. He knew White Bull was a man of strong and decisive character, and Vestal feared that if he approached the chief with an invitation to help him, White Bull might refuse. Once the old man made up his mind, he would never reverse himself, Vestal knew. So Vestal had waited, making no move toward White Bull. Sometimes he thought his patience would wear out. Often he had thought of approaching White Bull, but caution stopped him each time. His patience paid off, finally. The letter from White Bull said he wanted to see Vestal.

"I was delighted," Vestal wrote later in what was likely the understatement of the year. Vestal spent weeks seeking funds to finance the trip. But already many thousands of dollars in debt, and with a bad credit standing, he failed to get help. Twice before he had sought, unsuccessfully, to get Guggenheim Fellowships. In desperation, and armed with a large portion of what he needed for an outstanding biography, he applied once more to the Guggenheim Foundation. Next, he signed a contract with Houghton Mifflin Company, publishers of three of his four books, for the Sitting Bull biography.

The winter months likely were agonizing for Vestal. Priceless information appeared available if he could just get some financial backing. He did not expect to succeed with the Guggenheim Foundation, but simply knew no place else to try. Yet he worked hard all winter on his research notes.

Vestal's luck grew with his success, however. The following March the Guggenheim Foundation awarded him a $2,500 grant "to devote himself . . . to a study of the plains Indians, their foes, allies and neighbors" and "to a biography of the Indian leader, Sitting Bull." The grant was for fifteen months, starting June 1, 1930. [1]

Just a month later the University of Oklahoma granted

[1] Letter, Guggenheim Foundation to Campbell, Mar. 7, 1930.

Vestal an equivalent sabbatical leave, with $1,000 salary. [2]

Fifteen months off and $3,500 – Vestal could have asked for no more.

The next few weeks were busy ones for the Campbell family, centering around plans and preparations for the trip. Walter decided he would spend about four months completing the research, first among the Indians, then in Washington in the Library of Congress and the War Department. Isabel and the girls would meet him in New York in September, and the four of them would go on to France for the remainder of his leave. He believed that he could write the biography faster there, far from home. And there was a certain prestige in writers going to France in those days of the "lost generation" involving such literary greats as Ernest Hemingway, F. Scott Fitzgerald and others. Also, Walter, Isabel and their eldest daughter, Malory, all suffered from hay fever and asthma which was aggravated by pollens in Oklahoma. Vestal thought the climate in France might help them recover from the ailment.

The Campbells left their girls with relatives for the summer. Isabel went to Hollywood to contact various individuals connected with writing and movie production. Vestal packed his car with his well-worn camping equipment and headed for the northern plains. He picked up his cousin, Dallas, and drove on up through Nebraska and into South Dakota. Vestal's anticipation grew with each passing mile, as might be expected for one nearing the realization of a long-held dream. It was a wonder some of his anticipation did not bounce out of him, however, once they left the main road and took to the back roads of the primitive area. From the last city they drove a hundred miles over what passed for roads, stopping only

[2] *Ibid.*, to Campbell, unsigned, from Oklahoma University, Apr. 1, 1930.

at the sub-agency near White Bull's camp. When Vestal
told the white employees why he was there, they objected
vigorously to his project.

"Don't you know White Bull is the man who killed
Custer?" one of them demanded. [3]

Vestal knew that at the Custer battlefield ceremony
in 1926 White Bull had admitted he might have been
the one who killed Custer. The army was convinced
that he was at least among those who killed the last of
Custer's command, those whose bodies were found around
Custer's. In acquiring his already voluminous data on
the Custer fight Vestal had picked up some additional
indication that White Bull was Custer's killer. Now, the
vehemence of the agency employees and their conviction
that White Bull was the man, made Vestal more determined to check the incident until he was certain. If what
the agency employees claimed could be verified, Vestal
could achieve a major historical scoop. He and Dallas
wasted no time moving on to the nearby small Sioux
village of Cherry Creek on the banks of a creek by the
same name. Here was the promised land – or village – a
cluster of shacks and teepees that housed the people
of Chief Joseph White Bull.

Well versed in the ways of the plains Indians, Vestal
knew better than to approach White Bull that first day.
Their first meeting had to be properly arranged. Instead,
he and Dallas set up their camp near the village and
opened a few cans of food. [4]

---

[3] Letters, Campbell to Savoie Lottinville, Dec. 13, 1953; to Karl F.
Zeister, July 15, 1957; and to Paul Reynolds, Dec. 6, 1952. It is possible this incident and the interview of the following evening occurred
in 1932 rather than 1930 as reported here. Most of Vestal's papers
indicate 1930. Dallas McCoid who accompanied him in 1930, but not
in 1932, does not recall either this incident or the interview of the
following night.

[4] Letter, Campbell to his wife, June 6, 1930.

As Vestal entered the village the next morning, White Bull came out to meet him, smiling, grasping him by the hand and shoulder. He was a tall, husky, virile man in his late eighties. Vestal had been worried about winning the old chief's confidence, or that White Bull might limit the topics to be discussed. But the warm reception dispelled his fears. He developed an immediate liking for the chief, and later described him as the only man equal to his stepfather, J. R. Campbell.

"My friend," White Bull began, "you may ask me anything. I will tell you the truth. I am not afraid. The man who lies is a weakling." [5]

In this manner began what Vestal considered the most important series of interviews he ever conducted. That night the Sioux held a dance in a big, double log cabin to welcome him. It was a cold night so the door was kept closed but a mob of white men gathered outside and booed and whistled loudly for an hour or so to express their hostility toward Vestal's project. Ignoring the racket, Vestal presented White Bull with an old cavalry saber and a red shirt of the type worn by the University of Oklahoma men's pep club, the Ruf-Neks. Then Vestal took White Bull aside and asked him if he had killed Custer. White Bull admitted that he had killed the soldier whom others had identified as Long Hair. [6]

After further questioning, White Bull described what happened in detail, saying: When only about twenty soldiers were left on their feet, he and other Indians rushed in on foot to finish them off. As he approached one soldier, the man hurled his rifle at him. White Bull easily avoided the missile and charged in on the soldier, who jerked out his pistol. They wrestled for the weapon

[5] *Ibid.*, and autobiographical data.
[6] Letters, Campbell to Savoie Lottinville, Dec. 13, 1953; to Karl Zeister, July 15, 1957; and to Paul Reynolds, Dec. 6, 1952.

until White Bull wrenched it away and hit the soldier with it. The soldier fell to the ground, and White Bull shot him in the head and in the heart. When the battle was over, White Bull's cousin, Bad Soup, pointed to the body of that same soldier and said "That is Long Hair."

"I don't think my cousin would deceive me but I never saw Long Hair before the battle so that is hearsay and should not go into your book," White Bull told Vestal. [7]

Vestal later questioned many others who had seen the fight. All verified White Bull's version in every detail. All those who viewed the body that day said he was the soldier killed by White Bull in that particular fight. Now Vestal knew why White Bull had been chosen to lead the Sioux across the battlefield during the anniversary celebration of the fight. Who had a better right to the honor than the man who had killed Custer?

Throughout all his research among the Indians, Vestal always emphasized that he did not want any hearsay. What he learned from White Bull and members of his band was really eyewitness testimony of the first order, but White Bull did not see it that way. Vestal could not change his mind, and knew that he must respect the old chief's wishes. Also, the demonstration outside the cabin earlier in the evening showed the bitterness many whites still felt toward those responsible for the Custer defeat. Vestal feared if he published the account, some hot-head might harm the old man. Reluctantly, he decided he would never publish the story as long as White Bull lived. [8]

Most of the interviews with White Bull took place in the one-room cabin of the old chief, a room barren of anything but a large trunk, cooking utensils and blankets. White Bull spread blankets on the dirt floor for them to sit on. Most of each day they sat there cross-legged with only a brief interruption for a noon meal.

[7] *Ibid.*   [8] *Ibid.*

From One Bull, Vestal secured the domestic and religious side of Sitting Bull's life. From White Bull he now learned the political side. White Bull had fought in seventeen battles with his famous uncle and had been with him most of the time in political activities. [9] He was twenty-six when he surrendered to the army in 1876, soon after the Custer battle. Three years later he learned to write the Sioux language and compiled a written record – illustrated with drawings – of all the important battles and events of this nation within living memory. [10] No white man had ever seen those records. Now White Bull took from the trunk a hundred pages he had written, and to Vestal revealed their contents, through an interpreter.

With White Bull talking, many other Sioux wanted to prove their own courage by telling what they had seen and done. After only a few days, Vestal was stiff and sore from the ordeal, but White Bull never tired. He was one of the most intelligent men Vestal had ever met, with an infallible memory, a quick wit, and a great sense of humor. He not only sat and talked endlessly, but much of the time used both hands and sometimes his whole body illustrating his stories in the wonderful mimicry of the sign language, giving Vestal a moving picture of everything he described. When telling how the soldiers fired volleys, he imitated the sound of the firing by rapidly clapping his hands. When telling how an Indian shot an enemy, White Bull would draw an imaginary bow, loose an imaginary arrow, then smack the back of one hand into the palm of the other to indicate a hit, afterward throwing himself into the posture and grimace of the dying man. "It was all most graphic, the poetry of emotion," Vestal wrote. And it helped him check the interpreter whenever in such rapid-fire talk unfamiliar words were used. [11]

---

[9] Autobiographical data.　　　　　　[10] Vestal, *Warpath*, p. vii.
[11] Autobiographical data.

Vestal wrote his wife:

> This is the cream of my trip. My book is made, if
> nothing else were added. He [White Bull] was in 17
> battles with Sitting Bull and I have full details. He
> has ledgers full of data – with the names of all warriors,
> casualties and coups for every battle.   .   .   We talk
> 9 hours a day. Best of all, White Bull is not trying to
> make a hero of Sitting Bull. He knows he was one, and
> is content with facts. [12]

White Bull was almost deaf and listened through a
long, flexible ear trumpet. This enabled others in the
cabin to make sly remarks about him which he could not
hear. When he described how he led a charge, someone
nearby would mutter, "I was there but I did not notice
him out in front." The spectators, especially Vestal, enjoyed the horse play. "It is a scream," Vestal wrote.
"Sometimes things get rather tense, and the old men
have tears in their eyes as they tell of past suffering,"
Vestal wrote. "One man told yesterday how his mother
was killed by the soldiers and he was shot down when
he was only five years old." [13]
Often Vestal would tire during the interviews. Each
time he did so, White Bull would catch his horse and
ride around the village to show he was still fresh and able
to go on, even though he was eighty-six years old. This
impressed Vestal as much as anyone else. [14] He wrote:

> I have sat on the floor of White Bull's cabin so much
> my buttocks are sore, but he is giving me stuff worth
> any amount and I can't tear myself away.   .   .   The
> old man is fond of me, loves to talk, and is anxious to
> have me stay on indefinitely. I tell him history con-
> nected with his own, and it is pathetic to see his eager-
> ness to listen. How he can tell a story – what panto-
> mime, what mimicry of voice and expression.   .   .

[12] Letter, Campbell to his wife, June 6, 1930.
[13] *Ibid.*, June 10, 1930.   [14] Autobiographical data.

He will tell anything I ask. Yesterday he rehearsed his matrimonial history – 14 women – and marriages lasting from 9 days to 3 months and upwards. [His fifteenth wife joined in laughter at these discussions, and at White Bull's pantomimes on his sex life.] [15] Four times he tried to have 2 wives at once – always with unhappy results due to jealousy. . . One pair was so jealous that when he went to bed one woman clung to his arm and leg on one side, the other on the other, so that he couldn't sleep and was all cramped and stiff in the morning. He acted it all out for me. It was a scream! [16]

At one point White Bull gave Vestal a Sharps rifle which he had taken from a buffalo hunter during the warpath days.

Vestal usually honored his informants publicly, and also provided them with the meat for an occasional feast. To one he would give a scarlet woolen shirt, to another a sheeplined coat or hat. Each time the old warrior would be pleased and take his gift into his cabin, then send for Vestal in order that – after the custom of the Indians – Vestal might dress him in the new outfit with his own hands. Sometimes at a dance Vestal would make a little speech paying tribute to his informants and explaining to the Indians once more what he was trying to do with his research.

To White Bull, Vestal gave a cavalry saber and belt. This gift aroused the old warriors to such enthusiasm that they immediately started an old-time war dance which the younger men had to sit out. As Vestal sat watching, White Bull

came and stood before me, sternly fixed me with his eyes and held the tip of his eagle wing fan against my breast for fully three minutes. I looked him in the eye as a

---

[15] Letter, J. D. McCoid to Ray Tassin, June 25, 1962, in author's possession. [16] Letter, Campbell to his wife, June 11, 1930.

warrior should. Thereupon he invited me to join the
dance of the old-timers. It was all in the grand old
manner of the buffalo days. [17]

As the days passed, the friendship of Vestal and White
Bull matured. So did White Bull's desire to show his
appreciation for what Vestal was trying to do for his
people. One day they sat eating lunch in White Bull's
cabin – boiled jerk, boiled prunes and milk pudding.
White Bull was preoccupied during the meal. Then he
announced that he wanted to honor Vestal by adopting
him as his son, just as One Bull had done the previous
year. Accordingly, White Bull called in all those who
had been hanging around the cabin during the interviews.
To those assembled, White Bull said he was adopting
Vestal because he was recording the true story of the
Sioux for all to see and read in the city of the Great
White Father [Washington, D. C.].

The name White Bull bestowed on Vestal was Ocas-
tonka, meaning "His Name Is Everywhere," or "Famous."
The intention of White Bull was to show that Vestal was
spreading White Bull's fame everywhere with his book. [18]

During the interviews Vestal

did not do all the listening. They [the Sioux] were interested in the white man's motives, and at times demanded that I tell what the white men had said about
Indian campaigns, sometimes keeping me talking for
hours. I told them the truth, and I never expect to have
keener or more attentive listeners. Those old men
wanted to know why the white men came against them;
most of them had not the faintest idea what the wars
were all about. [19]

Vestal would have liked to remain there indefinitely,
but his time was carefully budgeted. At the end of June

[17] Autobiographical data.
[18] Telegram, Campbell to his wife, June 12, 1930.
[19] *Dallas Morning News*, Dec. 25, 1932.

VESTAL AND WHITE BULL

Standing in front of White Bull's cabin. The saber was a gift of Vestal in appreciation of White Bull's friendship and assistance to Vestal's research of the Sioux Wars.

he said farewell to White Bull and drove on north, seeking other eyewitnesses to the feats of Sitting Bull. He stopped in Fort Yates briefly, and visited the nearby birthplace and grave of Sitting Bull, which were only five miles apart.

As in past years, Vestal often talked old warriors into taking him to historical sites unknown to anyone except the Sioux – site of battles, large and small, and other events important in Sioux history. Each time,

> when we reach the spot we are seeking, we located the exact site, dig a narrow hole five feet into the ground, drop in a bottle containing a paper giving the facts, and fill in the hole. In this way I am enabled to mark important historic sites without expense. For before we leave we take a compass bearing and notes on the site. [20]

Just how many sites are marked in this manner is not known, but Vestal's notes on his trips contain many such compass bearings. [21] Perhaps someday historical societies or others might find the notes useful in erecting monuments at some of the more important sites.

One of Vestal's favorites among the old Sioux chiefs was Gray Whirlwind, "the jolliest old buck I ever knew." The last time Vestal saw him he was ninety-six years old.

> I found my old friend far out on the grass out of sight of any house, sitting alone in his tent while his children and grandchildren and great-grandchildren were busy at the harvest [of tipsin roots] all about.
>
> He made me welcome. We talked on until midday.
>
> The flap of the tent was open, and I could see for miles across the grey-green Dakota prairie. The tent, pitched only a few hours before, inspired a carefree feeling, since the grass inside it had not yet been trodden down. The very weather seemed to agree with the old man's jollity.

[20] *Ibid.*   [21] Sitting Bull data, Campbell Collection, *loc. cit.*

While we sat there talking of the old days, a furry half-grown puppy came bouncing in and flung himself upon me. He was sure the whole world was his friend, and the rest of the morning he was in my lap or on my feet every moment. I had to pet him to keep him from breaking up the meeting.

At noon my interpreter turned to me and said, "the chief wishes to honor you. He wants you to stay for dinner."

Of course, I was pleased at that, more particularly as it was many miles to a restaurant and I wished to continue my talk.

"Tell the chief," I said, "that I shall be very glad to accept his hospitality."

The interpreter hesitated. Instead of addressing Gary Whirlwind, he spoke to me again. "He is going to feed you that puppy," he said, eyeing me expectantly.

Now I knew that to be invited to a dog-feast among the Sioux was like being invited to a turkey dinner by a white man, and I knew too that dog meat has always enjoyed the reputation of being the finest flesh available on the prairie. I appreciated the honor done me. But I said to the interpreter, "Tell the chief we have to hurry back to town." I might eat dog and like it, but I'm damned if I will eat a dog I have just been playing with. [22]

Vestal and Dallas wandered all over the Dakotas, Montana and portions of Canada that summer. They located One Bull living in a cabin in a beautiful, remote and almost inaccessible valley near Regina, Saskatchewan, Canada.

The visit with One Bull was brief, but eventful for Vestal. Soon after his arrival, Vestal complained of a headache. One Bull's wife took a round and flat stone from under the bed, put it in the fire, heated it through, then wrapped it in a cloth and laid it on the bed. "Sit on

---

[22] Stanley Vestal, *The Missouri*, pp. 217-18.

that," she said. Vestal followed instructions. As the heat mounted up his backbone the headache disappeared [23]

Naturally this event brought on a discussion of cures and medicine men. One Bull remarked that he had Sitting Bull's medicine bundle, then asked if Vestal would like to see it. Vestal responded quickly before the opportunity was lost. So One Bull opened the inevitable trunk always found in an Indian cabin. From it he took the bundle which the Sioux believed possessed great magical powers. It consisted

of a yard of unbleached muslin thirty inches wide, dyed a deep orange yellow. In each corner is painted a conventional green dragonfly – the symbol of swiftness and agility in escaping enemies. In the middle of the cloth, between the horizontal blocks representing heaven and earth, stands an elk eight inches tall. The elk is outlined in green, with red spots on the body. Both elk and dragonflies face the beholder's left.

Wrapped in this cloth is also a bit of calamus root, and the tail of a white-tail deer mounted on a short stick, with a string attached with which to fasten it to the painted cloth. The deer tail contains the power of the fleet animal it was taken from, and adds to the speed of the charm. With these objects there is a pair of inch-wide wristlets of buffalo hide with the brown wool left on, having thongs tying them around the wrists. These wristlets were evidently cut from a painted buffalo robe, for there are traces of the robe design on the flesh-side of the skin, in red, yellow and blue.

When Sitting Bull wished to use this charm, he usually went to some lonely hilltop and made a sacrifice, either by cutting himself and letting some blood flow, or by hanging a piece of scarlet cloth to the top of a stick planted in the ground. Then he tied on the wristlets, fastened the deer-tail to the top of the medicine-

[23] Autobiographical data.

cloth, and sang the song taught him by the visionary elk:

> I have a good friend [meaning God] above;
> I have a good friend above;
> I have an elk-friend above;
> On earth I speak for a nation.

This song is apparently a reminder to the god who promised aid in the vision, and a prayer for help for the Sioux nation.

After singing this song, Sitting Bull took hold of the cloth by its upper corners, and holding it spread out, struck the ground with it four times. In his vision, he had been promised that this would make the wind blow. The harder he struck the ground, the harder it would blow.

If, on the other hand, he wished to make it rain, he had only to chew a small bit of the calamus root and sputter the saliva upon the cloth, at the same time waving it in the air. [24]

While Vestal inspected the medicine cloth closely, One Bull completed his account of how the charm worked. Then he said that he had seen it used only twice, both times in 1878 when the Sioux needed extra help in combat with their enemies. It worked both times, One Bull said. [25]

Enthralled, Vestal wanted to buy the bundle but One Bull shook his head. Some of the younger Indians in the family backed Vestal, however. One Bull said he hated to part with it because the Sioux had no other protection against the army's bombers. Finally, and with great reluctance, he agreed to lend it to Vestal on the condition that it be returned when the Sioux developed a need for its great powers.

One Bull and his neice, Mrs. One Bull Brown, both cautioned Vestal against using the bundle just "to see if it works." Use it, they told him, only when he had

[24] Vestal, *New Sources of Indian History*, pp. 144-45.   [25] *Ibid.*

faith in its powers. Then it would bring rain, or make the wind blow, according to which verse he used.

Vestal wrote his wife that he was going to try it out "when I reach *pavement.*" [26]

After Vestal and Dallas left the camp, they went to Regina, Canada, for a few days in the provincial archives. When they were ready to leave, they found themselves unable to do so because

> it had been raining all the time we were there. Since there was no pavement between the cities, the local authorities said we would not be able to leave for at least a week, as the barometer was dropping. That evening, in a very serious mood, Walter and I went to the edge of the city and he tore the red lining out of his tie as an offering [he was supposed to offer some blood] and he said the verse and waved the cloth four times before and after the verse, as per instructions. That night a wind came up and dried the roads and we drove out of town on top of the ruts. . . If he [Walter] didn't believe in the cloth, one could not tell it by his attitude. [27]

As the summer neared its end, the wanderers spent a few days in Ottawa where Vestal went through the Dominion archives checking out bits of information about Sitting Bull. Then the time came to leave Sioux country. He traveled eight thousand miles during the summer, averaging two hundred miles a day. By keeping a bed in the car and sharing the driving with Dallas, he was able to keep moving without camping much at night. "We only went into the ditch twice through falling asleep," he wrote. [28]

Also by this time, Vestal had visited every tribe in the United States and Canada that had any contact with

[26] Letter, Campbell to his wife, June 27, 1930.
[27] Letter, McCoid to Tassin, June 25, 1962.
[28] Letter, Campbell to Maurice Smith, Oct. 22, 1930.

Sitting Bull, except two minor groups where he got the work done by men who had spent their careers working with them. Altogether, he had traveled twenty thousand miles and interviewed more than one hundred men who had known Sitting Bull personally. He had read every available record and report in the archives of the Royal Northwest Mounted Police and Dominion government of Canada, and all the private papers of Major James McLaughin, the Indian agent at Standing Rock Agency when Sitting Bull was there.

Now, Vestal and Dallas went to Washington to wind up the job of research. Here they spent a week combing the Library of Congress, and records and reports of the War Department, the Bureau of Indian Affairs, and the Bureau of Ethnology.

Finally, in September they drove to New York where Isabel and the girls joined them. A week later, Dallas went home and the Campbell's started the long awaited trip to France.

Troubled Years

The Campbells spent the fall and winter months in a boarding house in Paris. Vestal and Isabel occupied themselves with their writing – he on the Sitting Bull biography and she on a novel – while the girls attended a private school.

But Vestal wanted his family to see more of France than just Paris, and to get more pleasure from the year than Paris could provide. In the early spring he moved them to southern France, where they lived in Cannes and Nice. This was the famous Riviera, a narrow coastal area of mild climate and beautiful scenery where many American literary figures of the day spent at least a portion of their time in the late 1920s and early 1930s.

Vestal described the Riviera as "a good place to write, because nearly everyone else is playing around and doesn't bother you while you work. And when you quit working, there is always someone to play with."[1]

Vestal provided some of the entertainment for others while in southern France. He and his family were living in a hotel at the time, and apparently were relaxing on the sunny terrace. They had made friends by then. As Americans usually do when on foreign soil, this group exchanged back-home tales. At one point Vestal told his new friends of Sitting Bull's medicine bundle which One Bull had given him. But when he described what happened in Regina, Canada, the only time he tried the charm, his audience became skeptical. Even the French

---

[1] Autobiographical data.

waiters smiled at the superstitious American who appeared to believe in such nonsense.

Somewhat irritated at the reaction, Vestal excused
himself and hurried up to his hotel room, picked up Sitting Bull's medicine bundle and returned to the terrace.
To the amusement of those watching, Vestal opened the
bundle and proceeded to go through the ritual taught
him by One Bull. The bright sunshine burned down on
the Terrace while Vestal performed. Finishing, Vestal
bundled up the charm and waited. Within minutes, the
sun vanished, black storm clouds appeared, and the area
was drenched with the heaviest rain of the season.

Vestal's delight was about what one would expect it
to be. But there was one drawback. None of the waiters
would come close to him. They wanted nothing to do
with one who possessed such mystical powers. [2]

Vestal planned the Sitting Bull biography as two volumes and had almost finished the first one when financial
troubles caught up with him again and changed his plans.
He had decided to stay in France into the 1931-32 school
year in order to finish the second volume. Two events
back home combined to prevent this. One was the depression which followed the stock market crash of 1929,
getting worse each month. The other was the inaugura-
tion of a new governor of Oklahoma.

Governor William H. "Alfalfa Bill" Murray took office
in January 1931, and immediately launched an administration generally regarded as anti-education. "His pet
aversion is the state university," Vestal wrote. [3] One of
Murray's first acts in office was to drastically cut salaries
for Oklahoma University faculty members, and eliminate
all sabbatical salaries. He also complained publicly about
one Oklahoma University professor, cavorting in France

[2] Letter, Mrs. J. D. McCoid to Ray Tassin, Apr. 18, 1962; also,
personal interview with Foster Harris and Fayette Copeland.
[3] Letter, Campbell to his wife, Sept. 6, 1931.

WALTER AND ISABEL IN FRANCE, 1931

on public money instead of earning his pay at home. This left Vestal without the funds he needed, and forced him to come home and resume teaching. [1]

Vestal and Isabel decided that she and the girls would remain in France, but that he should return home. Their plans were for him to teach one semester and try to get enough royalties from his writing to finance his return to France. Accordingly, he sailed for the United States September 5, 1931.

A few days at sea were enough to convince Vestal that he should not have left his family behind. He began writing his wife urgent requests for her to take the next ship home. Reaching New York September 13, he delayed his travel long enough to take the Sitting Bull manuscript to Houghton Mifflin and call on various magazine editors and book publishers checking markets and looking for story assignments. Results were discouraging. Publishers were buying very little, and at low rates. "I was told that five-cents-a-word authors now take two cents," Vestal wrote Isabel.

With growing discouragement and loneliness, Vestal boarded a train for Oklahoma. He reached Norman September 20, and found the effects of the depression devastating. Businesses were closed or closing, houses stood vacant. "Nobody has a cent," he wrote Isabel. "[Governor] Murray is talking of cutting us another 10 per cent [in salary] to feed the poor. . . I've never seen anything like it in Oklahoma, and it hasn't rained for months." [5]

Vestal rented a garage apartment for bachelor living, and began pounding his typewriter, still hoping he could beat the poor magazine market. But France seemed a long way off.

---

[4] *Ibid.*, to Frank Reid, June 2, 1932.
[5] *Ibid.*, to his wife, Sept. 22, 1931.

A slight financial reprieve came to Vestal after his arrival home. Houghton Mifflin had paid him an advance on *Sitting Bull,* and he could get no more money from the firm until after the book was published. But the firm decided to permit advance publication of the book as a serial in *Adventure* magazine. From the additional sale Vestal received $500 which he wired to Isabel so that she and the girls might remain in France at least until December. Then Houghton Mifflin paid him another $500 as an advance for a biography on White Bull. This amount he applied to his gigantic debts.

Much of the material for White Bull's story would be overflow from the Sitting Bull work, but additional research would be required. Financing this research would be another matter. Vestal, a veteran at attempting to finance research, despaired once more. Even one of his stature as a writer could not find financial backing in that third year of the depression.

"There must be someone or some corporation who can see the urgency of this research," Vestal wrote. "The old men and their memories may not survive another long winter." [6]

In his determination to get the money he needed, Vestal wrote numerous book reviews and articles for *The Saturday Review of Literature, Adventure,* and other publications. The total received was not great, but it helped.

At the same time, Vestal wrote a number of other universities seeking a better paying job, but found nothing suitable. In those depression years, jobs at any salary were hard to find.

Vestal's dream of returning to France faded with the passing weeks. Isabel and the girls sailed for home December 8.

Publication of *Sitting Bull: Champion of the Sioux*

---

[6] *Ibid.,* Oct. 12, 1931.

in the spring of 1932 firmly established Vestal's status
as the top historian of the plains tribes. "The combination of documentary and eyewitness testimony produced
a type of history . . . imaginative and exhaustive."
His "ascent as a writer was rapid thereafter." [7]

Vestal's faith in the biography was more than justified
by the acclaim it brought him. And it just missed selection as Book of the Month, which would have solved his
money problems. He learned of this near miss when he
received a letter from the famous newspaperman William
Allen White, editor and publisher of *The Emporia*
(Kansas) *Gazette.* White was on the board which
selected the Book of the Month, and wrote Vestal he was

> delighted with the book. I thought it should have been
> the book of the month. I believe the reason why it was
> rejected was that certain of our readers felt you were
> a bit prejudiced, that you were too ardent in cham-
> pioning the old man. It didn't seem so to me at all. [8]

The book did show Vestal's firm conviction that the
Sioux were wronged by the white men just about every
way possible. He believed that, despite frequent treaty
violations by the whites between 1851 and 1874, the
Sioux bore no hatred for the white man at that time.
During his period Sitting Bull rose to head war chief
of the Sioux nation by his exploits against other tribes
which coveted Sioux horses and buffalo. Then General
Custer entered their sacred Black Hills. His report of
gold there brought in a swarm of prospectors and open
war followed. The climax to this was the battle on the
Little Big Horn River in 1876, when Custer's Seventh
Cavalry was nearly wiped out. Sitting Bull and his nation
fled to Canada, but gradually returned. He was among
the last to submit to reservation living. For nine years

---

[7] Savoie Lottinville, "Walter Stanley Campbell," in *American
Oxonian,* Oct. 1958, p. 243.

[8] Letter, William Allen White to Campbell, May 21, 1932.

in captivity he struggled to prevent white men from stealing Sioux land. He was murdered in 1890 by reservation police. [9]

The book sold well enough that spring to finance a summer trip to the Sioux country. Vestal spent most of his time there with White Bull, finishing his research for a biography of the old chief.

Most every day for weeks Vestal quizzed White Bull in the latter's cabin on Cherry Creek, through an interpreter, John Little Cloud. As on previous trips, he secured information previously unknown outside the tribe. This time, Vestal sought White Bull's story as well.

White Bull was almost as famous among the Sioux for his visions as had been his Uncle Sitting Bull before him. But he was reluctant to tell Vestal about them because each time he mentioned them a fierce thunderstorm occurred. After much persuasion, White Bull finally agreed to discuss them, but first he sent everyone from his cabin except Vestal. He started talking about 4 p.m., with a cloudless sky outside. When he finished three hours later, he and Vestal ate supper then went outside. Black thunderclouds filled the sky. A storm broke loose with fury, but drenched only the cabin and a few yards around it. No rain fell on the nearby cabins. The wind was so strong that Vestal had to move his car to keep it from rolling over the bluff into Cherry Creek. He was greatly impressed, but White Bull took the storm for granted. [10]

When the interviews were finished and Vestal prepared to leave, White Bull made a farewell speech that Vestal remembered vividly. White Bull said that up to that day, the happiest moment of his life had been the day in 1926 when he led the Sioux nation across the Custer battlefield to meet the Seventh Cavalry.

[9] Stanley Vestal, *Sitting Bull: Champion of the Sioux, passim.*
[10] Autobiographical data.

Now you have taken down the story of my life. You
will make it into a book, my friend. At the Custer
Battlefield I was honored for one day. But when our
book is published, my name will be remembered and my
story read so long as men can read it. You have done
this and I think you have made this the happiest day
of my life. [11]

Vestal shared the feeling, for now he had the raw
material for another superb book. He finished the manuscript in the fall of 1933 and it was published the following spring by Houghton Mifflin.

Warpath was intended as more than just a biography
of White Bull, however. Vestal's stated purpose was to
cover the wars of the Sioux within living memory. The
two purposes went together however, because

research among plains Indians inevitably takes the form
of collecting the biographies of individual informants.
The Redskin fought for his own glory, and always thinks
of a fight in terms of his own personal achievements.
The individual horseman was the military unit; and a
battle was simply a series of single combats. . .
Chief Joseph White Bull, . . . was the ideal figure
for my purpose. [12]

White Bull distinguished himself in many campaigns,
including the Fetterman "massacre" in 1866 and the
Custer "massacre" ten years later when he killed Custer.
After going on the Sioux reservation, he replaced his
father as head chief of the Minniconjou and thwarted
many efforts by the whites to steal Indian land.

Although *Warpath* contained much of the overflow
material from Sitting Bull, Vestal still had enough material left for a third volume on Sioux history. This he
worked into *New Sources of Indian History 1850-1891*
published in 1934 by the University of Oklahoma Press.

A miscellany of material about the Sioux, *New Sources*

---

[11] Vestal, *Warpath,* pp. 255-56.   [12] *Ibid.,* p. vi.

is more a job of editing than writing but it was well received among historians. It contained hundreds of statements made by and letters written by Indians, Indian agents, army officers and others pertaining in some way to the history of the Sioux during the forty-year period covered by the book. The letters and documents included were found by Vestal during his five years of research among the Sioux. The book contains some of the finest published material about the Sioux ghost dance, warfare, treaties and similar things. It was edited and organized with considerable skill, but is not the sort of book that would prove popular or be commonly read among the general public. It is better suited as research material. Among publications praising the book was *The Saturday Review of Literature* which described it as "a long needed contribution to a great phase of our history." [13]

During 1933 and 1934 Vestal turned out a tremendous volume of short material, both articles and short stories, for magazines. A number of these were published in *Blue Book, Conflict, Space,* and *Adventure*. They covered – as might be expected – incidents in Sioux and Cheyenne history. None of the work was anything Vestal ever bragged about. It was written to make money as quickly and easily as possible, and added little if any thing to his prestige.

In the spring of 1934 Vestal heard that White Bull had died. He wrote the agent at Cherry Creek for verification. The agent turned the letter over to White Bull, who wrote Vestal saying, "Someone has told you a lie. I am still on my feet yet. I sure enjoyed dancing all night New Year's Eve." For a man of ninety-one years, that was quite an accomplishment. [14]

[13] Oliver LeFarge, "Sitting Bull and the Sioux Tribes," in *Saturday Review of Literature,* Apr. 20, 1935, p. 635.
[14] Letter, Campbell to Mrs. C. R. Phelan, May 2, 1934.

Hay fever and asthma continued to trouble Vestal, Isabel and Malory in the 1930s, particularly in 1934. Consequently Vestal welcomed an offer to teach writing at a twelve-week summer session of New Mexico Normal University, at Las Vegas, where the climate was high and dry. The family grew to love New Mexico, especially the Santa Fe area. At the western end of the historic Santa Fe Trail, the city still possessed the glamour of the Old West. Also, nearby Taos was the home of Vestal's boyhood hero, Kit Carson, and other mountain men; it abounded with writers; small tracts of nearby land were still available for homesteading, and the beauty and variety of the landscape appealed to Vestal.

Vestal had for many years talked to Isabel about the possibility of homesteading somewhere. This ambition was purely a sentimental one, rooted in family tradition, he wrote. Other generations of his family had done so, and it seemed incumbent upon him to keep up the practice. Buying land seemed a prosaic affair. He was proud of the log cabins in his past, as Europeans may treasure the memory of their ancestral castles. Although cabins are not very grand, he wrote, they are heroic, and certainly more comfortable than castles. And so he wanted to homestead. He and Isabel decided that New Mexico was the region in which to do this.

Early in August, Isabel walked into the Santa Fe land office and inquired whether any land was vacant for homesteading. She found a seventy-acre tract about eight miles from Santa Fe. They drove out to the land – if bouncing over boulders and ruts can be called driving. Actually, the bad road pleased Vestal because this meant they would have few visitors if they built a home there.

From the main "road" to the claim they had to climb up a steep mountainside covered with brush and trees. On top, at an altitude of 6,500 feet, it seemed that all

New Mexico was visible. This was exactly what they wanted. Piñon and great pine trees covered the seventy acres. Vestal described it as a mountain top "lavishly adorned with rocks, granite and quartz, every size from a grain of sand to a grand piano, blooming with cactus and yucca." [15] Vestal recorded his enthusiasm in these words:

> One must have been brought up on the plains to appreciate what a place like that may mean to a plains-man. Where I grew up, in Western Oklahoma, one might almost say that the public feeling toward trees was one of worship. A man who wantonly cut down a tree was regarded as far more reprehensible than the man who shot his neighbor. And for rocks – well, apart from soft sandstone and crumbling gypsum, we had no rocks. Rocks were, if anything, far more rare and precious than trees. And so, when I laid eyes on that hillside – all rocks and trees – I knew that I had found the place for me. And I was pleased to note that, though wild-flowers abounded, there was mighty little grass. I have pushed too many lawn mowers in my time to derive the slightest pleasure from the sight of a green lawn. For my part, I think the French idea of making one's lawn of gravel is simply swell. [16]

To make the site even more ideal, another of Vestal's boyhood heroes, Ernest Thompson Seton, lived just across the road. Vestal could see the Seton land from his own hilltop.

Vestal filed his homestead claim August 28, 1934, in Santa Fe. Soon after, the president of the United States issued an executive order withdrawing from settlement all the unsettled land still owned by the federal government. When Vestal learned this, he likely felt kindly toward a Democrat for the first time. He wrote: "I

---

[15] Autobiographical data.   [16] *Ibid.*

believe myself to be the very last homesteader, the last of the pioneers." [17] Nothing could have pleased him more than to be able to make such a claim.

To satisfy the minimum residential requirements for proving up on a homestead, it was necessary to live on the claim at least seven months a year for two years. The Campbells solved this problem by Isabel remaining on the claim for part of the winter months. Vestal and the girls returned to Oklahoma University.

For his eighth book Vestal selected an area totally different to anything he had done before – an off-beat murder mystery. The scene was the great Chateau in the French vineyards near Bordeaux where he was billeted during World War I. For his story line, Vestal used a detective who solved crimes by stimulating himself with various kinds of wines. By this time Vestal was something of an authority on the wines mentioned in the story, and this provided the most interesting part of the book. But this setting and story line were not the natural element for Vestal. [18]

Little, Brown and Company published the book March 22, 1935. It sold 1,633 copies the first day, and very few after that time. By stepping out of his element, Vestal produced the only book-length failure of his writing career. Except for later textbooks on how to write, he stuck with what he knew, loved and could produce best – stories about the Old West and the he-men who made it what it was.

---

[17] *Ibid.*   [18] Stanley Vestal, *The Wine Room Murder, passim.*

Growing Fame

The only writing Vestal did during 1935 was a large volume of short material, while casting about for a new series of books. In his search for material, and to be close to his homestead, he returned to New Mexico Normal University again that summer to teach writing for twelve weeks.

Building a home on his claim occupied much of Vestal's time that summer. To call in a contractor to build a house on a claim would have outraged all the finer feelings of any genuine pioneer, Vestal wrote. A homesteader must plan, supervise and have a hand in the actual building, or lose all his self-respect. So he and Isabel besieged their friends in Santa Fe with questions about how to build roads, whether they should dig or drill a well, build of adobe or stone, use a cistern or tank, and that sort of thing. Estimates and plans kept them busy for the first part of the summer.

At first Vestal and Isabel wanted to build the house of adobe and call it "Dobe Walls," after one of his books. But they were told there was no adobe on the place, and to haul in adobe bricks would be expensive. Logs were out of the question, for the same reason, since Vestal was determined not to cut down a single tree on the claim. So they voted to build of stone. Finally, they hired some Mexican workmen, made a trail up the mountainside to the claim, and selected a site for the house.

The Campbells engineered the laying of the foundation and the Mexicans built the walls. The workers were amazed at Vestal's alarm lest a tree should fall, and were even more astonished to find that he was very particular not to disturb any of the stones within a hundred yards of the house. But they obediently followed his notions and hauled in the stone from a distance. Vestal failed, however, to make them adopt all his ideas about the stone. It seems he picked chunks of white quartz for their beauty. The mason would look at the stones, mutter profanely to himself, and then surreptitiously cast them aside.

But the workers were faithful, thoughtful and agreeable. The Campbells fell in love with them. "In short, we had a picnic," Vestal wrote. The sand they had expected to haul from a considerable distance, but their foreman discovered plenty of it in the arroyo behind the house. Adobe was found there also, after they had begun the walls with stone. It made excellent bricks, which they used for the corner fireplace and the partition inside. Vestal wrote, "It was decidedly satisfactory to find that practically all materials used in the house were found nearby and were not manufactured or carted in from a great distance." He had strong sentimental objection to this.

When the Campbells tired of the job, they went in to Santa Fe in twenty minutes. The city's charm never ceased to impress them. They liked its continental atmosphere, its serious interest in the arts, its history and its Indians, its metropolitan tourists, and its leisurely social life. Its climate seemed to rival that of the Riviera. "It came to us with pleasure that we were residents there," Vestal wrote. "We were building a home."

Sheets of iron for the roof were used as lean-tos at night. Here the Campbells lived while their house took shape. They found the nights in New Mexico quite different from Oklahoma. On the plains there was a ceaseless hum and buzz of insects. On their homestead, there was only silence or the sound of the wind in the pines.

Day by day the fourteen-inch granite walls went up, the door and window frames were placed and built around. Doors and windows were hung, and professional roof builders brought in from Santa Fe to add the galvanized steel roof. Finally they cleared away the rubbish and viewed the completed structure, a twenty-eight by eighteen-foot rectangle, a bit lop-sided.

A log stable and corral completed the construction. A name for the place was provided by the workmen. They told Vestal the hill had always been known as Cerro Pajarito, the Hill of the Birds. The Hill of the Birds. The Campbells kept the name.

One thing remained to be done. Vestal wanted privacy so he could write. He had a proper notice burned in buckskin and posted on trees warning trespassers to stay off the claim. This was how Vestal became the last of the pioneers, if his boast was correct.

Once again Isabel spent the winter at Cerro Pajarito to satisfy residential requirements for homesteading. Vestal took the girls back to Norman for the 1935-36 school year. When he arrived there, he found a letter notifying him of his selection to Who's Who in Oklahoma. The next month he was selected for membership in the American Military Foundation. [1]

Vestal wrote only short material during that school year, except for some work on textbooks for use with the experimental writing course he offered in addition to his regular classroom load.

The summer of 1936 found Vestal back at his homestead, where he and Isabel kept busy writing while the girls did the housekeeping and cooking. He signed a con-

---

[1] Letters, Lyle H. and Dale Boren to Campbell, Aug. 15, 1935; and Campbell to William C. Brown, Oct. 10, 1935.

tract June 15, 1936, with Houghton Mifflin for his next book, *Mountain Men*, a history of fur trade industry during the days of Kit Carson, James Bridger, Joe Meek, and their companions. [2]

That autumn Isabel became increasingly depressed over their financial condition and her mounting pile of rejection slips to her writing. She told Vestal that if her latest novel failed to sell, she would quit writing and get a salaried job.

Since the early days of their marriage the Campbells had been a writing team. In fact, a mutual interest in writing had originally drawn them together. And each published a first book the same year, 1927. After that time, however, Isabel did not match her husband's success. She never did sell another book, and sold very little short material. This mystified Vestal, for he regarded her literary style as superior to his own. And who could judge better than one with his success? Each new failure added to her depression.

From Isabel's failure, however, Vestal re-learned an old lesson about writing for a particular market. Then, as in later years, there was an excellent market for both fact and fiction about the Old West. And Vestal's material, coming first hand from those who lived the events he wrote about found quick acceptance. By now publishers were contacting him asking him to write for them. But Isabel fought a very limited, highly competitive market for contemporary life stories. Where Vestal's market was wide open, her market was just about closed in those years when readers were interested in escaping from the reality of the times.

In the twelve months preceding that November, Vestal had earned $5,236, nearly half of it from his royalties. The value of that sum in the middle of the depression

---

[2] Campbell diary, June 3, 1936.

was considerable, yet it did not reduce his indebtedness greatly. Isabel became more nervous and depressed. [3]

Vestal made final proof on his homestead December 1, 1936, and received his permanent deed. In the remainder of his life he was as proud of this accomplishment as any he ever achieved.

Mountain Men, published in 1937 by Houghton Mifflin, was an exceptional piece of historical literature about the fur trade business already covered in *Kit Carson* and *'Dobe Walls*, and to be covered again in two other biographies. But there was little duplication in it and the other four books.

Mountain men roamed the western part of the United States and into Canada from 1822 to 1838, trapping beaver. The hard drinking, hard fighting bunch fought some Indians and married others, explored new territory and in general opened up a large portion of the nation to later settlement. The replacement of silk hats for beaver ended their way of life but not their contribution to America.

Without a doubt, Vestal accurately captured the spirit of a way of life that helped open the Old West to post-Civil War settlement. He did not paint romantic pictures of these men, nor hide their faults. He showed them as rough, brawling, somewhat loose-moraled frontiersmen – but he-men. [4] Publication of this latest book helped Vestal get selected for membership in the Oklahoma chapter of Phi Beta Kappa "in recognition of achievement as a writer, teacher, and productive scholar." [5] It also brought him the friendship, at least by mail, of another famous writer of the time, Robert Penn Warren. They corresponded many times in the next few years.

[3] *Ibid.*, Feb. 11, 1937.
[4] Stanley Vestal, *Mountain Men, passim.*
[5] Letter, Grace Ray to Campbell, Mar. 29, 1937.

The drought of the 1930s which turned the Great Plains into the tragic dust bowl had an odd side effect on Vestal. When Chief Oscar One Bull had first shown him Sitting Bull's medicine bundle a few years earlier, and Vestal sought to buy it, the old chief had foreseen a future need for it. He loaned the bundle to Vestal after getting the promise that it would be returned if the Sioux ever needed it. In 1937 One Bull wrote Vestal that the Sioux were suffering greatly from the drought and that he needed the bundle to make rain. Vestal promptly returned it. The great drought did not last much longer, but Vestal never recorded whether he believed the bundle might have helped.

The Campbell's oldest daughter, Malory, was acutely ill with asthma in May, so they became anxious to spend the summer in the high altitude of their homestead. Vestal sought and received a summer research grant from Oklahoma University. Before they left Norman, Isabel's latest book was rejected. This story, she had told Vestal, would be her last if it did not sell. Its failure and Malory's illness added to her depression. [6]

The family left for New Mexico June 4, where Vestal and Isabel both worked on his latest book, *Revolt on the Border*, a novel about Santa Fe during the war with Mexico. When not working on it, they visited their many friends, including Lynn Riggs, by then Vestal's most famous former student.

Vestal also took off long enough in July for a brief visit in the Dakotas with Sitting Bull's two nephews. This turned out to be the last visit with One Bull and White Bull. For a Sunday outing, Vestal drove the two chiefs to the Mount Rushmore Memorial in the sacred Black Hills. He parked across the gulch from the colossal

[6] Letter, Campbell to Oklahoma University treasurer, June 25, 1937; and Campbell diary, May 12, 19, 1937.

carved heads of Washington, Jefferson, Lincoln and Theodore Roosevelt.

Although impressed by the carvings towering above them, the old chiefs had to have their fun. They dared each other to get in the basket and ride across the gulch on the cable which led up to the stone portraits. Of course, no Sioux chief would think of passing up a dare.

When Vestal asked what they thought of the carvings, both said they thought Sitting Bull's head should be up there also, since he was the great defender of these sacred mountains of the Sioux and the most famous man ever born in South Dakota. This time they were not joking. [7]

Back in New Mexico, Vestal resumed his novel and his textbook on professional writing. But Isabel's health occupied his thoughts much of the time. He described her as "in a nervous tailspin over the kids and her stories." The condition was aggravated by anemia, and worry over debts.

In October, 1937, Vestal signed a contract with Houghton Mifflin for the novel, *Revolt on the Border*, and then concentrated on his textbook on writing. Within two weeks, however, his financial plight drove him to take on another project for Houghton Mifflin, a history entitled *The Old Santa Fe Trail*, which he had been researching in Santa Fe. "I need the money so badly," he wrote. "Creditors are hunting for my blood." [8] Within a year this was to prove disastrous for him.

[7] Campbell diary, entries of July 14, 19, 1937.
[8] *Ibid.*, Oct. 12 and 16, 1937.

Training Professional Writers

Vestal established his unique school of writing at Oklahoma University in 1938. The department of English had for many years offered an elective course called "Creative Writing." This course was passed around from one member of the department to another, with no one willingly accepting the job of teaching it. According to Vestal, the purpose of the course was seldom clear in the teacher's mind, and the results in the main were unimpressive. Though occasionally, a student was able to publish something written in the course, he seldom could repeat the feat after the term ended. Success, when achieved, seemed to depend on collaboration with the professor who taught the course. When that collaboration was ended, the student found himself unable to write anything else salable. As a result, the student usually suffered a heart-breaking disappointment. The professor had an uneasy feeling that he had failed to give the student any real training or help, and the university suffered criticism.

The head of the English department in the late 1920s used Vestal's early success in writing as an excuse to assign him the task of teaching creative writing. Vestal knew he could not achieve any real success with just one course. Also, the course was aimed at teaching literary appreciation rather than how to write. "As time went on," Vestal wrote, "I became more and more unwilling to repeat it."

At the same time, Vestal's knowledge of literary history

and his own experience in writing made him confident that an effective program in writing might be developed. He believed that young men with a love for words and an earnest desire to write well could be taught how to do it. It seemed to him that the proper goal for writing courses, and the only valid test of their effectiveness, was the ability of students to regularly publish their work after graduation.

Eventually Vestal worked out plans for a system he believed would produce writers capable of publishing their work on their own, work which the instructor had never seen. In the autumn term of 1934 he decided to try out his system, on his own and apart from his regular teaching load. He submitted his plan to the president who heartily endorsed it, so Vestal put it into operation. [1]

The first step was to advertise in the student newspaper for students who wished to learn to write. Eight applied. Vestal selected four who seemed to have sufficient talent and enthusiasm for his experiment. One afternoon a week the four came to him for individual conferences. He gave them detailed personal instructions based on his own experiences, criticizing their manuscripts, trying out his ideas of teaching.

By the end of the school year, three of the four students had sold short stories, one winning a prize in a writing contest. This proved to Vestal's satisfaction that there was something valid in his method. Unfortunately, however, each of the students carried a full academic load and had too little time for writing. And Vestal, having tested his method, had no further interest in continuing his experiment at that time. However, he did continue as a part of his teaching load the lecture course in "Creative Writing" which he had grown to loathe.

[1] Letters, Campbell to W. B. Bizzell, Dec. 7, 1934, and Bizzell to Campbell, Dec. 19, 1934.

A national convention of teachers of creative writing was held in 1936 and the proceedings published in a pamphlet. President Bizzell sent a copy of the pamphlet to Vestal, who studied it carefully. In it, the teachers aired their disappointments, failures, and intense dissatisfactions with the old-style creative writing courses. Their experiences were similar to those of Vestal. First, they complained unanimously, their students did not learn to write, seldom published, and those successful in class were generally dissatisfied afterward since the teacher could no longer collaborate with them. Second, colleges regarded creative writing courses as advanced English composition or an unnecessary frill. Third, writing courses were generally taught by persons unable to sell their own writing.

As usual, Vestal had an urgent need for money at that time. Also, he had already worked out what he considered a sound method of teaching writers. Consequently, he decided to write a textbook on the techniques of writing – one that would serve as a course in writing and pass along in a few months of self-study what he had spent twenty-five years learning. He thought the book might make him some quick money, without additional research. Employing a part-time secretary, he started to work on the book. Since his office was shared by other teachers, he and the secretary usually sought out an empty classroom elsewhere in the building where he could dictate undisturbed.

Vestal was quite unwilling to have his textbook "stained with the connotations of the old name, 'creative writing.'" He felt that a method which purported to train people to write and publish on their own deserved the name of a profession. Accordingly, he called the book *Professional Writing*. It was not his purpose to train staff writers; that he considered the function of the school of journalism. His aim was to train free lance writers, applying the methods used at Oxford, and based on his own practical experience.

Vestal spent many years of apprenticeship learning what he put into this single volume. In the preface he said:

> This book should, if faithfully digested, spare the beginner months and years of blind struggle, and materially shorten his apprenticeship. . . It aims at showing the student what is to be done, how it may be done, and when to do it. [2]

To accomplish this goal, Vestal started with the most basic part of writing – how to select a subject about which to write. "A good subject is simply one which stirs the interest, emotion, and imagination of the writer," he said. [3]

Vestal explained the importance of having a particular market in mind for each piece of writing, and how to slant the work toward that market by analyzing the publication and understanding its readers. He recommended studying the methods – but not copying the style – of the literary masters. He showed how the writing techniques of the masters remained pretty much the same throughout the centuries although literary style varied greatly. Included also were instructions on determining the impression the writer wished to make on a reader, and how to achieve this effect by leading the reader through a series of emotional responses.

Vestal called the book *Professional Writing*, but he could just as well have called it "Professional Thinking Before Starting to Write" because that is what the book taught. The areas covered – selection of a subject, reader, model, market, and so on – all dealt with things writers needed to know and do before actually doing any writing.

---

[2] Walter S. Campbell, *Professional Writing*, p. vi.   [3] *Ibid.*, p. 7.

In other words, the book was designed to make one think like a professional writer rather than a literary critic or someone writing to amuse himself.

But the material merely told the prospective writer what to do. The most valuable part of the book came at the end of each chapter, where Vestal included a work program on the material covered in the chapter. He believed that by carefully working out each exercise, writers would develop truly professional attitudes and thereby avoid the many years of trial and error experienced by himself. Later success of Vestal's students proved him right. Later textbooks written by him and used by these students covered techniques of writing.

At this time Vestal had many friends among representatives of book publishers. One of these was Edward L. Skelley of the Macmillan Company, who occasionally talked to Vestal's students. Vestal cornered Skelley on one of his visits and tried to sell him on the idea of such a textbook.

"I must have talked his arm off," Vestal wrote, "for he showed a good deal of interest, offering to present my project to the editor of Macmillan." With this encouragement, Vestal raved on until Skelley "threw up his hands and said that I could do a better job selling and that I had better contact them myself." This Vestal did, securing a contract for the book. He polished the manuscript in the summer of 1937, while in New Mexico, and sent it to the publisher.

Vestal had assumed the book would be merely a textbook for the educational department of the publishing house. But Macmillan submitted the manuscript to two readers, one a college professor who insisted it would make the best textbook of its kind, the other a professional writer who was equally certain it would make an excellent manual for practical writers. Consequently, Macmillan brought out two editions in 1938, one for schools and one for the trade department, differing only in the preface. This meant considerably greater profit for Vestal, and greater recognition.

Even before the book was published it had a major effect on the future of Vestal. When he was a student at Weatherford in 1904-07 one of his best friends was Kenneth C. Kaufman, another member of Southwestern's first graduating class. When Kaufman and Vestal joined the English faculty at Oklahoma University they renewed their friendship. Kaufman also was associate editor of the University's international literary quarterly, *Books Abroad*, editor of *The Daily Oklahoman* Sunday literary page, and generally recognized as Oklahoma's foremost literary critic. After Vestal developed his ideas for teaching professional writing, Kaufman tried to get him to offer a regular course along the lines he used in training the four students on his own time. The English department objected to any type of commercial emphasis in writing so Vestal did not even try to start such a program. He already was the disgrace of the department because of his own commercial writing.

Kaufman let the matter drop until he saw the final draft of the textbook. His enthusiasm for the book renewed his campaign to get Vestal to use it as the basis for a course. About the same time Kaufman saw a newspaper photograph of four recent Oklahoma University graduates sitting in a writing class at another university taking work they could not get in Oklahoma. The wily Kaufman clipped the photograph, took it to President Bizzell, and pointed out that the four students had to go elsewhere for training in writing. Sooners should not have to leave the state for such training, he pointed out, especially not with a man like Vestal on the faculty. And besides, the training offered elsewhere was not getting results, according to the report from the National

Conference of Teachers of Creative Writing. Then he spent some time praising Vestal's new book and its unique approach to the training of professional writing.

All these arguments were too much for Dr. Bizzell, who agreed with Kaufman and immediately appointed a committee to organize a sequence of writing courses. Naturally Vestal was included on the committee, but the head of the English department was not, a factor that gave Vestal considerable advantage later.

After deliberating briefly, the committee voted unanimously to put Vestal in charge of the new courses. The president agreed. Although interested in the experiment and certain that something useful could be accomplished, Vestal feared that he might find his efforts hamstrung by academic restrictions and antagonism toward his professional approach. But the president insisted he take charge. Vestal said he was "unwilling to be a party to the fraud of the old-fashioned creative writing courses." The only way he would accept the new post would be if he were given an absolutely free hand to direct the training as he saw fit. The president granted him this authority.

Next, Vestal pointed out that in naming him for such an undertaking, the university was attempting to capitalize on the name he had made for himself as a writer on his own time while other professors were out playing golf. Therefore, he thought he should be promoted to full professor and get a pay raise. This, too, was granted. The amount was later set at $1,000 a year. [4]

Having agreed to give Vestal a free hand in directing the courses, the president and committee then began to tell him how to direct them. The president generously offered to establish a magazine on the campus in which students could publish their work. Vestal replied:

---

[4] Autobiographical data; and letter, Campbell to John DeLana, May 23, 1938.

> We will have no magazine. There are plenty of magazines in the country. If we set up a magazine on the campus, it will be edited by professors who will insist on academic and literary standards and so lead students into by-roads and away from the high road of publication. [5]

Vestal said he did not care where a student published nor what kind of material he wrote so long as he wrote it well and got it published. He would not tell them what to write, or make any decisions for them, but would only show them how to implement their own decisions. Again the president and committee approved of his stand.

Then the well-meaning group went right on with its suggestions. If there was to be no magazine, then they would offer prizes to the best writing by students. Vestal replied:

> No prizes, please. There is no prize which you could offer which will compare with the real prize of a sale to a good publishing house or a magazine of national circulation. Moreover, a local prize, like a local magazine, may set up false standards and lead my students astray from their main career. [6]

Once more Vestal prevailed, but the committee was not yet finished. They proposed to offer graduate credit for the courses, and again Vestal shook his head. He said:

> That will only result in attracting people with little interest in writing, who think it would be nice to take a few easy courses in creative writing after they get their bachelor degrees. I want nobody in my courses who is not hell-bent to write. We shall make all these courses for undergraduates. [7]

Final effort of the committee was a proposal to set up a separate department of professional writing and hire

---

[5] Autobiographical data.   [6] *Ibid.*   [7] *Ibid.*

a number of instructors. This, also, Vestal refused. He did not want his teaching time consumed with a lot of administrative work, so the sequence remained a part of the English Department. Also, he was determined to have no one help him who had not made a living writing. "I was not eager to have a great facade, for I had learned at Oxford that the object of education is to achieve results and that men are far more important than machinery to this end." [8]

A number of persons were considered for the post of Vestal's assistant, mostly amateurs at writing. But Vestal felt that until a man had published at least a million words in a variety of markets, he was not qualified to teach professional writing. He decided he wanted his old friend Foster Harris, if he could get the university to approve his choice. Back in the early 1920s Harris had been a student of Vestal's. Already a successful writer then, Harris went on to become a top pulp magazine writer after leaving the university in 1925. In 1937, *Writer's Yearbook* selected him one of the nation's top ten pulpateers. That same year he moved back to Norman, his wife's hometown.

The dean of the college of arts and sciences listened to Vestal's recommendation of Harris, but questioned the qualifications of one who had only a bachelor's degree. He suggested Vestal secure a list of the work published by Harris. Vestal returned to his office and relayed the dean's request to Harris, who looked depressed but said nothing. The next morning Harris came into Vestal's office clutching in one hand a sheaf of papers on which was typed a list of about 800 pieces of fiction and non-fiction he had published.

"W. C.," Harris said, "these are all I can remember on such short notice. Do you suppose this will do?"

---

[8] *Ibid.*

Chuckling, Vestal assured Harris he thought the list would be sufficient. Harris was approved for the job without further question as to his qualifications.

Vestal's choice turned out to be one of the wisest decisions he ever made. Dwight Swain, who became a third member of the team many years later, evaluated his colleagues in this manner:

> I suspect that the divergent characters of the two men themselves played a far larger role in their success than most people realize. That is, it seems to me that either Campbell or Harris, working alone, would not have had half the success that the two of them achieved together.
>
> Campbell was primarily an organizer, an analyst, a dissector of what might be termed the fundamental minutae of writing. Fact, logic and pattern were his tools. He knew that if a piece of writing achieved a particular effect, there was a reason for it, laid out in plain sight for all to see.
>
> With such an outlook his emphasis, too, was on analysis. He would tear the student's eyes off the cathedral that was a completed literary masterpiece and force him instead to look at the bricks and mortar that were the nouns and verbs that made it up. The framework that was pattern was torn out and exposed to view. The beauty of the emotional stained glass windows were dissected down to sand and coloring, words and connotations. He simply forced the student to learn the literary facts of life and find out how the successful practitioners of the writing craft did the job.
>
> Foster Harris was just the opposite of Professor Campbell. Where Campbell analyzed, Harris distrusted logic. Where Campbell directed the student's attention on hard facts, Harris demanded they forget the facts and start feeling. Where Campbell commanded attention to detail, Harris talked metaphysics.
>
> Harris considered structure as merely the outline for

a personalized fight between good and evil, right and wrong. He put the core of the story in the heart of the main character, and demanded that the writer solve it there by conscience, not logic. He gave fiction direction by insisting that every story is somebody's story, and then made the student tell the tale as that somebody felt it. In a word, he made the student forget the technique and pour out human life and emotion.

Both Harris and Campbell believed that the average fictional sentence should contain both a fact and a feeling, an action and an emotion, if the story was to keep moving. The same principle can be applied to their partnership. Campbell was largely factual in approach. Harris taught in terms of emotion. Together, they made up a dynamic unit, alive to the full meaning and potentialities of writing. [9]

The two of them searched for a third member of their team in the spring of 1938. Since neither had much experience in drama, they decided on Robert Whitehand, then teaching at the University of Iowa. But when the head of the Oklahoma University school of drama learned of their intentions, he hired Whitehand to teach play writing for the school of drama. Campbell and Harris decided this was just as well. It seemed more appropriate to them that the school of drama handle courses in dramatic writing, since it had the stage and the actors with which to produce their students' work. They decided to confine their teaching to the writing of fiction and non-fiction for books and magazines.

Together Vestal and Harris worked out their professional writing sequence. They were in accord on the basic purpose of the course – to help the individual writer find himself and learn to do the kind of thing for which he was best fitted. They never allowed others to tell them what to write, and they determined to never tell their students.

---

[9] Personal interview with Dwight V. Swain, 1962.

Vestal later described their concept in these words:

Neither Professor Harris nor myself had the slightest desire to produce writers like ourselves or to have our pupils imitate our own work. We have not tried to form a school of writers, but rather a school for writers. Each pupil is encouraged to be himself. As a result they have never formed coteries or joined "Movements."

The classes are informal because we find that makes for efficiency and understanding, but the atmosphere is one of hard work and has no smell of the tea party to it.

We make no attempt to impose our own tastes and preferences upon our pupils. They may write anything which does not violate good taste and the postal regulations. For my part I have always endeavored to enjoy as many kinds of literature as possible, and I honor good work and a good workman in whatever kind of writing he elects. Accordingly, we make no decisions whatever for our pupils, but merely try to show them the factors which they must consider, before making decisions of their own. Since a writer must do his own work himself, he must learn to make his own decisions and to accept the consequences as his own responsibility. For when everyone else is regimented from the cradle to the grave, the free-lance writer will still be his own man. For otherwise he cannot produce. [10]

Defending the concept of the program, Harris said the usual creative writing courses

are taught from the wrong viewpoint, from that of the critic rather than the creator. They teach the student how to judge and appreciate an omelette rather than how to lay an egg – and unfortunately, the best judge of an omelette on earth can tell a hen nothing whatever about producing the necessary ingredient. [11]

[10] Autobiographical data.
[11] Letter, Foster Harris to L. N. Morgan, Nov. 24, 1938.

VESTAL AND STUDENTS IN HIS OFFICE-CLASSROOM

Perhaps the most important single principle of the system was the use of a modified version of the tutorial system Vestal learned at Oxford. Each Oxford scholar had his own tutor who guided him through his study program. Examinations were given by a board on which the tutor could not serve. As modified for the writing program, Vestal and Harris served as individual tutors, while book publishers and magazine editors served as examiners. As the Oxford tutors went all out to get their students ready for examinations, so must they, Vestal and Harris agreed. And they would allow rejection slips or sales contracts to determine their worth as tutors.

Eventually six courses in professional writing evolved in the sequence, not all the first year. The first course, taught by Vestal, was based entirely on his first textbook and was aimed only at giving the student a professional viewpoint toward his craft. It did not distinguish between fiction and fact writing, because in developing a professional point of view there was no difference. "At the end of this first course," Vestal noted, "the student is potentially a writer and thinks the way a writer thinks." [12]

The second course, also taught by Vestal, continued where the first left off. It covered the techniques of writing fiction and non-fiction, since many of the techniques were the same, but the emphasis was on fiction. He taught how to create living and breathing characters, build plots, write dramatic scenes, show instead of tell about settings, and so on. As was true of the first course, the second one included seemingly endless work programs in which the students dissected published works to see how others had done the same thing. Then they tried the various techniques themselves.

---

[12] Autobiographical data; and statements by Foster Harris and Dwight Swain during personal interviews.

Two advanced courses were set up for Harris. The first was a lab-type course, with no classroom lecture. Instead, each student came to him for one hour a week for individual criticism of writing. Word by word, like a gruff old city editor giving the business to a cub reporter, Harris took apart each piece of writing. His second course, added later, was purely a lecture course on plotting and technique. Like Vestal, he wrote his own textbook for the course. Although it overlapped somewhat the second course taught by Vestal, the approach was so different that there was no real duplication. He did not analyze scenes, settings and characterizations as did Vestal. Instead, he was concerned mostly with overall effect of the plot and how to achieve it.

The fifth course, taught by Campbell, was based on the techniques peculiar to non-fiction writing. The sixth course, novel writing, was switched around and eventually became the course taught by the third member of the team, Dwight Swain. All three taught the individual criticism course, simultaneously.

In this manner the professional writing courses were first established in the spring of 1938, to be offered the following fall semester. As Vestal expected, the English Department bitterly opposed bringing such commercialism into the classroom. But President Bizzell ignored the protests and kept his promise of a free hand to Vestal.

An Eventful Year

Although Vestal's life was marked with many highlights, 1938 undoubtedly was the most eventful single year in his life. It saw him publish two books, establish his professional writing school, and experience one of his most tragic losses.

In the spring Houghton Mifflin published Vestal's fourth and final book-length fiction, the historical novel *Revolt on the Border*, which had the same background as most of his previous work. John Martok, an American trader and buffalo hunter, was on the Santa Fe Trail when the Mexican War started in 1846. He hurried home to Santa Fe to protect his family. Enroute he met and fell in love with an American girl he escorted part of the way. When they reached Bent's Old Fort, they encountered the girl's husband, a brutish American army officer who later tried to steal Martok's land. Various complications arose in Santa Fe after General Kearny took possession of New Mexico. Martok eventually killed the bad-guy husband, clearing the way for true love.

As usual, Vestal's fictional story line was something less than outstanding, but the writing techniques were his usual high quality. Also once again, the principal value of the book was in its historical background, its depicting of a way of life. Like two of Vestal's three previous novels, it was more fact than fiction. This helped the book, however, for the presentation of historical fact was Vestal's most outstanding talent. [1]

---

[1] Stanley Vestal, *Revolt on the Border, passim.*

Several additional honors came to Vestal that same spring. He was chosen to address the annual conference of the American Library Association in June in Kansas City, Missouri. By now his services as a speaker were in frequent demand by literary, historical, and other groups. He enjoyed it immensely, although it did cut down on his writing time. Memberships in various groups also came to him as a result of his writing success. Among the more important were the League of American Writers and the British *Who's Who*.

Vestal had his heady moments over setting up his school of professional writing, and unhappy moments over Isabel's health and depression. In June he sent her and the girls to Santa Fe to spend the summer, hoping the change might help her. He remained behind to teach summer school, and planned to join them in August.

Between the spring and summer semesters, Vestal and Harris held a professional writing short course as a prelude to the regular professional writing program to start next fall. Burton Rascoe, a literary critic, was the only speaker of the one-day event attended by about thirty persons, most of them drawn to the campus just for the short course. The university provided a $100 budget and no fee was charged for attendance. Despite the meager program of that first short course, it went over big with those attending. Consequently, Vestal and Harris decided to stage it annually and expand it to several days, bringing in numerous professional writers, editors and publishers, and representatives of book publishing houses. They foresaw immediate success for the expanded offering.

In August Vestal joined his family in Santa Fe, and found Isabel in an extremely nervous state approaching a breakdown. He stayed out on the homestead while Isabel and the girls remained in town with a woman friend of Isabel's, where they had spent the summer.

VESTAL, PAUL I. WELLMAN, AND J. FRANK DOBIE, 1938

Vestal finished interviewing old timers for data about *The Old Santa Fe Trail,* his current project, but worry about Isabel interfered with his work. He wrote her sister that she had been depressed for many years over her failure as a writer and had worried too long about Malory's health. "Then, too," he said, "I am to blame. A professor is not always a good businessman. . . If a bill collector comes to the door, Isabel goes all to pieces."[2]

When the time arrived for the family to return to Norman for the fall term, Isabel insisted Walter take the girls home while she remained in Santa Fe for a rest. She said she just could not face their creditors in Norman in her present state. Reluctantly Vestal consented.

Isabel's absence broke up the family into four units, Malory, now 19, and a student at the university, moved into a sorority house. Dorothy, a senior in high school, boarded with family friends. Vestal stored their furniture and rented a small apartment for himself. The necessity of scattering his family in this manner put Vestal in a bleak mood. But the worst lay just ahead.

A few days after his arrival home Vestal received a letter from Isabel stating she wanted a six-month separation to be followed by a divorce.[3] It is not hard to imagine the shock Vestal felt as he read the letter. That he loved his wife to the point of worship is undeniable. His first instinct was to rush back to Santa Fe, but his teaching duties made this difficult. He telephoned Isabel's doctor who advised him to delay a trip out there until her nervous condition improved. This would not take long, the doctor said. For the next three weeks he corresponded with Isabel, and this exchange of letters helped pinpoint her reasons for wanting a divorce.

Isabel blamed their troubles on the strain of her health due to overwork and Walter's debts, his actions on those

---

[2] Letter, Campbell to Mrs. A. C. Plage, Aug. 20, 1938.
[3] Letter, Isabel to Campbell, Sept. 3, 1938.

occasions when he drank liquor, inadequacy of their living quarters in Norman, her extreme dislike for Norman which she said "is poison to me and I will die before I live again the kind of life I have to live there," her hatred for many of their Norman associates whom she described as "those Norman bitches," and finally, her need to regain her health and devote herself to literature. "I am an artist, not a household slave," she wrote. [4]

Vestal admitted contributing to the situation through his debts. But he also blamed what he called Isabel's psychotic condition brought on by menopause and anemia; and undue influence on her by her daily companions in Santa Fe who he said were "unhappy people who have failed at marriage," particularly the divorcee with whom she had been living since June. [5]

Later in September, Isabel's doctor told Vestal by telephone that her health was improving and that Vestal might come out and see her. Vestal drove to Santa Fe, and found her extremely nervous and tense, and withdrawn. But they talked for a long time and eventually she began to relax. Determined to save his marriage, Vestal promised to rectify the things to which she objected. And he succeeded, for she agreed to call off her plans for a divorce. They parted happily that night after agreeing to have dinner together the next day, Sunday.

The dinner was a happy affair for the couple, but the evening ended in an argument that caused Isabel to renew her plans for a divorce. Vestal pleaded once more, this time uselessly. He wrote:

> I went back to the ranch to bed broken-hearted. Next morning I called on her to say goodbye. She was in a state of collapse, but let me see her. I did everything I knew to make up again, and unsaid everything

[4] *Ibid.*, Sept. 14 and 18, Oct. 17 and 28, and Nov. 7, 1938.

[5] Letters, Walter to Isabel, Sept. 7, 9, 10 and 16; Oct. 7, 8, 21, and 31; and Nov. 9, 1938.

I had said to trouble her, but she would not change. She said there would be a divorce after all. Still, she let me kiss her goodbye, and fondled me, and did not deny it when I told her she loved me. When I got home I was a nervous wreck. I wrote her again and again, blaming myself and making love to her. But she never answered. The woman where she stayed threatened to have the law on me, if I ever set foot on her premises again. [6]

A week after Vestal returned home Isabel filed a divorce suit on the grounds of incompatibility, "which merely means that we cannot get along together," she wrote the girls. She neither asked for nor received alimony, but Vestal sent her $50 a month "because the girls like it that way." [7] Vestal continued to write Isabel trying to get her to change her mind. She never did, and the divorce was granted in 1939. He continued to partially support her for ten years, then for a time increased this financial help to full support when she went through another lengthy illness.

Perhaps due to his marital difficulties, Vestal buried himself in his writing for the next few years. He completed the narrative history book, *The Old Santa Fe Trail*, in the fall term of 1938 and sent it to the publisher. Also, he and Foster Harris launched their professional writing program. So many students wanted to enroll, Vestal had to screen out all but the most promising. The first group sold more than seventy manuscripts.

Vestal had expected to find talent rare and fortitude plentiful. Instead, he wrote, "I discovered that talent was abundant and fortitude rare. Too many persons lack any real desire to write well. They quit trying when they discover that good writing means hard work." [8]

Success drove Vestal to additional effort. At the end

[6] *Ibid.,* to Mrs. A. C. Plage, undated.
[7] *Ibid.,* to Isabel, June 16, 1944.   [8] Autobiographical data.

of the school year he set up correspondence courses covering the same material. At first he was a little dubious about trying to teach writing effectively by mail, but soon found that the percentage of students selling copy was just as high in the correspondence group as among resident students.

Numerous literary figures were impressed by the new approach to teaching writing and wrote Vestal letters of praise after that first successful year. Among them, Sherwood Anderson said: "I like very much the set-up of your course." [9] From Louis Bromfield came the remark: "I can think of nothing better than to be able to turn over to you the number of ambitious writers who are constantly writing me." [10] Irvin S. Cobb added: "I shall be very glad to recommend your Correspondence Study Department to any literary aspirants whom I regard as promising." [11]

During this same busy period Vestal addressed numerous meetings, such as the annual convention of the Texas Institute of Letters and various historical societies. And he produced about thirty short works, mostly for *Southwest Review* and for *The Boys' World*. Most notable were "Sailing Over the Prairies," later reprinted in *A Treasury of Western Folklore, 1952*; "Dakota Courtship," widely reprinted for many years, and included in *The Best Short Stories of 1940*; "The Warriors Road," reprinted in *Best Short Stories for Boys and Girls in 1939*; "Make Yourselves Wolves" reprinted in *Best Short Stories for Boys and Girls in 1940*; and "The Listeners-under-the-Ground," published in the anthology, *Best Short Stories from the Southwest*. Whenever Vestal's cash shortage became critical, which was often, he turned out a short work for quick money. Some of the short fiction are

---

[9] Letter, Sherwood Anderson to Campbell, Sept. 20, 1939.
[10] Letter from Louis Bromfield, Oct. 25, 1939.
[11] Letter from Irvin S. Cobb, Oct. 31, 1939.

classics, however, and far superior to his book-length fiction.

Equally successful was Vestal's twelfth book, *The Old Santa Fe Trail*, published in 1939 by Houghton Mifflin. It resulted in his selection to *World Biographical Encyclopedia*, and charter membership in the Society of American Historians. Among the favorable reviews was the praise of the *New Republic* which said: "He knows the old southwest and tells good stories about it." [12] Houghton Mifflin issued four printings, and Bantam Books published a paperback edition.

The Old Santa Fe Trail followed no particular chronology of time. Instead, Vestal employed a geographic story line, beginning where the trail did, in Missouri, and progressing westward. The story covered important points along the way where historical events occurred at various times in the history of the trail. Various historical characters were brought into the story as they were related to the trail and nearby areas. As usual, Vestal skillfully drew a picture of the people who lived this bit of history. [13]

Vestal signed contracts in 1939 for a second textbook on writing with Doubleday and Company, and for a biography of the explorer Pierre Esprit Radisson for Houghton Mifflin, both to be delivered the following year. The textbook required little more than final typing, for it was based on the lecture notes and methods used by Vestal in the second of his writing courses. The biography required some additional research, although much of the material he already possessed. He first became interested in Radisson during his Oxford days, where he spent so much time reading Radisson's lengthy diary he found in

[12] "A Reader's List," in *New Republic,* Nov. 1, 1939, p. 377; and assorted unidentified newspaper and magazine clippings in Campbell Coll., *loc cit.*

[13] Stanley Vestal, *The Old Santa Fe Trail, passim.*

the library there. Although this happened about three
decades earlier, Vestal either remembered clearly what
he had read or he had a good set of notes. Now he read
what he could find in American libraries, which wasn't
much, and wrote numerous persons who had papers relating to the exploits of Radisson. Historians in Canada and
Minnesota, knowing Vestal's talent for that sort of writing
and possessing information about Radisson, had been the
ones who convinced Vestal he should do the book. Now
he called on them for help. Much of the material came
from his own vast knowledge of the fur trade era, however. [11]

Despite these projects, and a growing number of students in his writing courses, Vestal continued to turn out
short work and speak to groups of various types, particularly historical societies. In the spring of 1940, soon after
he published his second textbook, he was selected for inclu-
sion in *Twentieth Century Authors*, a dictionary-type
listing of biographies of the more important contemporary
writers in the world.

Vestal's first textbook sought to prepare students to
write by making them think and work like professional
writers of both fact and fiction. The second textbook,
Writing Magazine Fiction, took up where the first left
off, but dealt only with fiction writing techniques. The
first of three parts was devoted to the methods of creating
fiction, the scene, the plot and setting, and basic methods
of writing good narration and dialog. Part two covered
the variations in writing techniques for different types
of stories, the short-short story, the short story, novelette,
and the serial. Part three was devoted to a study of
markets and how to slant to them. *Writing Magazine
Fiction* was widely acclaimed then and in succeeding
years. [15]

---

[11] Letter, Campbell to Ira Rich Kent, Apr. 20, 1939.

[15] Walter S. Campbell, *Writing Magazine Fiction, passim.*

King of the Fur Traders was published by Houghton Mifflin in 1940 with the usual acclaim. [16] As usual, Vestal avoided romanticizing his characters, either the Indians or the fur trade king, Pierre Esprit Radisson. Instead, he presented exhaustive detail to show life as it was on the early Canadian frontier. Though often brutal, the Indians also were kind to fellow tribesmen, with fierce and courageous fighting traits. While a youngster, Radisson was a prisoner of the Mohawks and learned their ways. In later years he discovered Lake Superior and the Mississippi River, was the first to explore and chart what is now Wisconsin and other parts of that area, and was the key man in establishing the Hudson's Bay Company which dominated the fur trade in Canada for many decades.

One can almost see Vestal's delight as he recorded the deeds of the adventurer. This was his kind of man. But the most important value of this work was its depicting a way of life. [17]

[16] *New York Herald Tribune,* Nov. 17, 1940, book section; and assorted, unidentified newspaper and magazine clippings in Campbell Coll.

[17] Stanley Vestal, *King of the Fur Traders, passim.*

Busy Years

A major literary figure by 1940, Vestal received a vast volume of mail from across the nation. Thousands of letters came in praising his work, particularly his biographies and histories. Some asked for his sources of information. A few challenged his accuracy. Others asked his advice on writing and were referred to his books or correspondence courses. Numerous also were invitations to speak around the nation – especially to historical societies – teach short courses and judge writing contests. These cut down on his writing time, but he enjoyed them and participated often.

But the most significant gauge of Vestal's stature was the fact that he no longer had to seek out publishers. They came to him with requests that he write for them on specified subjects. One of these was Erskine Caldwell, who had just been hired to edit a series of books on American folkways to be published by Duell, Sloan and Pearce of New York. Caldwell asked Vestal to lead off the series with a book on the short grass country. Vestal was committed to too many other projects at the time, but agreed to write the book for later in the series. Houghton Mifflin was Vestal's regular publisher, having printed nine of his fourteen books. They were reluctant for him to write for a rival firm, but agreed to permit it.

After the 1940 summer school, Vestal took a long tour of the short grass country and bordering regions both for research and pleasure. He started at the University of Colorado, where, at a writers' conference, he shared the lecturing duties with a friend, William McLeod Raine, one of the outstanding western novelists of the day. In between other speaking engagements and tours of the area, he did research in the Colorado State Museum in Denver. Mid-August found him traveling through Colorado interviewing old trappers and Indian fighters. In Wyoming he toured the Jackson Hole Country of Old West fame, interviewed old-timers in Montana and eventually reached the Oregon Trail Association meeting in Cody, Wyoming. Here he spent what he called "one of the happiest weeks I ever had." The primary reason was an airplane flight over many old Sioux battle grounds. He described the flight as "an old fellow's joy – an easy, beautiful resume of his past research." He returned to Denver for another week in the museum, then went home for the fall school term.

In the two years since the end of his marriage Vestal had tried on several occasions to bring about a reconciliation. [1] Loneliness became worse for him in the fall of 1940. Both his daughters lived in a sorority house and he lived alone. Christmas that year was especially bad for him. Isabel had by then recovered her health and was working in Santa Fe. He longed for her so greatly that on the day after Christmas he decided to try one last time to get her to return to him. He wrote her a letter pleading for her to meet him somewhere and discuss the possibility. For more than a month he awaited her reply. Finally it arrived. She refused to even discuss the matter, saying she was determined to live alone for the rest of her life. [2] In none of Vestal's vast records is there any indication that he ever again attempted to change her mind.

Vestal's bachelorhood had another effect than that of

[1] Various letters from Campbell to his wife in 1938 and 1939.
[2] *Ibid.,* Jan. 30, 1940.

VESTAL VACATIONING ON HORSEBACK

loneliness. It made him the romantic target for some of his female students, particularly some of the middle-aged housewives, much to his discomfort. One of the romantically inclined women blamed him for her nervous breakdown when he failed to respond to her advances. Another was a neurotic woman in her fifties who, according to Foster Harris, "looked like the wrath of God" and became quite violent when Vestal avoided her clutches. On one occasion the husband of an elderly female student came around the campus asking if it was true that Vestal made love to all his female students. That, he said, was what his wife had told him. Vestal, the hardy outdoorsman, the rugged individualist, the captain of field artillery, the close associate of famous Indian war chiefs, had only fear for the females. [3]

The romantic incident that bothered Vestal most involved an unmarried female from Dallas who was much younger than he. She attended his classes one semester, then went home and began writing him letters. Over a period of weeks the letters became more romantic until she finally wrote him that she was coming back to Norman to marry the man she loved, even though her family objected to her giving herself to a much older man. [4]

Vestal was so scared he hid out for three weeks. Even Foster Harris could not find him. [5]

Harris blamed some of the romantic incidents and other classroom difficulties on Oklahoma City psychiatrists, and the fact that the writing business attracted so many "crackpots." The psychiatrists had the habit of telling their mental patients they needed a creative outlet for therapy, and recommended the professional writing courses at OU. "We never knew anything was wrong until they went through the ceiling," Harris said. Fortunately,

[3] Interview with Foster Harris.
[4] A series of letters to Campbell in the autumn of 1941.
[5] Interview with Foster Harris.

the screening process turned back many of the more unstable ones, but a few always appeared normal until something in class "triggered an outburst." [6]

Vestal's fifteenth book, *Short Grass Country*, was published in 1941 as the third in the series on American folklore by Duell, Sloan and Pearce. As usual, it won considerable acclaim. *The New York Herald Tribune* praised it as an exceptional collection of anecdotes and legends about cowboys, Indians and pioneers. [7] William Allen White described it as a "must book for anyone who wants to understand American civilization." [8]

The short grass country, also called the high plains, included the western half of Oklahoma and Kansas, the Texas panhandle, and the eastern third of New Mexico and Colorado. Vestal's book covered the history of the region and its people, starting with the first residents, the Indians, followed by the cattlemen who arrived next, then the farmers and the businessmen. From buffalo hunts and cattle drives to county-seat wars and dust-bowl days, each major event of history was brought into the work. The dominant theme was the development of rugged individualism, first among the plains tribes, and later among the whites who settled the country. [9]

To the plains Indians, Vestal wrote, war was "a glorious holiday, a splendid adventure, and a lot of fun. It was his vacation from the hard drudgery of hunting." The "warlike spirit was inevitably communicated to the white men who moved into their country, who hunted, lived and fought with them. A man who did not enjoy battle did not last long on the plains." [10]

"After the Indian wars, a wave of banditry swept the West. White men, no longer able to hunt buffalo or fight

[6] *Ibid.*
[7] *New York Herald Tribune* book section, Nov. 30, 1941.
[8] Letter, William Allen White to Campbell, undated.
[9] Vestal, *Short Grass Country. passim.*   [10] *Ibid.*, pp. 21-22.

redskins, turned to stealing horses." And there was no
law outside the immediate vicinity of a camp, village
or town. As a result, everyone carried his own law in an
open holster or rifle boot. In this period communities
fought each other over which would be the seat of county
government. [11]

Vestal's admiration for these plainsmen is clearly the
strongest thread of the book. They were his kind of
people. In presenting their way of life, he climbed one
more rung up the ladder to literary greatness.

During World War II, Elmer Davis, a fellow Rhodes
Scholar at Oxford and head of the U.S. Office of War
Information, asked Vestal to write an article on "The
American Southwest" for use in a magazine published
for overseas use. This Vestal did willingly, without pay.
Like a true professional writer, however, he turned out
a number of articles about the war for regular consumer
magazines.

Many servicemen were trained at the University of
Oklahoma during the war, and at the two naval bases
in Norman. They comprised most of the male students
of Vestal during the period. Some went on to considerable
success as writers. One of these was the navy chaplain
who, during the attack on Pearl Harbor, uttered the
famous words: "Praise the Lord and pass the ammunition." With the help of Vestal and Harris, the chaplain
wrote a book about his exploits entitled *Pass the Ammunition.* It became one of the best sellers of the war. [12]

Vestal often was asked why he chose the Old West
as his field of writing. He detested much of the material
printed about the Old West, the blood-and-thunder yarns,
"the curse of Diamond Dick on the pioneer, of Hiawatha

[11] *Ibid.,* pp. 234, 241, 244.
[12] Letters, Campbell to Capt. Seth King, Dec. 1, 1944, and to Lt.
Col. Hal Muldrow, Jr., Apr. 10, 1944.

and the Land-of-the-Sky-Blue-Water on the Indians. I hope to have avoided these falsenesses, anyhow," he wrote. He believed the people of the Old West "deserved better of the country they made than that. I can see no sense in pretending to be an illiterate cowboy, or slobbering around over hard-boiled old sob's like Satank [a Kiowa Indian chief]." He wanted to tell the truth and write about Western life in an intelligent manner. [13]
Vestal believed:

> The Southwest, and particularly the High Plains, had a history and a tradition at once the oldest in North America and the newest in all the states. Moreover, it seemed to me that the Plains and the Southwest generally had a tradition of vital importance to American culture, something that we must cherish and understand to appreciate if we are to make the most of our life here. That tradition is something that Americans cannot willingly let die.
>
> Naturally this tradition seemed most clearly expressed in the heroic age of the Old West. Therefore, that heroic age became my chosen field, and I endeavor . . . to write of the things I know and love, trying to set forth the truth, the significant and glamorous truth, about the Old West. It is my aim to help others understand and enjoy those things which mean so much to me. [14]

Vestal also detested those who wrote about "the scum of the earth as if it were a virtue to do so," and he was especially critical of foul language in writing. Of the latter, he wrote, "I might publish an appendix containing all the dirty words some readers love so well. But they can be read gratis on any backhouse wall – and the backhouse is where readers who like them belong." Instead,

---

[13] *Ibid.,* to John Mosely, Jan. 17, 1927.
[14] *Ibid.,* to John W. Rogers, Dec. 22, 1944.

he wrote only about people and places he respected and loved. An examination of his published work makes this apparent.

By the time Vestal was an established professional writer, he found himself praised by some for taking the side of the underdog in his books about Indians. "That had never occurred to me," he wrote. "I simply tried to state the case of a lot of people I liked and admired." He avoided an attitude of condescension, and just accepted the Indians as people. He had no interest in fighting a cause for the Indians, even though he knew about numerous atrocities committed by soldiers against Indians. He said *Sitting Bull* was "not animated by love for the underdog – but shame for my own people."

Finally, Vestal said he wanted to write Indian history from the Indian point of view. Too many others had written it from the white man's viewpoint, and Vestal knew the two versions were quite different. He blazed a new trail in this respect.

Normally a stiff, reserved, lone wolf type – at least on the surface – Vestal took little interest in socializing. Spare time was too precious. But occasionally he attended a party with close friends and loosened up a little after what Foster Harris called "a few snorts of white lightning." At one such gathering in the Harris home, Vestal drank a large quantity of "white lightning" and reached a stage Harris described as "quite cheerful." Although Vestal lived in the same block, Harris was not certain Vestal could get home alone so he escorted him. When they reached his front yard, Vestal decided he wanted to "Indian rassle." Harris objected because another faculty member who lived across the street was a Baptist deacon and a teetotaler. The more Vestal insisted, the louder he became, so Harris finally relented. "We went at it with the appropriate grunts and groans," Harris said later, but his attention was only half on the contest. He kept glancing across the street. Fortunately, the deacon went to bed early. [15]

Prior to 1942, all eight of Vestal's biographies and histories, and three of his four novels, were related to each other. They dealt with the traders, hunters and Indians who in turn had dealt with each other. Often many of the historical characters appeared in several of the books. Houghton Mifflin then talked Vestal into writing a biography of the same sort of frontiersman, Bigfoot Wallace, but one in no other way connected with Vestal's previous work. Published in 1942, it was more of a library type research effort, and included only a limited amount of material from original sources. [16]

The New York Times described *Bigfoot Wallace* as "a factual volume about an excessively fictionized person. It is not the equal of Mr. Vestal's earlier fine biographies on frontier folk, but the fault is more Bigfoot's than the author's." [17] *The Saturday Review of Literature* devoted nearly a full page to a laudatory review, calling it a "vivid and entertaining tale." [18]

In the book Vestal described Bigfoot as a sort of combination Will Rogers and Sergeant York, one of the greatest of the American frontiersmen, and probably the favorite Texas hero. Wallace went to Texas from Virginia in 1836 and for four years was a frontier hunter and Indian fighter. He joined the first company of Texas Rangers in 1840, serving until he went on the Mier expedition in 1842. The invasion of Mexico by ambitious Texans ended in disaster. Wallace was among those captured and imprisoned for two years. In 1846 he was commissioned

---

[15] Interview with Foster Harris.　　[16] Autobiographical data.

[17] *New York Times*, Aug. 23, 1942.

[18] E. DeGolyer, "A Virginian in Texas," in *Saturday Review of Literature*, Aug. 8, 1942.

first lieutenant in the war against Mexico, helping to take Monterrey. He returned to Texas for service as a captain in the Rangers, fighting hostile Indians in the frontier country. [19] Vestal's worship of frontier he-men was as obvious in this book as in his earlier work. Likely the book helped him get two honors later in the year. He was inducted into membership in the Oklahoma Hall of Fame and was included in *Who's Who in the Western Hemisphere.*

About this same time a national radio network offered Vestal $300 a week to write its weekly "Lone Ranger" programs. His income from all sources was then less than that amount, but Vestal did not want to write what he called "blood and thunder horse operas," and he felt the work would take too much of his time. It would keep him from producing any other writing. Consequently, he declined the offer.

Vestal had long wanted to write a textbook from the lecture notes he used in his non-fiction writing class. In the spring of 1943 he received a letter from A. S. Burack, editor of *The Writer* magazine which also published books about writing, asking him for such a textbook. Instead of signing a contract, however, Vestal turned the matter over to Paul Reynolds, a New York literary agent of high repute, for negotiations. Except for his first book, Vestal had never tried an agent. He preferred to negotiate directly, and agents could not sell anything he could not sell. Besides, publishers came to him so selling was no problem. But he had decided that the real value of agents was not in selling, but in getting better terms. Vestal decided to try out Reynolds. This was the beginning of a long and successful business association for both. Reynolds did negotiate a better contract and get more advance royalties on the book, then handled all Vestal's books published at later dates. Two years later, the

---

[19] Sanley Vestal, *Bigfoot Wallace, passim.*

pleasant association prompted Vestal to write: "A good agent is the author's best friend. . . . Agents and publishers are businessmen, know each other, and are accustomed to working together." [20]

Writing Non-Fiction, published in 1944, was to fact writing what the earlier *Writing Magazine Fiction* was in its area – a step by step manual on writing techniques. [21] By the following year the book was used by many colleges and universities as a textbook, and the number increased in succeeding years. The book made no spectacular entry, but gained wide respect among writers and teachers of writers.

Vestal's next book turned out to be his best. Up to that time, the most successful series of books published in the nation was the Rivers of America series of Farrar and Rinehart. Vestal described his connection with the series in these words:

> Soon after the series was launched it occurred to me that I might reasonably hope to do a book for it. There were plenty of rivers and I knew a good deal about a number of those in the West. I had also been permitted by Houghton Mifflin, my publisher, to do a book in the American Folkway Series entitled *Short Grass Country* for Duell, Sloan and Pearce. This regional series was going strong and I brought out my book in 1941. With that beginning in mind I wrote to the editor of the Rivers of America Series if I could possibly be of service by doing a book for her.
>
> The editor turned me down flat. I was a little at a loss and for a time considered that she may have been displeased with me since we had engaged in controversy in book reviews. Probably I did the lady an injustice, but at any rate I was not permitted to do a River book. I was not even permitted to suggest a topic

---

[20] Letters, Campbell to Paul Reynolds, May 18, 1943; to A. S. Burack, Oct. 13, 1944; and to Mrs. I. M. Draper, June 11, 1945.

[21] Stanley Vestal, *Writing Non-Fiction*, p. 4.

or present my credentials. I therefore dropped the project from my mind and thought no more about it. What was my surprise somewhat later to receive a letter from Farrar and Rinehart asking me if I would undertake to write *The Missouri* for their series. At that time, unfortunately, the original editor of the Series had died and a new editor was in charge. At the first opportunity I visited Farrar and Rinehart, was turned over to Mr. John Farrar, Mr. Carl Carmer, and Stephen Vincent Benet. I gathered that Benet was the man who had suggested my name to the committee.

Of course, I was very keen to get this assignment, as I realized that it would be a splendid opportunity. In fact, that subject was the plum of the whole series. *The Missouri* was one of the longest rivers in the country, a river with a violent and a unique personality and any amount of varied history along its banks. I learned that the original editor had kept this subject for herself and her untimely death had prevented her from doing anything on the book.

The four of us had a friendly chat and planned the strategy and tactics of the book in the office of Farrar and Rinehart.

At that time I was very happy to have such a distinguished author as Benet sponsoring my undertaking. At that time he was not in good health, having had a severe illness and being within a few months of his death, but he was very gracious as indeed all three were and we had a very pleasant conference that afternoon. It seemed that a book on the Arkansas River had received a very bad press because the author had filled most of his space with stories about one end of the river, neglecting other portions. In some of the other River books the authors had wandered far afield too. Accordingly I was advised to treat every part of the river fair and for the most part to stay within sight of the water.

But Houghton Mifflin who had published most of my books up to that time I found were unwilling to let me do another book for another publisher. They felt that one regional book off their list was enough for me. For my part I could not forego such an opportunity by turning down a subject so well suited to my hand, I thought, and so when Houghton Mifflin said, "No," I felt compelled to say, "Good-bye."

I proceeded to go home and get my research, making bales and bales of notes and planning the book. It was planned to be somewhat more than 80,000 words in length. Now in order to "play fair with every part of the river" I sat down and did a little figuring. I knew I had 2,500 miles of river and 300 years of history which equalled 750,000 mile years to be covered in a little more than 75,000 words. That is to say, each word must theoretically cover ten mile years. This meant that if I spent 100 words on an incident in the book, I had used up an allowance of 100,000 mile years – that is to say, everything that could happen in 100 miles of river in ten years' time. It was clear that the choice of materials was my first problem, and that I must choose things that were important and significant or memorable in some way. Yet I wished to interpret as well as record. So my work was cut out for me. And after I had gathered and sifted my materials and gone to writing, I found that I had a tremendous surplus of excellent material. This, of course, was an advantage, as a book is much better cut than padded. But I soon found that at the rate I was going, every time I wrote a chapter I had to throw one away. In fact, I still have enough chapters written for the book and afterward rejected to make another book of the same size. Perhaps someday I shall write another volume entitled "Missouri Overflow."

The Missouri River is a river with hair on its chest, forever doing things, and I wanted to present its personality effectively. I also realized that the river had three major aspects: highway, boundary, and outpost.

As it was a highway and everybody went up the river from the mouth, I proceeded in the same manner, starting at the mouth and moving up to the source, arriving there in the last pages of the book. I had followed this strategy in planning an earlier volume, *The Old Santa Fe Trail.* . .

Hervey Allen, author of *Anthony Adverse* and many other fine historical novels, was acting as editor of the series. [22]

Not since his biographies of Sitting Bull and White Bull did Vestal devote so much research to a book. He exchanged hundreds of letters with librarians, historical societies, old-timers and others who might contribute the smallest fact to the story. One series of letters did nothing more than provide him with the exact measurements of a dugout canoe mentioned in the book. But he wanted the exact measurements and was willing to go to whatever length was necessary.

Of course, much of the history of the Missouri was related to the history of the Sioux Indians and the fur traders with whom many of Vestal's previous books dealt. This material he already had. And he went through the routine process of reading all printed material he could find relating to the river.

The book was a collection of stories about the people and events connected with the history of the river. As a highway, as described in part one, the Missouri carried fur traders from St. Louis to the far northwest. The Lewis and Clark expedition was along the river, as were the migration to Oregon and various gold rushes along sections of it.

As a boundary, the Missouri had a bloody history. First came the religious wars between Mormons and the people they called "gentiles" in Jackson County, Missouri. The Mormons were driven across the river and out of the state. Guerrilla warfare preceding the Civil War was waged between Kansas and Missouri partisans, with the

[22] Letter, Campbell to Earl Vandale, Oct. 12, 1949.

river as a boundary between their territories. The Big Muddy was the boundary between woodlands, lakes and farms on the east banks, and the plains and the ranches on the west side. It was about the center of North America, the point where the west began, a barrier between two different cultures, two climates, two ways of life.

As an outpost, the Missouri was equally distinctive, Fort Yates and the Standing Rock Reservation for the Sioux nation were on the west banks of the river in North Dakota. From here were launched many of the expeditions into the far west. Here Sitting Bull surrendered and later was killed. From Fort Abraham Lincoln, also on the west banks, George Custer launched his 1874 expedition into the Black Hills and his 1876 trip to his death on the Little Big Horn. [23]

The Missouri was a typical Vestal book in at least one respect. It emphasized the rugged, masculine character of the men connected with its history. He said:

> The south dreams of the past, the east sees visions of the future, but the plainsman is happy here and now. He is not very well-to-do. Sometimes his life is one of extreme difficulty. Yet all he asks is a little more of the same – more rain, more grass, more cattle – not another kind of life. . .
>
> His tradition is one of freedom, of loyalty, almost feudal to his boss, of courage, fun, and respect for decent women. He feels that he is different from, and superior to, most men, and emphasized his status by a lingo and humor all his own. . .
>
> Nobody, probably, in North America so fully embodies the old American Independence and the old American romantic faith in the natural rights of men. [24]

Since Vestal believed this, and measured up to these traits himself, it is no wonder that he admired and respected the plainsmen.

---

[23] Stanley, Vestal, *The Missouri, passim.*   [24] *Ibid.,* pp. 164-66.

The key to Vestal's notion about the proper way to treat Indians is found in one passage of the book when he discussed the success of the French in dealing with them. Vestal said: "In Indian country, the Anglo-American tried to make himself monarch of all he surveyed; the Frenchman simply made himself at home there." [25]

Rinehart was so impressed with the book that the first printing was almost twice as large as any of the previous twenty-five books in the Rivers of America Series. Literary critics were equally as sold on the book, giving it more praise than any of his previous work. [26]

The Missouri without doubt was Vestal's most successful book to date, both in acclaim and money earned. His royalties for the year totaled $6,500, much of it from *The Missouri*.

Some prestige writing came Vestal's way that same year, when, at the editor's request, he produced sixteen biographical sketches for *The World Book Encyclopedia*. The articles covered various plainsmen, white and red, all well known to Vestal.

Honors continued to pile up for Vestal. His work was frequently quoted and used in various anthologies. Hundreds of letters were sent to him suggesting ideas for books and novels. He answered as many as he could, and usually included a sales pitch for his latest book or his textbooks. Another of the honors in 1945 was his induction into the International Mark Twain Society for his "contribution to literature."

With this success Vestal could afford to be amused by a news story in *Time* magazine praising another writing school because its students and graduates had pub-

[25] *Ibid.*, p. 65.

[26] *The New York Herald Tribune*, Jan. 28, 1945; "American Rivers," in *Time*, Jan. 29, 1945, p. 99; and numerous newspaper and magazine clippings, mostly undated and unidentified, Campbell Coll.

lished twenty-five stories up to that time. Just one student trained by Vestal, Harland Mendenhall, had by then published 426 stories.

From E. P. Dutton and Company Vestal received an advance of $1,500 for a history of Oklahoma University as one in a series on American universities. What Vestal had in mind was an anecdotal history. His collection of notes on the subject indicate it would have been highly amusing. One of the incidents he planned to use involved a war between a university vice president and faculty members over who could use toilets in the administration building. Those who did use the toilets, the vice president decreed, would have to come by his office for toilet paper, and he would issue only four sheets per person per trip.

An unfortunate circumstance prevented the publishing of the book, so what might have been an excellent piece of humor was never written. First, Dutton made a public announcement about the contract soon after it was signed. This infuriated Vestal, who always insisted on no publicity until a manuscript was completed. Consequently he delayed starting the book until Dutton eventually dropped the series because the first books were too dry to sell well. Vestal eventually agreed to cancellation of the contract and refunded his advance.

Another project later abandoned was a book on wildwest shows. During his research Vestal wrote a brewery for a reproduction of a painting on Custer's last stand. Copies once hung in saloons all over the frontier. The brewery found a copy in the company archives and sent it to Vestal. Foster Harris wanted to hang the picture in the office of the writing school, but Vestal lacked the courage to do so. It had a beer advertisement printed under the battle scene. Vestal hung it on the wall behind some filing cabinets for awhile, then eventually took it home.

A few years later Vestal told Harris he would give him the picture, if he would help him look for it and the unfinished wild-west-show manuscript. Both were supposed to be stored with eleven trunks of papers in the attic of a downtown commercial storage warehouse. Harris, wanting the picture, agreed and soon regretted the bargain. "It must have been a hundred and forty degrees in that attic," Harris said, "and we damned near had heat stroke." For several days they prowled through the trunks without finding the manuscript or the picture.

Vestal later found the picture under his bed at home and gave it to Harris. To this day, Harris swears Vestal knew where the picture was all the time and just wanted someone to help him go through the trunks of paper. [27]

For the fall school term of 1945 Vestal used a research grant from the university for extensive travel and research. He started with a brief rest in Virginia and some fishing trips with his old Oxford roommate, Frank Reid, then a prominent lawyer in New York. Next he went to Washington for research in the Library of Congress, seeking material for his next book, a biography of perhaps the most famous of all frontiersmen, Jim Bridger. He had a contract with William Morrow and Company for the book.

Vestal's youngest daughter, Dorothy, then lived in Washington. For Thanksgiving they went to New York where Malory, the oldest daughter, worked on *Mademoiselle* magazine.

Near the end of the year Vestal finished his research and flew home to Norman. He described the preceeding twelve months as his happiest since 1928. His income for the period was $14,320, the largest amount he ever received in a single year up to that time, thanks mostly to *The Missouri*.

---

[27] Interview with Foster Harris, 1962.

The Early Post-War Years

After its beginning in 1938, the professional writing program at Oklahoma University enjoyed a steady but not spectacular growth and success during the first few years. Serious minded World War II veterans, determined to make up for their lost years, added the spectacular element in the early post-war years. Some of the veterans received training before and during the early part of the war, then settled down to writing after separation from service. Others trained after the war. Non-veterans found themselves hard pressed to keep up, although many did.

A few years after Vestal and Harris established the writing program they began keeping records of sales by their students and graduates. They listed only verified sales reported voluntarily by the writers, so not all sales were recorded. Still, the result was an average of more than one sale per day in 1946, including twenty books. By this time Vestal estimated about fifty per cent of their students had become selling writers, about twenty per cent of them full time. This included only free-lancers and not staff writers trained by the school. *The Writer's Digest* was impressed enough to call it "The best college resident school for teaching writing in the United States." [1]

That same year Vestal added another first-rate biography to his growing list, the story of *Jim Bridger*. It contained the same lively literary style as his previous biographies, and achieved the same success. The Westerners,

[1] Autobiographical data; *Daily Oklahoman*, May 12, 1946.

an organization of Old West historians with headquarters at Northwestern University in Evanston, Illinois, selected it as one of the ten best western books published that year.

According to Vestal, no frontiersman who explored and helped conquer the west deserved the name pioneer more than Bridger. It was Bridger who helped train Kit Carson, Joe Meek and others in the art of trapping, hunting and Indian fighting. A top guide and scout for the army and other groups, Bridger also was the best explorer among the mountain men, having discovered Yellowstone Park, the petrified forest, Great Salt Lake and South Pass. [2]

Vestal's sketch of the life of the legendary frontiersman was a labor of love as well as money. And it made him an average of over one book a year for twenty years.

Vestal traveled extensively in the summer of 1946, vacationing, lecturing and tending to both family and business matters. He took a trip to Boulder, Colorado, where he conducted a week-long writer's conference. While there he stayed in the home of a friend, Gayle Waldrop, director of the University of Colorado School of Journalism. In late July he rode a train to Chicago to conduct another writer's conference. So many students wanted to attend a class taught by the famous Stanley Vestal that its sponsors had to rent the Studebaker Theater to hold it. Next came a week of lecture to a group of Baptist periodical editors at the Ridgecrest Baptist Assembly near Asheville, North Carolina.

In August, Vestal went to New York to attend the wedding of his oldest daughter, Malory, to John Ausland, a career foreign service officer. The wedding, held in Grace Church, New York City on Vestal's fifty-ninth birthday, was something of a reunion of family and

---

[2] Stanley Vestal, *Jim Bridger, passim.*

friends. Vestal was especially happy over getting to see two of the guests, playwright and former student Lynn Riggs, and Joe Brandt, a one-time president of Oklahoma University and then director of the Princeton University Press.

While in New York Vestal was honored with a luncheon given by the editors of *The Saturday Review of Literature*, and with an evening party in the apartment of Stanley Rinehart, publisher of *The Missouri*. Most Rinehart staff members were there, but it was the publisher's mother – Mary Roberts Rinehart – who delighted Vestal. A famed writer herself, she was "a gracious little woman who from her experiences among the Blackfeet could match my Indian stories perfectly," Vestal wrote. [3]

Officers of Vestal's old army regiment held a reunion in Oklahoma City after the fall term of school started in 1946. Host to the party was Governor Robert S. Kerr, who had served as a second lieutenant in the regiment. "It was very pleasant to see the men again after 27 years," Vestal wrote. [4]

Bennett Cerf, president of Random House book publishing company, visited the writing school in 1947 and praised it highly. He said later, "Stanley Vestal and Foster Harris have uncovered many promising young writers." He also called Vestal "The Sage of Oklahoma." Vestal wrote Cerf that the latter remark "roused unextinguishable laughter among some of my colleagues . . . who insist that I immediately grow a beard." [5]

Two novels, written in 1947 by graduates of the school, later set records still unbroken by Vestal-trained writers. Movie rights to William Brinkley's World War II novel, *Don't Go Near the Water*, sold for $340,000. *Tokyo Romance*, written in English by Earnest Hoberecht, Tokyo

[3] Letter, Campbell to Earl Vandale, Oct. 12, 1949.
[4] *Ibid.*, to Mrs. Harvie McCoid, Sept. 30, 1946.
[5] *Ibid.*, to Bennet Cerf, Feb. 3, and May 14, 1947.

Bureau chief for United Press news wire service, was published in Japanese and set an all-time sales record of several million copies. Hoberecht received $80,000 in royalties in 1947 alone. [6]

Growth of the writing course each June and correspondence courses the year around kept pace with the residence program. By 1947, Vestal's non-resident students comprised twenty per cent – and averaged 230 continuously – of all correspondence students at the University of Oklahoma. Students from every state had been trained by mail during the ten-year history of the writing program, and Vestal found their success matched that of the resident students, although only three of the six courses were offered by correspondence.

Since first offered ten years earlier, the short course had grown to a twelve-hour-a-day, four-day program usually attracting about 250 persons. The record attendance was five hundred. After the first two years, Vestal and Harris decided to add a small registration fee for the short course to keep down the number of "somnolent benchwarmers whose indifference lowered the enthusiasm of the meeting." They wanted only those present who were determined to write.

The short course itself was somewhat unique, if for no other reason than the large number of professional writers and editors who helped stage it. These usually totaled three to five magazine editors, three or four book publishers or editors, and three to six writers. The first day was devoted to marketing, featuring talks by a literary critic, a bookseller, a publisher, an editor, and a representative of the Oklahoma University Press. These speakers told how literary products might be marketed and promoted. The program for the second day was devoted to writing non-fiction, both for books and magazines; the third day to fiction, and the final day to poetry. Talks

---

[6] Autobiographical data.

VESTAL, EARNEST HOBERECHT, AND FOSTER HARRIS, 1947 Hoberecht, author of the best-selling book *Tokyo Romance*, was a former student of Vestal and Harris.

given by the speakers were informal, informative, illustrated by anecdotes and personal experiences, and packed
with advice. Each evening was devoted to a round table,
or panel, to answer questions turned in during the day
or asked from the floor that evening. Any question about
the field of writing and selling was acceptable. The panel
each evening included the professionals who served as
speakers that day.

Representatives of many publishing houses usually attended and examined manuscripts brought to the short
course by those attending. Many manuscripts were picked
up here and later published.

Two things made it possible for Vestal to go on leave of
absence in the fall of 1947. First was a Rockefeller
Foundation award for work on the advancement of literature in the south. Second was his promotion to research
professor. In addition to being the top honor for a teacher at Oklahoma University, the research professorship
meant a $1,000 annual increase in salary and reduction
in teaching load to half-time.

In October the superintendent of the Cheyenne River
Agency in South Dakota notified Vestal that Chief Joseph
White Bull had died earlier in the year. The tough old
chief was 104 years of age, having lived seventy-one years
after he had killed Custer on the Little Big Horn River.
Although Vestal had not seen White Bull for ten years,
he felt as if he had lost a member of his family. In a
sense, he did, since he was White Bull's adopted son.

This was the end of the Old West era for Vestal, since
White Bull was just about the last survivor of that heroic
period of American history. His death released Vestal
from a vow not to reveal who had killed Custer for fear
someone would harm the old man. But the biography of
White Bull had been published fourteen years earlier and
was out of print. Vestal may have tried to get a new
edition printed, but there is no evidence that he did. It

was to be many years later – only twenty-two months before his own death – that he found a way to get White Bull's story before the nation's Custeriana fans. [7]

Vestal's twentieth book, *Warpath and Council Fire,* was published in 1948 by Random House of New York. In a way it was a summary of all his previous books about the Indians, based on forty bloody years of Indian wars stretching from the soon-to-be-violated Treaty of Fort Laramie in 1851 to the final defeat of the red men at the Battle of Wounded Knee in 1891. Vestal described it as "the result of 40 years research much condensed." [8] The book covered the major battles of the plains Indians, plus stories about such scouts as Kit Carson, Jim Bridger and Buffalo Bill; the Indian chiefs, particularly Sitting Bull and Roman Nose; the trader, Colonel William Bent; soldiers, such as Custer, Phil Kearny, Nelson A. Miles, William Tecumseh Sherman, and Marcus Reno; and others. [9]

The New York Times said of *Warpath and Council Fire* that "No better summarization could be made of the conditions which caused the plains wars." [10] The Westerners Chicago Corral selected it as one of the ten best westerns in 1948.

The principal value of the book over the previous volumes which covered much of the same material was its exploration of the reasons for the Indian wars. Also, Vestal was more objective and less pro-Indian in this summary volume. For the first time in all his writing he pointed out that the United States had acquired legal title to the plains from the French and Mexicans before most of the plains tribes moved there. Also, the Indians

------

[7] *Ibid.*; and letters, G. W. Spradling to Campbell, Oct. 15, 1947, and Campbell to Spradling, Oct. 21, 1947.
[8] Letter, Campbell to John D. DeLana, June 17, 1948.
[9] Stanley Vestal, *Warpath and Council Fire, passim.*
[10] *New York Times*, Aug. 1, 1948.

themselves took possession of the land from weaker tribes, and were paid for it by the whites who had already paid for it once before. Despite this, the book showed Vestal thought the plains Indians were less to blame for the forty years of war than were certain whites, and treaties broken by whites.

The Minnesota Massacre of 1862, in which hundreds of whites were killed, started the plains wars even though the plains Indians were not responsible. Various other "massacres" followed, from the Sand Creek Massacre of Cheyennes to the Little Big Horn defeat of the Seventh Cavalry. Only after the army was given control of Indian affairs were the plains tribes finally overwhelmed. [11]

In 1948 Vestal's students and graduates kept pace with his success by recording their best year to date, publishing twenty-five books, three serials, sixteen novelettes, one hundred seventy-four short stories, eighty-two articles, two plays, two screen plays, two booklets, one book-length condensation in *Reader's Digest*, and thirteen poems. As usual, this annual report did not include any staff written material, and many free-lance sales were never reported.

Vestal's family increased by two in 1948. His oldest daughter, Malory, "presented me with my first grandchild on June 14, a seven and a half pound girl, Ann Malory," he wrote. His reaction was typical of a new grandfather. Less than a month later he hurried to Princeton University for the Wedding of his youngest daughter, Dorothy, to a psychiatrist, Dr. Enoch Callaway iii. After the marriage Vestal found himself strutting at the huge reception in the Princeton Inn. He also got to visit with Isabel.

Vestal went to New York and spent a month with Frank Reid, his Oxford roommate, working on a book and taking an occasional fishing trip. On one trip to the

---

[11] *Warpath and Council Fire.*

mountains in Canada they fished in a private preserve. That night Vestal suffered a heart attack and almost died. For six months he was in a condition he described as "creeping around." Reid took care of him part of this time, or he might not have survived.

Even when recovered, Vestal was supposed to curtail his activities. Then sixty-one years of age, he began thinking about retirement and whether to do so in four years or wait until he had to when he was seventy. Retirement would mean a great loss in pay, because he received $8,500 a year for teaching one hour a day. And where would he live? The homestead near Santa Fe would be a cheap place to live, was in a good climate and would provide him with the privacy he needed for writing. But the place would be lonely, high altitude was bad for a heart ailment, he would have to buy a new car, and he would have to do his own housekeeping.

Vestal-trained writers once again set records in 1949, with more than five hundred sales. And 1950 was more of the same. The Board of Regents at Oklahoma University was so impressed with this success that a special enrollment fee was added to the regular tuition for the writing courses.

Vestal's fourth and final textbook, *Writing: Advice and Devices*, was published that same year by Doubleday and Company of Garden City, New York. The first textbook taught the student to think like a writer, while the second and third ones taught actual writing techniques for fiction and non-fiction. The fourth one, a supplement to the two books on technique, showed Vestal's attention to detailed analysis of the work of masters. It explains how to isolate, analyze and learn devices used to produce desired effects on the readers. [12] It was well received by critics and readers.

---

[12] Stanley Vestal, *Writing: Advice and Devices, passim.*

Somehow Vestal found time for numerous lectures over the country during 1950, at the University of Indiana, a teacher's college in Superior, Wisconsin, Catholic University in Washington, D.C., and others. But the trip which he liked most to recall was one to a college at Canyon, Texas, an area plagued by an extended drought. As he approached the town, Vestal noticed a black storm cloud off in the distance. He started his lecture that day by telling the audience that the Sioux had given him the power to make rain and that he was going to use that power to produce a downpour on the area. He neglected to mention that he had long since returned Sitting Bull's medicine bundle to One Bull. Of course, the audience took the remark as a joke. People in west Texas had almost forgotten what rain looked like. But after the lecture, as Vestal was leaving town, the black cloud swooped in on the community. "It must have been a cloud burst," Vestal wrote. The incident helped make his summer tour a success. [13]

---

[13] Autobiographical data.

The Golden Years

A new era for the professional writing courses was near when Vestal returned to the campus in the fall of 1950. The courses had never been popular within the English Department, where many faculty members believed the commercial approach to writing did not belong in a liberal arts program. Some also resented Vestal's financial success and recognition, and his free hand in conducting the program which they believed should be under the full control of the department. Some of the faculty remained Vestal's staunch friends and backers, but in general the atmosphere was hostile.[1]

When Foster Harris was promoted in recognition of this contribution to the program, certain members of the department complained because other faculty members had not been promoted at the same time.

Dr. Fayette Copeland, director of the school of journalism, was a former student and long-time friend of Vestal's. As the strain between Vestal and his departmental colleagues increased, Copeland suggested switching the program to the school of journalism. Dr. Ed Meacham, dean of arts and sciences, and the president of the university liked the idea. After weeks of consideration, Vestal agreed to the change, and it was made June 1, 1951.

Since Vestal's early days among the Sioux it was not uncommon to see Indians stalking across Norman campus looking for "Makes-Room." Often they came to sell him

[1] Interviews with Foster Harris and Dwight Swain.

Indian art objects because he could not resist buying them. And as he traveled around Western Oklahoma and elsewhere in Indian country he also picked up such objects, mostly things he had wanted but could not afford to buy in earlier years.

At a Cheyenne powwow near Clinton, Oklahoma, Vestal saw a squaw setting up a teepee. Desire to own such a set of teepee poles overcame him, and he bartered with her until she sold them to him. The set included twelve poles thirty to forty feet long. The squaw was supposed to ship them to him, but they failed to arrive. He wrote her, and learned that her brother claimed the poles were his. Vestal had to pay for them a second time. Then he had trouble getting them back to Norman. He finally had them shipped by special truck at considerable expense.

While attending another powwow at Pendleton, Oregon, Vestal found another set of poles – numbering eighteen – he liked even better. He bought them and notified the railroad to ship them to Norman. When he arrived back home, he told his secretary to pay the shipping fee out of petty cash, a fund of a few dollars he kept available for such use. But the railroad had its troubles also, and had to ship the poles by special railroad car due to the length. The cost was more than a hundred dollars. And trouble with the poles was not yet over. Vestal could not find any place to store them. Finally he had to put them under the seats of the football stadium, where they remained through the years. He never did use them. [2]

As a youngster among the Cheyenne, Vestal often admired the bow of an Indian friend, but the Indian would not sell it to him. Through their fifty years of friendship Vestal often tried to purchase the magnificent weapon, always with the same results. When the Indian died at the age of eighty-three, his widow sold the bow to Vestal.

-----

[2] Interview with Foster Harris.

"I have seen old bows in captivity but this is the finest," Vestal wrote. "I almost took it to bed with me like a kid with a new toy. It is not often that one obtains something one has wished for for half a century." [3]

Something he had wanted for fifty years and finally secured was a buffalo hide. He sat down and wrote an essay about the role of the buffalo robes in the lives of Indians, and said that all great warriors and chiefs possessed them. "But I, biographer of Sitting Bull, White Bull, and author of many a chapter and article story about Indians, I had none. But today I acquired it." [4]

One such purchase Vestal soon regretted. He had always wanted a coonskin cap, and finally bought one while lecturing in Kansas. Proud of his new possession, he placed it on his bed post. He awoke in the middle of the night, saw two gleaming eyes without realizing they were part of the cap, and fled the room in terror.

For more than twenty years Vestal's Indian friends wrote of their extreme poverty, particularly during the winter months when Dakota weather dropped below zero. He wrote many letters to relatives and friends asking for old clothes "for my Sioux relatives." The financial plight of the Sioux infuriated him, all the more so because he could do so little about it. They were entitled to better treatment, he thought.

Vestal's income for 1950 totaled only $12,226, most of it from his salary. Royalties added up to only a little over $2,000. Perhaps that was one reason for his bitterness over his failure to sell movie rights to any of his books. But the major reason for this feeling was the fact that several times studios produced movies about Old West characters soon after Vestal published biographies about them. And some of the dialog would be the same as that secured by Vestal first hand and published no-

[3] Letter, Campbell to Mr. and Mrs. John Franks, Jan. 5, 1956.
[4] Autobiographical data.

where else. In March of 1951 he reported seeing a movie with several lines taken directly from one of his books. [5]

Many Vestal-trained writers fared better with movie sales. The record was the $340,000 for William Brinkley's *Don't Go Near the Water*. This was the sort of jackpot the optimistic Vestal always expected but never hit. His students did so with fiction. Studios seldom bought non-fiction.

In 1950 Vestal began work on a history of Dodge City, Kansas, perhaps the best known of Old West cities. He prowled through old court records, newspaper files, and freight company records, and exchanged hundreds of letters and interviewed numerous old-timers who could provide information about the city. His usual exhaustive research included many trips to the Kansas and Oklahoma historical societies and museums. He sought out the material with the thoroughness that was his trademark.

In September of 1951 a third member was added to the professional writing faculty, unexpectedly. Five years earlier Dwight V. Swain came to Oklahoma University for summer study. Before the war he had been earning a living free-lance writing, a profession he had learned the same way Vestal and Harris had learned it, on his own. He had little regard for schools of writing, but he thought the discipline of regular work would help him

> burnish the rust of the war years off my own techniques, thus speeding up the process of getting back into the steady production of pulp fiction.
>
> To be frank, the work under Professor Campbell rang few bells with me at the time. A one-month abridgement of his regular course in magazine fiction, it called for such vast numbers of "finger exercises" and analytical disections of magazine stories as to have taxed a

---

[5] Campbell diary, Mar. 11, 1951, and letter to William Bean, April 29, 1957.

literary Hercules. I could see its value, but felt it took far more time than was warranted.

My association with Foster Harris was another story. As an old pulp writer himself, he talked my language. His comments were both pointed and pungent, and from the start I couldn't help but recognize the insight and worth of his theories on fiction structure.

Best of all was my association with the other members of the class. Most of them were veterans like myself, and all were imbued with a wonderful fierce determination to become writers, no matter how long or hard the road. Night and day they wrote, wrote, wrote. And when they were not actually writing, they were studying it or talking about it. All in all, I never hope to meet a finer group of men.

But the summer was merely a pleasant interlude so far as I was concerned. By the time the session ended I had hit my pre-war stride once more. Shortly thereafter, I hied myself away to the wilds of darkest Arkansas, and there settled down to enjoying an Ozark view.

Through the years that followed, however, news of my friends at Norman kept catching up with me. Cliff Adams – who had sold his first yarn to *Fight Stories* while we were at the university – climbed all the way to *The Saturday Evening Post* and other big slicks with some of the best western and war stories I have ever read. Bill Scott began to hit Collier's as if it were a wired slot machine. Jim Propp took his place as a regular contributor to the *Toronto Star Weekly* and the western pulps, Cord Nelson and Larry Becker broke into the detective books.

It was incredible No matter how competent the Campbell-Harris team might be; regardless of the effectiveness of their methods, I still found it hard to understand how any course could turn virtual beginners into selling writers in so short a time. I knew that most college writing courses would have been shocked and delighted at even one sale a year. Yet the successes I have mentioned were only those of my own particular friends. In spite of relatively small classes, literally dozens of other Campbell-Harris students of the period were selling also.

The more I thought about it, the more curious I became. Increasingly, I pondered as to just what unique touch or approach or technique or theory it was that distinguished OU's professional writing courses from the others. I even promised myself that if I ever had the time and opportunity to investigate them properly, I'd make it a point to find out the how and why of their achievement. [6]

Swain's chance to learn this "how and why" came in 1951 when he accepted a job at Oklahoma University as script writer of industrial films produced by the university. Soon after school opened that fall, Foster Harris became ill. Unable to teach his courses, and faced with a long convalescence, Harris recommended that Swain replace him. When Harris returned to the job, Swain remained on the faculty.

The year 1951 saw another record set by students and graduates of the school. A total of 641 sales included twelve books, 252 short stories, eleven serials, thirteen novelettes, 106 articles and 101 poems. The average of $100,000 a year continued. [7]

Harper and Brothers of New York published *Queen of Cowtowns: Dodge City* in January 1952, and the following month had to come out with a second printing. A Pennant edition paperback reprint followed in 1954 and a Bantam edition paperback was published in 1957. A British paperback publishing house came out with a paperback edition in 1957. A sizeable portion of the book's success likely came from many favorable interviews.

[6] Interview with Dwight Swain, 1962.
[7] Letter, Campbell to C. S. Boyles, Jan. 29, 1952.

The praise was justified, for the book really captured the flavor and spirit of what Vestal called "the Wickedest Little City in America." Starting as a whiskey camp serving Fort Dodge, the city was a stop-over on the Old Santa Fe Trail, a center for buffalo hunters and hide buyers, and with the arrival of the railroad became "Queen of Cow Towns." It took some of the top gun-hands of the Old West, including Bat Masterson and Wyatt Earp, to keep the lid on the town. Most of the best known men and women of frontier times came there at one time or another. [8]

Dodge City is another of Vestal's books which will remain in print for a long time, not only because it is enjoyable reading but because it so accurately portrays a golden era of American history.

In the summer of 1952 Vestal became a traveling man again, visiting his children and grandchildren in the east while researching his final biography in the Library of Congress. This was a book about Joe Meek, another of the mountain men who helped open up the west. Publishers honored Vestal with dinners, and everywhere he lectured to overflowing crowds. But when he returned to Oklahoma University in September and found all his classes overflowing, and his correspondence students numbering more than three hundred, he decided "There is such a thing as building too good a mouse trap." He had little time to himself anymore. [9]

The biography, *Joe Meek*, published in 1952 by Caxton Printers, Caldwell, Idaho, was perhaps Vestal's most underrated work for several years. But it gained in stature until the University of Nebraska Press reprinted it in 1963. With *Kit Carson* and *Jim Bridger*, it formed a trilogy – biographies of the three most important moun-

[8] Stanley Vestal, *Queen of the Cowtowns: Dodge City, passim.*

[9] Letters, Campbell to Dr. G. L. Cross, June 12, 1952; and to Mrs. Harriet Horst, Nov. 3, 1952; Campbell diary, Sept. 11, 15, 1952.

tain men – trapping for beaver, hunting, exploring and selected as one of the ten best westerns of the year by *The Rocky Mountain News* of Denver, Colorado, but for the most part received little acclaim at that time.

A comrade of Jim Bridger and Kit Carson, Meek shared many of their experiences in the era of the mountain men – trapping for beaver, hunting, exploring and fighting Indians. After the final rendezvous of the trappers in 1839, he went to Oregon Territory and helped establish the first provisional government. He was the first territorial marshal and foremost among the Indian fighters there. [10]

[10] Stanley Vestal, *Joe Meek, passim.*

Oxford Revisited

Vestal's interest in Oxford never lessened with the passing years, and he felt a deep sense of gratitude to the program and the university. When former Rhodes Scholars were first permitted to serve on selection committees, starting in 1926, Vestal immediately became a member of the Oklahoma committee and retained membership for thirty years. He often wrote letters of congratulations to scholarship winners, usually recommending they try for Merton College. Ten of the thirty-one Rhodes Scholars from Oklahoma during his tenure were admitted to Merton College. He also kept in touch with Oxford officials.

Every twenty-five years the Rhodes Scholars held a reunion at Oxford, but Vestal was unable to attend the first one after his graduation. [1] He knew the second one, in 1953, would be his last chance but he lacked the necessary funds for such an expensive trip. But in the spring of 1953 Bantam Books, a paperback publishing house, bought reprint rights to *Dodge City* and *The Old Santa Fe Trail* for $3,000 each. With this windfall, he contacted Frank Reid in New York and the two made plans for the trip to England.

Reid and Vestal boarded the liner "Britannic" June 17. The reunion began immediately, for about forty Rhodes Scholars were aboard the same vessel. Among them were Senator William Fulbright of Arkansas, who for many

---

[1] Stanley Vestal, "Oxford Revisited," in *Southwest Review*, Spring 1955, p. 151.

years served on Rhodes Committees with Vestal. Vestal wrote that the ship was just about the right size "for such a party – big enough to escape from people who bore you, small enough to find the friends you are looking for – with a bar at each end." The trip over was a continual round of "teas, cocktail parties and jolly dinners. It was wonderful to sail with so many old pals aboard." [2]

They arrived in Liverpool June 26, a gray and foggy day. As a diplomatic compliment to the Rhodes Scholars, their luggage was passed unopened by the customs inspectors. Had they opened Vestal's suitcase, they would have found eighteen and a half pounds of tinned beef. Like the plains Indians, he did not care much for vegetables and he was taking no chances on the British meat shortage making a vegetarian out of him.

Vestal expected many changes at Oxford after forty-five years, and found them. He arrived two days before the reunion and was appalled by the run of traffic along the once quiet streets. The Queen Mother was in town for a wedding, which added to the congestion created by the reunion. Also, Oxford was now a big industrial center. Stone buildings once gray with coal smoke were now buff or honey colored, thanks to electricity. Vestal did not object to the latter change.

Vestal and Reid secured rooms, and then set out for the campus. Vestal's first goal was his old college, Merton. He was eager to see it again, especially his old rooms and certain parts which had not been open to undergraduates when he had been a student there. But the porter was out and his boy dared not leave the lodge. While Vestal and Frank talked to him one of the dons came in and volunteered to show them around. He was Professor J. R. R. Tolkien, author of *The Hobbit* and *The Lord of the Rings* trilogy, well-known fantasy books.

---

[2] Letter, Campbell to Frank Reid, Apr. 24, May 1 and 12, 1953.

Tolkien took them everywhere, including the room where the queen lived when King Charles lived at Oxford. The tour concluded with Danish lager in the don's rooms.

For two days Vestal and Reid wandered about, taking many photographs and sightseeing. The little courtyard where once stood a row of outdoor toilets had been replaced by a rose garden. "Sic transit gloria latrinae," Vestal wrote of this. The old inn where Shakespeare had often stayed had been replaced by a Woolworth store. One of the strangest sights was to see young women about the university grounds wearing caps and gowns. "There were no undergraduettes in the old celibate days," Vestal wrote.

Registration for the reunion was held in Rhodes House, followed by a reception that night in three large tents. Meeting old friends again was pleasant, but "the drinks were so soft (nothing stronger than sherry) that everybody was perfectly sober. In fact, nobody could get tight at any party – the whole reunion was as orderly as could be."

The next day Vestal attended morning prayer wearing a cap, gown and hood as suggested by the booklet given him at the registration desk. Hardly anyone did likewise. The usual reunion tours and teas followed. At dinner that night nine hundred guests crowded into a tent "big enough for a circus." This time caps and gowns were worn by most. Naturally Vestal came without his. The following night the scholars attended dinner in their own colleges. This time Vestal was determined to come properly dressed. His booklet said dinner jackets would be worn. "I turned up in mine. Then I found everyone arrayed in gowns." He tipped a servant to get his from the hotel, and waited for it before joining the other diners.

About a hundred persons attended the Merton dinner.

Vestal received one of the most honored chairs, "probably because of seniority." The first course – melon – caused him a bit of trouble. Before he touched it, a servant came around with a silver dish containing a light brown powder intended for the melon. Vestal sprinkled some on and put a bit in his mouth. Then he almost choked. He had forgotten the habit of Britons of salting melons with ginger, just as he had forgotten the results.

The final night of the reunion, July 2, a reception was held at Rhodes House. Vestal was announced as Mr. Campbell, then greeted by the Oxford secretary as Stanley Vestal, which pleased him greatly.

After the reunion, Reid bought a car and the two old friends left on a 2,400-mile tour of the islands. The car gave them some trouble, since the steering wheel was on the left side, American style, but had to be driven on the left side of the road, British style. They solved this problem by Reid driving while Vestal sat on the right acting as navigator, watching the road, signs and maps.

At Stratford-on-Avon they rented rooms in the Shakespeare Hotel, with windows overlooking the gardens of Shakespeare's home. They visited his grave, birthplace, chapel and gardens, and the cottage of his wife. Through rural England they eased along at thirty miles an hour, enjoying "magnificent scenery" despite narrow and winding roads. Wales and Ireland they found windier than Oklahoma. Ireland was the greatest disappointment of the trip for Vestal, for he had thought of it as "the home of fighting men, dashing lovers, drunks, etc." But he saw no drunks, only one fight and that between two small boys, and "absolutely no sign that either sex took the least interest in the other. Nobody held hands or even walked together." [3]

Near the end of their touring, Vestal was invited to

---

[3] *Ibid.*, to Malory Campbell, July 15, 1953.

address two London writers' clubs. He could not pass up the opportunity. They sailed for home August 25. Vestal visited briefly in the east with his daughters before returning to Norman.

In the school year following Vestal's return from England his students and graduates continued selling their manuscripts to the top markets in the country. Sales reported to him boosted the totals since 1938 to 150 books, and about nine thousand articles and short stories published in more than 950 different magazines. The school had by this time trained about two thousand writers from all over the world.

At the same time Vestal was working on the only book he ever hated to write. Ironically, it turned out to be his last book. A year earlier, when he first started it he said he intended to cut down on his writing

> if I ever live to finish this damn book for the University Press. Why I was such a fool as to ask for that job ought to be a mystery. I will keep it so because my real motive was to compel the Rockefeller Foundation to give me a grant after they had twice struck my name from those invited to attend one of their conferences. This may have been done by somebody at ou. But, at any rate, I wasn't going to stand for that. [4]

So, because his pride was injured, Vestal undertook the writing of *The Book Lover's Southwest*, a survey of literature of the southwest. Finally published in 1955 by the University of Oklahoma Press, it was mostly just reviews of books of the region, books which Vestal rated best. He intended it to be good reading, and not just a bibliography. Many of the books were merely listed by title, author and publisher. But Vestal evaluated the better ones at some length. The book was divided into chapters on biographies, histories, description and inter-

---

[4] *Ibid.*, Oct. 9, 1952.

pretation, humor, juveniles, oratory, satire, science, fiction, poetry and song, folklore and drama. [5]

"Most of the well-written books fall into the field of non-fiction," Vestal wrote. For that reason, the work dealt mostly with non-fiction. His own reading preference was for "anything good of its kind." For satisfaction he preferred non-fiction, for distraction, fiction. But his favorite book was fiction, one not connected with the southwest, *The Three Musketeers*. "I have read it once a year for thirty years," he wrote. [6]

The Book Lover's Southwest received wider acclaim than one might expect for what amounted to a reference book. Of course, Vestal's vast knowledge of books about the southwest made the work more interesting than it might have been if written by others. And it was quite a scholarly achievement.

Years earlier Wallace and Eloise Thompson, Oklahoma University graduates interested in books and the general cultural level of the southwest, set up a fund with the University of Oklahoma Press. The fund could be applied to any work the Press thought particularly deserving, in order to turn out a better book than would normally be economically possible. This book was one chosen by the Press as worthy of such special treatment.

Vestal never wrote another book, although a revised and much more successful edition of *Sitting Bull* was published the following year.

---

[5] Stanley Vestal, *The Book Lover's Southwest, passim.*
[6] Autobiographical data.

End of the Trail

The final four years of Stanley Vestal's life –1954-57 – were not radically different from the final four decades, but he enjoyed them more and did little writing. Except for finishing *The Book Lover's Southwest* in 1954, he spent the years pretty much as he wanted to spend them. With royalties coming in regularly, and more than $9,000 a year received for half-load teaching during the regular school years, he could afford both the time and money to do what he wanted. The indebtedness that had plagued him most of his life had long since vanished. And he was honored everywhere he went.

In the summer of 1954 Vestal traveled about the northern portion of the Great Plains interviewing old Indians, poking around museums and historical sites. Most of July he spent in the historic Jackson Hole country of Wyoming with Reginald and Gladys Laubin, a couple he had helped when they were writing a book about Indian teepees. [1] The Laubins lived in a log cabin, but had two teepees nearby. Highlight of the summer came early in August when Vestal went to Sheridan, Wyoming, to attend the American Indian Days pageant. Many thousands of Indians were there for three days of dancing, racing, and other contests. Vestal found some old friends among them, and many other Indians to whom Stanley Vestal was a magic name.

---

[1] For the Laubin book, *The Indian Tipi*, Vestal wrote the Foreword and the first chapter on the history of the tipi. The book was published in 1957, the year of Vestal's death.

Seventy-two Indian girls wearing buckskin competed for the Miss Indian America title. The winner, a Sioux girl from Fort Yates, South Dakota, "went to Atlantic City and stole the show at the Miss America contest although she couldn't compete because Indians don't like for their women to exhibit themselves in bathing suits." Some of the officials talked Vestal into agreeing to judge the Indian contest the following year.

A trip to New York to visit Frank Reid, and to Baltimore to visit Dorothy and family, concluded the summer. Over the Christmas holidays he and Reid took a twelve-day Caribbean cruise.

The next year, 1955, was pretty much of a repeat for Vestal. Crowded spring classes gave way to an overflow crowd at the June short course. Then he headed north again for another summer of research, travel, and speaking engagements. In Denver he talked to a writer's club, visited Gayle Waldrop at the University of Colorado in Boulder, then went in to Salt Lake City "where I was able to show them their labels were wrong on certain Indian items in the museum."

At the cabin of the Laubins near Moose, Wyoming, Vestal found fifteen Sioux and Arapaho families in tee-pees. After talking to them, he continued his roaming. Addressing writers, interviewing Indians, prowling through museums and libraries, Vestal traveled in Canada, Montana, and back to Wyoming. Just for kicks, Vestal went into one library and proceeded to autograph all his books he found on the shelves there. This "made the girl at the desk pop out her eyes."

In Sheridan, Wyoming, Vestal and the other judges of the Miss Indian America contest interviewed seventy-eight Indian maidens before selecting Miss Rita Ann McLaughlin as winner. She was the part-Sioux granddaughter of Major McLaughlin, the agent in charge of the Standing Rock Reservation when Sitting Bull was killed there. Vestal blamed the major for Sitting Bull's death, "but his granddaughter well deserved the honor" of winning, he wrote.

Once again, Vestal concluded the summer with a trip east, fishing with Frank Reid and visiting Dorothy and family.

Vestal continued addressing conferences of writers and historians across the country during the school year, mostly for his own pleasure. He also wrote short material, probably for the same reason. He produced a series of thirty-minute radio scripts for "The American Story" program sponsored by the American Society of Historians over the Columbia Broadcasting System. Included were "The American Indian" in 1955, "Kit Carson" and "Dakota Courtship" in 1956, and "Jim Bridger" in 1957. [2]

For Vestal 1956 was another year of honors. In March he was inducted into Western Writers of America, a four-year-old organization of the top writers in that field. President of the group at that time was Bill Gulick, one of Vestal's most successful students.

The American Council on Education in Journalism inspected the Oklahoma University Journalism School curricula that spring and Vestal's program was one of the few in the nation to receive an "excellent" rating. [3]

In April Vestal received the National Achievement Award from The Westerners "in recognition for his untiring efforts in the preservation of the cultural heritage of the American West through his research, teaching and writing." A banquet was given in Chicago in his honor, attended by sixty of the nation's leading American West historians. Vestal entertained his audience with stories about Indian warfare. After the banquet he was interviewed over a national radio network.

Finally, the Rhodes trustees published a book listing

[2] Autobiographical data.   [3] *Sooner State Press,* Jan. 11, 1958.

Rhodes Scholars who achieved the greatest distinction. Vestal was among those listed, but as a novelist. He reacted with this statement: "It is the fate of most writers to be known, if they are known at all, for something to which they never attached much importance, and which is no particular credit to them." [1]

The fame of the Vestal-Harris-Swain team drew nearly three hundred persons to the writing short course in June 1956. Like royalty, Vestal reigned supreme amidst adulation. Coming from many distant points, those attending brought numerous books by Vestal for him to autograph.

Vestal began his usual summer trek by attending the annual convention of the Western Writers of America, meeting that year in Santa Fe. He met many old friends and some new ones, and was most pleased to see his former student, Bill Gulick, presiding over the session.

Next Vestal conducted writing conferences at Portales, New Mexico; at the Southern Baptist Convention annual assembly at Glorieta, near Santa Fe; and at the University of Colorado in Boulder.

The Miss Indian America contest drew ninety-one entries in August, with a Pawnee girl from Utah winning. As a judge, Vestal held a portion of the spotlight and enjoyed it, as usual. Before leaving Sheridan, he could not resist buying a "handsome war bonnet. I have no use for it and have no place to keep it, but I have one, at any rate." [5]

After a brief visit in Gallup, New Mexico, Vestal concluded his summer touring with his usual trip east to see Dorothy and family, and going fishing with Frank Reid.

Soon after his return to Norman in September, Vestal

---

[1] Letter, Campbell to Dorothy and Malory Campbell, Feb. 9, 1956.
[5] *Ibid.*, to Mrs. J. D. McCoid, Oct. 5, 1956, and to Randy Steffen, Oct. 30, 1956; and Campbell diary, August 2-5, 1956.

completed a revision of his 1932 edition of *Sitting Bull*. The University of Oklahoma Press wanted to reprint it as the forty-sixth volume of its Civilization of the American Indian Series. Vestal did not expect to receive much from the old book, especially from a university press. But it gave him an opportunity at last to tell Chief Joseph White Bull's first person account of how he killed Custer. This chapter of the book also was printed in the February 1957 *American Heritage*. Prestige normally was much greater than profit for articles in the hard cover magazine, but this article – published as the lead story and featured on the cover – caught the attention of the Associated Press wire service. A news story about it was sent across the world by the AP's far-flung wire network. [6]

The widespread publicity boomed sales of the book. One month Vestal's royalties totaled more than $5,000. He always regarded the book, even the first edition, as his best piece of research and writing. Certainly it was his most successful, most highly regarded, and most controversial. Publication of the new edition, along with the *American Heritage* article and AP release, brought him a flood of mail from Custer lovers, Custer haters, historians and cranks. Vestal enjoyed even the critical letters. "You should see some of my fan mail," he wrote. "You would think I was the man who killed Custer, or was at least an accessory." [7]

Vestal packed a lot of living into his last summer. He flew first to Denver for research on the Apache chief, Geronimo, for an article requested by *Harper's Magazine*. Next he flew to the Western Writers of America convention at Great Falls, Montana. Two publishers approached him with projects, one wanting him to write a book on *The Day Custer Was Killed*. Another wanted

---

[6] *Ibid.*, to Mrs. A. W. Constant, Mar. 21, 1957; and Associated Press dispatch, *Daily Oklahoman*, Feb. 11, 1957.

[7] Letter, Campbell to Mrs. A. W. Constant, Mar. 21, 1957.

a biography of the Old West painter, George Catlin, based on his adventures among the Indians. Vestal signed a contract for the Catlin book. But he was there to enjoy himself, and did so, even joining in a picnic near the Great Falls. After a night in Calgary, Canada, an old cow town with an old-fashioned railroad hotel right on the tracks, he flew to Vancouver. The next day he chartered a small plane and flew to nearby Wallace Island where David Conover, a correspondence student of Vestal's, owned a fishing resort complete with cottages and boats. By mail they had arranged to exchange manuscript criticism for boat fishing trips

As might be expected, Vestal found some Indians to talk to on a nearby island. But the ways of the white man had reached the village. All of the children were enthusiastically fishing off a footbridge, and chewing something at the same time. Each time one caught a fish, he ran over and deposited it in a submerged fish trap, then ran back to fish some more. The owner of a small store nearby explained to Vestal that he traded the children bubble gum for the fish they caught.

When Vestal took the boat to Seattle, he became chilled and had a bad time getting up the ramp to the customs. All summer he had carried three different kinds of heart pills, and needed them on several occasions. This was one.

After completing some research in the historical museum at Helena, Montana, he went to Sheridan, Wyoming, for the All American Indian Days and helped judge the Miss Indian America contest for the third and last time. Contestants, numbering 107, represented fifty-seven tribes. The Oklahoma contingent was so large a separate parade was held for it.

From Sheridan Vestal went to the Custer Battlefield in Montana, accompanied by his old friend, Maurice Frink, head of the Colorado Historical Society, and by

Casey Barthelmess, an old cowman and son of a famous frontier photographer. With his heart ailment bothering him more, and his seventieth birthday that month, Vestal knew he had little time left. At the administration building of the national park he learned that his military service made him

> eligible to be buried in the military cemetery there, which is a beautifully kept grave. I don't yet know of any spot of which I have more interesting recollections than the Custer Battlefield. I knew so many men who fought there. . . It might be nice to believe I was buried there . . . on that historic hill with the magnificent views around. [s]

From the battlefield the three drove through the Cheyenne country to Miles City, then to Busby, where they stopped to photograph Firewolf, son of a famous Cheyenne chief by the same name. While making the photos, a messenger came from the house next door saying they had pipes to sell. When they went over to see the pipes, the seller turned out to be Last Bull, an old friend of Vestal's. But a bigger surprise awaited Vestal. For the past one hundred years the southern Cheyennes had been the custodians of the four sacred medicine arrows of the Cheyenne. But the previous year the keeper of the arrows, an alcoholic, had sold them to the northern Cheyenne. Vestal knew they were in Montana, but had been unable to learn which Indian had them. After Vestal photographed Last Bull, the old warrior asked, "Would you like to see the medicine arrow bundle?"

Vestal's response was about as prompt as might be expected of him. Last Bull picked up his axe and led his guests to a tent house next door. The medicine arrows could not be kept in a regular house. The bundle,

[s] *Ibid.*, to Dorothy and Malory Campbell, July 11 and Sept. 25, 1957.

about eight inches thick and four feet long, was hanging on the rear wall above an old envelope on which someone had scribbled "Don't touch the medicine." Last Bull would not let them see the arrows, but he untied one end of the bundle and let them see the wrappings, three of cloth, one of buffalo hide. And they could see the nose of the coyote skin next to the arrows. Vestal had seen the arrows forty-four years earlier when they were exposed to the view of the males of the tribe in western Oklahoma. [9]

On the road once more, Vestal and his two companions continued to visit historic sites and museums. They even visited Crow Rock, a natural fortification of sandstone where the bloodiest fight in all Sioux history was fought. They took numerous photographs of the area. Casey, who had a lively sense of humor, carved in large letters on the rock "Sitting Bull, 1869."

At the Pine Ridge Reservation they found a Sun Dance in progress. For once, Vestal did not stay up all night to see it. He tired too easily now, and had had a long day.

From the far west, Vestal went to Chicago for three weeks' research in the Ayer Indian Collection of the Newberry Library. He regarded the collection as the best in the country. Here he secured data for the *Harper's* article on Geronimo, and for the biography of George Catlin, the painter. Then, as usual, he concluded the summer with a trip to Baltimore, New York and Washington for visits and research. But his heart bothered him so much he cut his eastern stay short and went home.

September began Vestal's forty-second and final school year at Oklahoma University. Now seventy, retirement would be mandatory the following June. By then the prospect of retirement began to appeal to Vestal, for he realized it would give him more time for writing. He had several book projects in mind, including an autobiography,

---

[9] *Ibid.*

STANLEY VESTAL IN HIS OFFICE

the Catlin biography for which he had a contract, and several others. But in his mind also was the knowledge that the end of his life was not far away. Hardly had the fall semester started before he made inquiries on how to get buried in the Custer Battlefield National Cemetery.

One final honor awaited Vestal that fall. The state was celebrating its fiftieth anniversary, and the Library of Congress staged an exhibition to commemorate the event. Featured speaker was one of the state's most famous citizens, Stanley Vestal, flown to Washington for the ceremony.

Only three days later Vestal walked up the ramp of the football field at Norman to watch a game long awaited by himself and many other Oklahomans – another contest with Notre Dame. He was a rabid Oklahoma University football fan long before the teams of Coach Bud Wilkinson rewrote the record books in the ten preceding years. In fact, he seldom missed even a routine game. And the clash with Notre Dame was something special. Oklahoma went into the game with the longest winning streak in football history, forty-seven victories in a row, covering more than four seasons. A few days earlier a national sports magazine published an article on why Oklahoma could not be beaten. Like others, Vestal looked forward to the slaughter of the Irish. Soon after the game started a cold wind began whipping the length of the stadium. Perhaps it was an omen. Nothing seemed to work for the Big Red football team. Late in the game Notre Dame scored seven points, and Oklahoma fought to the final second trying to score. In the excitement, Vestal's "old ticker got uneasy." Of the defeat, Vestal wrote: "This fell like the sky upon the crowd, and it was very depressing to me." After the game he found it difficult to get back to his office just two hundred yards from the stadium.

The following Wednesday Vestal's heart condition got worse. He dismissed his classes and went to bed for a week. By December he was back at his routine, but not feeling well.

For Christmas that year Vestal visited a niece in Oklahoma City. Christmas night he suffered another heart attack and died in an Oklahoma City hospital. After the funeral services three days later in Norman, he was buried in the Custer Battlefield National Cemetery.

A few years before his death Vestal sat in his office one day talking to a friend. His secretary working nearby overheard the conversation. Eventually the talk got around to the hereafter, and what one might expect there. After the friend left, Vestal's secretary said: "I know what you'll do in the hereafter."

"What?" the amused Vestal asked.

"You'll be interviewing old Indians." [10]

Perhaps he is.

---

[10] Campbell diary, undated entry in 1952.

Bibliography
and Index

Bibliography

PUBLISHED WORKS OF STANLEY VESTAL
BOOKS

Campbell, Walter Stanley. *The Book Lover's Southwest.* Norman: University of Oklahoma Press, 1955.

——. *Professional Writing.* New York: Macmillan Co., 1938.

——. *Writing: Advice and Devices.* New York: Doubleday and Co., 1950.

——. *Writing Magazine Fiction.* New York: Doubleday and Co., 1940.

——. *Writing Non-Fiction.* Boston: The Writer Inc., 1944.

Garrard, Lewis H. *Wah-To-Yah and the Taos Trail,* edited by Stanley Vestal. Oklahoma City: Harlow Publishing Co., 1927.

Laubin, Reginald. *The Indian Tipi . . . with a History of the Tipi by Stanley Vestal.* Norman: University of Oklahoma Press, 1957.

Parkman, Francis. *The Oregon Trail,* edited by Stanley Vestal. Oklahoma City: Harlow Publishing Co., 1927.

Seger, John Homer. *Early Days Among the Cheyenne and Arapaho Indians,* edited by Stanley Vestal. Norman: University of Oklahoma Press, 1924, 1934.

Sibley, Henry Hastings. *Iron Face: The Adventures of Jack Frazer,* edited by T. C. Blegen and S. A. Davidson, with foreword by Vestal. Chicago: The Caxton Club, 1950.

Vestal, Stanley. *Big-Foot Wallace.* Boston: Houghton Mifflin Co., 1942.

——. *'Dobe Walls.* Boston: Houghton Mifflin Co., 1929.

——. *Fandango: Ballads of the Old West.* Boston: Houghton Mifflin Co., 1927.

——. *Happy Hunting Grounds.* Chicago: Lyons and Carnahan, 1928.

Vestal, Stanley. *Jim Bridger.* New York: William Morrow and Co., 1946.

——. *Joe Meek.* Caldwell, Idaho: Caxton Printers, 1952.

——. *King of the Fur Traders: Pierre Esprit Radisson.* Boston: Houghton Mifflin Co., 1940.

——. *Kit Carson.* Boston: Houghton Mifflin Co., 1928.

——. *The Missouri.* New York: Farrar and Rinehart, 1945.

——. *Mountain Men.* Boston: Houghton Mifflin Co., 1937.

——. *New Sources of Indian History, 1850-1891.* Norman: University of Oklahoma Press, 1934.

——. *The Old Santa Fe Trail.* Boston: Houghton Mifflin Co., 1939.

——. *Queen of the Cow Towns: Dodge City.* New York: Harper and Brothers, 1952; Bantam Books, 1957.

——. *Revolt on the Border.* Boston: Houghton Mifflin Co., 1938.

——. *Sallow Moon,* by Walter D. Merton (pseud.). Privately printed, ca. 1937.

——. *Short Grass Country.* New York: Duell, Sloan and Pearce, Inc., 1941.

——. *Sitting Bull: Champion of the Sioux.* Boston: Houghton Mifflin Co., 1932; Norman: University of Oklahoma Press, 1956.

——. *Wagons Southwest.* New York: American Pioneer Trails Assn., 1946.

——. *Warpath.* Boston: Houghton Mifflin Co., 1934.

——. *Warpath and Council Fire.* New York: Random House, 1948.

——. *The Wine Room Murder.* New York: Little, Brown and Co., 1935.

ARTICLES BY STANLEY VESTAL

"The American Southwest." *U.S.A., Overseas Magazine,* Feb. 1944.

"Amerindian Traits." *Southwest Review,* Autumn 1942.

"Ballad of Kit Carson." *American Mercury,* July 1925.

"Ballads of the Old West: Belle Starr, Boggy Depot, Cynthia Ann." *American Mercury,* Apr. 1926.

"Battle of the Little Big Horn." *Bluebook,* Aug. 1933.

"Best Seller Making." *Saturday Review of Literature*, Oct. 16, 1954.

"Brave Alone." *Boys' Life*, June 1937.

"Buffalo Scout." *Boys' World*, Apr. 24, 1938.

"Buffalo Trail." *Boys' World*, Apr. 16, 1939.

"Bullet Proof." *Conflict*, Sept.-Oct. 1934.

"Cash of Gold." *Boys' World*, Nov. 6, 13, 20, 27, Dec. 4, 1938.

"Characterization," by Walter S. Campbell. *The Writer*, Dec. 1939.

"Cheyenne Dog Soldiers." *Chronicles of Oklahoma*, Jan. 1921.

"The Cheyenne Tipi," by Stanley Campbell. *American Anthropologist*, Oct.-Nov. 1915.

"The Culture is Here." *Southwest Review*, Summer 1926.

"The Custer Massacre." *Bluebook*, 1933, month unknown.

"Cynthia Ann" (poem). *Literary Digest*, Apr. 17, 1926.

"Dakota Courtship." *Southwest Review*, Jan. 1939.

"Death of Satank." *Southwest Review*, Oct. 1926.

"Drama League – Strong, Masculine." *University of Oklahoma Magazine*, May 1922.

"Dream to Pattern." *The Writer*, June 1942.

"Duel with Yellow Hand." *Southwest Review*, Autumn, 1940.

"The Eagle Catcher." *Boys' World*, Sept. 17, 1939.

"Early Days Among the Northern Cheyenne." *Westerners Brand Book* (Chicago), Aug. 1949.

"El Rancho Magnifico." *Saturday Review of Literature*, Sept. 14, 1957.

"Facts About Rhodes Scholarships," by Walter S. Campbell. *University of Oklahoma Magazine*, May 1922.

"Feast Maker." sold to *Boys' World*, Feb. 20, 1938.

"The Fetterman Massacre." *Bluebook*, 1933, month unknown.

"First Families of Oklahoma." *American Mercury*, Aug. 1925.

"Fuss and Feathers." *Westerners Brand Book* (Chicago), May 1956.

"Good Medicine." *Boys' World*, May 7, 1939.

"Good Thunder." sold to *Boys' World*, July 24, 1936.

"Grass Money." *Adventure*, Aug. 25, 1932.

"Hats: Beaver vs. Silk." *Rotarian*, Nov. 1940.

"The Heart of a Chief." sold to *Boys' World*, autumn 1935.

"The Heart of Horseback." sold to *Boys' World*, Apr. 9, 1938.

"Hell's Line Riders." *West*, Feb. 6, 1937; and two others in this magazine, titles and dates unknown.

"The Histrionic West." *Space*, June 1934.

"How Good Were Indians as Shooters." *Guns*, Dec. 1950.

"The Hollywooden Indian." *Southwest Review*, Summer 1936.

"How Not to Write a Story." *The Writer*, Nov. 1940.

"How to Win a Rhodes Scholarship," by W. S. Campbell. *American Oxonian*, July 1926.

"Imitating the Indian." *Southwest Review*, Summer 1930.

"Indian Hoop Game." *Holiday Magazine for Children*, about 1905, issue unknown.

"Indian Summer." sold to *Southwest Review*, Oct. 22, 1938.

"Irish Flathead." *Catholic Digest*, Apr. 1945.

"January Thaw." *Omnibook Reader*, Dec. 1945.

"Jim Bridger." *Boys' Life*, Mar. 1947.

"John Colter's Race for Life." *Adventures for Americans* (anthology). New York: Harcourt, Brace & Co., 1956.

"Kit Carson." *Boys' Life*, Nov. 1945.

"Kit Carson's Last Smoke." *Southwest Review*, Apr. 1925.

"Last Laugh." *Boys' World*, Mar. 19, 1939.

"Last of the Pioneers." *New Mexico*, Nov. 1935.

"Listeners-Under-the-Ground." *Best Short Stories from the Southwest* (anthology). Dallas: Southwest Press, 1931.

"The Little Chief." *American Mercury*, July 1925.

"Little Soldiers." *Boys' Life*, Oct. 1936.

"The Lost Woman." *University of Oklahoma Magazine*, Mar. 1916; reprinted in *Magazine Digest*, Jan. 1940.

"Lynn Riggs: Poet and Dramatist." *Southwest Review*, Autumn 1929.

"Make Yourselves Wolves." *Boys' Life*, Feb. 1939; reprinted in *Best Short Stories for Boys and Girls*, Evanston, Ill.: Row, Peterson & Co., 1940.

"The Man Who Killed Custer." *American Heritage*, Feb. 1957.

"Material to Burn." *Southwester*, Feb. 1936.

"Medicine Hat." sold to *Rangeland Romances*, Mar. 5, 1940.

"Mistress White." *Southwest Review*, Apr. 1925.

"Modern Article Technique," by Walter S. Campbell. *The Writer*, Jan. 1944; and *The Writer's Handbook*. Boston: The Writer, Inc., 1953 and 1954 edns.

"Moki's Indian Love Song." *Rangeland Romances*, July 1940.

"Mountain Gardens." *New Mexico*, Feb. 1937.

"The Myth of British Omniscience." *Harper's Magazine*, 1954, month unknown.

"Name Your Poison." sold to *The Writer*, 1946.

"No Encore." *Southwest Review*, Oct. 1934.

"The Oklahoma Personality." *Sooner Magazine*, Feb. 1929.

"Oklahoma – An Indian Laboratory." *Sooner Magazine*, Dec. 1929.

"Oliver Wiggins." *Southwest Review*, Apr. 1925.

"One Genius in the Family is Not Enough Say the Campbells," by Isabel and Walter S. Campbell. *Sooner Magazine*, Oct. 1929.

"Our Oklahoma Tribe," by Walter S. Campbell. *Holiday Magazine for Children*, 1904, month unknown.

"Oxford Revisited." *Southwest Review*, Spring, 1955.

"Parable of the Buzzard." *Verse*, 1925, month unknown.

"Plains Indians and the War." *Saturday Review of Literature*, May 16, 1942.

"The Plains Indians in Literature – and in Life." *Trans-Mississippi West*. Boulder: University of Colorado, 1930.

"Post-War Opportunities for Discharged Servicemen in the Great Southwest." *American Legion Magazine*, Aug. 1945.

"Prairie Pictographs: Prairie Dog, Burrowing Owl, Rattlesnake, Spider, Buffalo." *Poetry, A Magazine of Verse*, Aug. 1928.

"Qualifications of a Writer." *Junior Historian*, Sept. 1942.

" 'Rapaho Girl." *American Mercury*, July 1925.

"Ree Horse Race." *Southwest Review*, Autumn 1931.

"Re-Tooling for the War Market," by Walter S. Campbell. *The Writer*, Aug. 1943.

"Saga of the Corncob Pipe." *Southwest Review*, Summer 1945.

"Sailing Over the Prairies." *Southwest Review*, July 1938.

"San Pascual." *American Mercury*, July 1925.

"Sans Arc." *Space*, May 1934.

"Settlers in the Territory." *Saturday Review of Literature*, Sept. 14, 1935.

"Significant Form," by Walter S. Campbell. *The Writer*, Jan. 1931.

"Sioux in Ambush." *Bluebook*, Sept. 1933.

"Sitting Bull." *Adventure*, Jan. 15, Feb. 15, 1932.

"Sitting Bull's Maiden Speech." *Frontier*, Mar. 1932.

"Sitting Bull's Nephews." *Indian Time*, 1951, issue unknown.

"The Soldiers." *This is the West*. Chicago: Rand McNally & Co., 1957.

"Son of the Prairie Raiders." *Ten Story Western*, Nov. 1936.

"Sooner Songs and Ballads: Saddle Songs, Kit Carson's Mule, Kit Carson of U.S.N., The Lost Trail." *Poetry, A Magazine of Verse*, July 1925.

"Squaw Dress." *Ten Story Western*, Nov. 1936.

"Squaw Pig." *Adventure*, Apr. 15, 1933.

"Strong Heart." *Adventure*, Feb. 1, 1933.

"Tenderfoot." *Ten Story Western*, Oct. 1936.

"The Tipis of the Crow Indians," by Walter S. Campbell. *American Anthropologist*, Jan. 1927.

"The Troubled Life of Billy Bonney." *Saturday Review of Literature*, July 21, 1956.

"They Dance in Oklahoma." *Southwest Review*, July 1935.

"Two Rhodes Scholars from Among Us," by Walter S. Campbell. *University of Oklahoma Magazine*, Nov. 1920.

"Two Smoke." *Boys' World*, Mar. 4, 1936.

"War Above Washita." *Big Book Western*, Jan. or Feb. 1937.

"War Paint." *Frontier*, 1925, issue unknown.

"The Warriors' Road." *Boys' Life*, Dec. 1937; reprinted in *Best Short Stories for Boys and Girls*. Evanston, Ill: Row, Peterson & Co., 1939.

"The West Rewrites its History," by Walter S. Campbell.

Saturday Review of Literature, July 16, 1955.

"Western Stuff." *Southwest Review,* Winter 1930.

"What Oxford Offers to an American," by Walter S. Campbell. *University of Oklahoma Magazine,* Mar. 1920.

"When Catlin Camped at the University," by Walter S. Campbell. *University of Oklahoma Magazine,* Spring 1926.

"White Bull." *'47, Magazine of the Year,* 1947, issue unknown.

"White Bull and One Bull." *Westerners Brand Book* (Chicago), Oct. 1947.

"White Redskin." sold to *Boys' World,* Apr. 8, 1936.

"Who Will Win the War?" *Woman's Home Companion,* Nov. 1942.

"Wild Horses," (serial). sold to *Boys' World,* Apr. 1, 1939.

"The Willow Bed," by Walter S. Campbell. *Holiday Magazine for Children,* July 1905.

"With a Little Salt." *Boys' World,* June 4, 1939.

"Wooden Indian." *American Mercury,* Jan. 1928.

"The Works of Sitting Bull." *Southwest Review,* Apr. 1934.

"Write – to be Read." *Baptist Leader,* June 1948.

"Writing Historical Fiction." *The Writer,* June 1941.

"Writing Non-Fiction," by Walter S. Campbell. *The Writer,* Oct. 1943.

"Your Intimate Subject." *The Writer,* Sept. 1940.

ENCYCLOPEDIA CONTRIBUTIONS

World Book Encyclopedia. Chicago: Quarrie Corp., 1945. Biographical sketches: Daniel Boone, James Bowie, Kit Carson, Chouteau Family, William Clark, William F. Cody, David Crockett, William G. Fargo, John C. Fremont, Simon Girty, Meriwether Lewis, James W. Marshall, Ezra Meeker, Z. M. Montgomery, Sitting Bull, and Marcus Whitman.

RADIO SCRIPTS

Columbia Broadcasting System: "The American Story" radio series, sponsored by American Society of Historians: 1955, "The American Indian"; 1956, "Kit Carson" and "Dakota Courtship"; 1957, "Jim Bridger."

GENERAL BIBLIOGRAPHY

BOOKS

Luce, Edward S. and Evelyn A. *Custer Battlefield.* National Park Service, Historical Handbook Series No. 1. Washington: Government Printing Office; 1949.

Twentieth Century Authors, First Supplement. New York: H. W. Wilson Co., 1955.

MAGAZINES

"American Rivers." *Time,* Jan. 29, 1945.

"A Reader's List." *New Republic,* Nov. 1, 1939.

DeGolyer, E. "A Virginian in Texas." *Saturday Review of Literature,* Aug. 3, 1942.

Dobie, J. Frank. "Kit Carson and Sam Houston." *The Nation,* June 6, 1928.

"Dr. Campbell's Wonderful School." *Saturday Evening Post,* Mar. 8, 1958.

Hoig, Stan. "Medicine Arrows." *Oklahoma Today,* Spring 1962.

LeFarge, Oliver. "Sitting Bull and the Sioux Tribes." *Saturday Review of Literature,* Apr. 20, 1935.

Lottinville, Savoie. "Walter Stanley Campbell." *American Oxonian,* Oct. 1958.

Nevins, Allan. "Kit Carson." *New Republic,* May 16, 1928.

Webb, Walter Prescott. "Real Wild West." *Saturday Review of Literature,* Feb. 23, 1952.

"Western Reappraisal." *Saturday Review of Literature,* July 16, 1955.

White, Len. "The Triumph of Stanley Vestal." *Sooner Magazine,* Oct. 1957.

NEWSPAPERS

Arkansas Democrat (Little Rock). July 25, 1954.

Dallas Morning News. Dec. 25, 1932.

Daily Oklahoman (Oklahoma City). May 12, 1946; Feb. 11, 1957; Jan. 7, 1958; Apr. 21, 1963.

New Orleans Picayune. Apr. 17, 1927.
New York Herald Tribune. Nov. 17, 1940; Nov. 30, 1941;
 Jan. 28, 1945.
New York Times. Mar. 25, 1928; Aug. 23, 1942; Aug. 1,
 1948; Feb. 10, 1952; Jan. 11, 1958.
Sooner State Press (Norman, Oklahoma). Jan. 11, 1958;
 Dec. 2, 1961.
Southwestern (Weatherford, Oklahoma). May 17, 1944.
Sunday Star (Washington, D.C.). Mar. 23, 1952.
Wilson County (Kansas) *Citizen.* Aug. 28, 1896; May 29,
 1898; July 1, 1898.
Four bundles of unidentified and mostly undated newspaper
 clippings in Autobiographical Data, Campbell Collection,
 Division of Manuscripts, University of Oklahoma Library,
 Norman, Oklahoma.

DIARIES

Vestal, Stanley (Walter S. Campbell). Unpublished note-
 books in the Campbell Collection, Division of Manuscripts,
 University of Oklahoma Library, Norman, Oklahoma, scattered dates in the following years: 1900, 1902, 1903, 1904,
 1908, 1909, 1922, 1924, 1925, 1927, 1928, 1936, 1937, 1940,
 1946, 1951, 1952, 1953, 1956.

LETTERS (UNPUBLISHED)
(Unless otherwise indicated: to W. S. Campbell; and
in the Campbell Collection, University of Oklahoma Library)

Alley, Mrs. Mildred. Nov. 16, 1942.
Anderson, Sherwood. Sept. 20, 1939.
Bizzell, Dr. W. B. July 20, 1929; Dec. 7, 19, 1934.
Boren, Lyle H. and Dale. Aug. 15, 1935.
Bromfield, Louis. Oct. 25, 1939.
Brooks, Stratton D. Apr. 29, 1916.
Campbell, Daisy (Mrs. J. R.). To Mrs. Sara Wood. July
 9, 1911.
Campbell, Isabel (Mrs. W. S.). To her daughters. Oct. 2,
 1938.
——. July 6, 1917, and various dates in 1917-19; Dec. 8,

1931; Sept. 3, 14, 18, Oct. 17, 28, Nov. 7, 1938; Jan. 30, 1941.

Campbell, James Robert. To F. J. Wylie. Mar. 12, 17, 18, 1908; to unknown person, Aug. 2, 1911.

Campbell, Walter Stanley (Stanley Vestal). To Martin Abernathy, Nov. 18, 1929; to Joseph Balmer, Feb. 10, 1947; to Dr. Bardemeir, June 19, 1949; to Leonard B. Beach, Sept. 29, 1947; to Wm. Bean, Apr. 29, 1957; to Harold Belknap, May 16, 1956; to W. B. Bizzell, Dec. 7, 1934; to C. S. Boyles, Jan. 29, 1952; to Stratton D. Brooks, May 23, 1914; to Mark H. Brown, Apr. 18, 1955; to Wm. C. Brown, Oct. 10, 1935; to Erik Brunstrom, Mar. 18, 1957; to A. S. Burack, Oct. 13, 1944; to H. D. Bugbee, Nov. 1, 1957.

——. To Dorothy and/or Malory Campbell. Sept. 6, 1929; Dec. 17, 18, 1947; Feb. 4, 1948; May 6, Dec. 4, 1950; Oct. 9, Dec. 8, 18, 1952; Mar. 19, July 13, 15, 1953; Sept. 14, 1955; Jan. 19, Feb. 9, 1956; July 11, Sept. 25, Nov. 4, 21, Dec. 8, 9, 1957.

——. To Isabel Campbell. Feb. 22, June 19, July 16, Sept. 12, 23, Oct. 19, Nov. 1, 4, 6, 8, 13, and various dates in Dec. 1918, and Jan. 1919; Feb. 2, 12, 21, 22, Mar. 9, 14, 16, 18, Sept. 18, 1919; Aug. 31, Sept. 1, 3, 1929; June 6, 11, 12 (telegram), 27, 1930; Sept. 6, 8, 11, 17, 18, 21, 22, 25, Oct. 12, Nov. 16, 26, 1931; Sept. 7, 9, 10, 16, Oct. 7, 8, 21, 31, Nov. 9, 1938; various dates, 1938-39; Dec. 26, 1940; June 16, 1944.

——. To Mr. and/or Mrs. (Daisy) James Robert Campbell. Nov. 8, Dec. 18, 29, 1908; Feb. 28, Mar. 3, 16, 28, Apr. 3, May 29, July 18, Sept. 28, Oct. 10, 1909; Feb. 10, June 7, 29, July 30, Aug. 14, Oct. 8, 1910; Jan. 19, Apr. 16, June 13, Sept. 6, 23, Oct. 1, Nov. 11, 1911; Jan. 16, Feb. 16, Mar. 8, 9, 28, Apr. 3, 27, Oct. 7, Nov. 3, 1912; Mar. 9, 30, Apr. 27, May 11, Nov. 8, 19, Dec. 13, and various other dates in 1913; Feb. 9, Apr. 5, various other dates in 1914; Oct. 17, and various other dates in 1915; Mar. 13, Oct. 17, 28, 29, Dec. 6, and various other dates in 1916; Jan. 6, 14, 15, Feb. 21, Mar. 6, 16, 20, Apr. 1,

21, May 20, 27, June 8, 17, July 12, 17, Aug. 4, 9, Sept. 8, 9, 20, 22, 23, Oct. 1, 2, 3, 29, Dec. 27, 1917; Jan. 8, 11, 13, 20, Feb. 14, 25, Mar. 15, various dates in June and July, Dec. 1, 1918; Mar. 9, 14, 1919; June 28, 1920.
———. To Bennett Cerf, Feb. 3, May 14, 1947; to Marchette Chute, Feb. 6, 1956; to Collector of Internal Revenue, Feb. 16, 1949; to Mrs. A. W. Constant, Mar. 21, 1957; to Marianne Conway, Mar. 29, 1946; to Dr. Fayette Copeland, Dec. 30, 1954; to Mrs. Fayette (Edith) Copeland, Jan. 4, 1949, Apr. 26, Dec. 17, 1956; to Earnest Cox, July 15, 1948; to Dr. George L. Cross, June 12, 1952; to John D. DeLana, May 23, 1938, June 17, 1948; to Mrs. I. M. Draper, June 11, 1945; to Fr. Augustine Edele, Feb. 17, 1947; to Editor, *Adventure*, Feb. 2, 1932; to Editor, *Boys' World*, Feb. 12, 1938; to Paul Eldridge, June 12, Aug. 20, 1946, June 16, Aug. 7, 1948; to Walter Ferguson, undated 1915, Nov. 25, 1929; to John Fischer, May 6, 1957; to Paul Flowers, May 5, 1947; to Mr. and Mrs. John Franks, Jan. 5, 1956; to Miss Dorothy Gardiner, Dec. 5, 1939; to J. H. G. Gibbs, July 31, 1942, Dec. 4, 1945, Feb. 19, Oct. 10, 1947, Apr. 2, 12, 1948; Oct. 18, 1949; to Thomas Gilcrease, Jan. 31, 1953; to Townsend Godsey, Sept. 14, 1954; to Mr. or Mrs. Harlan Greenfield, June 16, 20, Sept. 26, 1947, Apr. 15, 1948.
———. To Lowrey Harrell, Jan. 19, 1953; to M. J. Harrison, Sept. 9, 1954, Sept. 30, 1957; to E. A. Hawks, Dec. 20, 1939; to Thayer Hobson, May 29, 1947; to Mrs. Harriet Horst, Nov. 3, 1952; to Dr. R. T. House, Sept. 30, 1946; to Mrs. Lucille Houston, Oct. 1, 1954; to Cecil Hubbert, Sept. 14, 1956; to Ralph Hudson, June 11, 1947; to Ira Rich Kent, Sept. 10, 1929, Nov. 25, 1934, Mar. 10, 1938, Apr. 20, 1939, Jan. 20, Mar. 26, 1940, Mar. 5, 1942; to Capt. Seth King, Dec. 1, 1944, Aug. 1, 1945; to Josh Lee, Dec. 26, 1936; to Savoie Lottinville, Dec. 13, 1953; to E. S. Luce, Jan. 3, 1952; to Macmillan Co., Aug. 5, Nov. 24, 1939; to Frank A. Manny, Apr. 6, 1945; to Joe A. Martinez, Jan. 5, 1957; to Earl C. May, Oct. 4, 1941; to J. D. McCoid, June 6, 1947; to Mrs. J. D. (Harvie)

McCoid, Sept. 30, 1946, June 20, 1947, Oct. 5, 30, 1956; to Rudolph Mollard, Feb. 25, 1955; to or from H. L. Mencken, Apr. 18, 24, May 6, Aug. 14, Oct. 17, Nov. 25, 1925; to John Mosely, Jan. 17, 1927; to Lieut. Col. Hal Muldrow, Jr., Apr. 10, 1944; to National Inventors Council, various dates in 1942; to Mr. and Mrs. Kenneth Ogilvie, Dec. 19, 1957; to Sidney Ohmart, Mar. 18, 1953.

———. To Norberto C. Padillo, June 4, 1949; to Col. Wm. Paxton, Dec. 9, 1949; to Mrs. C. R. Phelan, May 2, 1934; to Waite Phillips, June 29, 1929; to Mrs. A. C. Plage, Aug. 20, Oct. 8, 1938; to Gene Price, Apr. 22, 1949; to T. M. Purdy, Mar. 14, 1947; to Frank Reid, June 2, 1932, Apr. 24, May 1, 12, 1953; to Paul Reynolds, May 18, 1943, Jan. 30, Sept. 4, Dec. 7, 1945, Nov. 10, 1948, Jan. 18, May 5, 1949, Dec. 6, 1952, Oct. 14, 1957; to Don Rickey, Sept. 25, 27, 1955, Nov. 30, 1956, Sept. 25, 1957; to John W. Rogers, Dec. 22, 1944; to Don Russell, Jan. 10, Dec. 4, 1956; to Ernest Thompson Seton, various dates in 1902-05; to Courtney Smith, Oct. 12, 1930; to G. W. Spradling, Oct. 21, 1947; to Randy Steffen, Oct. 30, 1956.

———. To Janet Thompson, Oct. 6, 1936; to Thomas Thompson, Mar. 12, 1956; to J. R. R. Tolkien, Dec. 3, 1953; to Treasurer, Univ. of Oklahoma, July 25, 1937; to Mrs. Robert L. Turner, Sept. 13, 1946, Feb. 16, July 16, 1948; to Earl Vandale, Oct. 12, 1949; to Ralph Velick, Oct. 2, 1957; to Gayle Waldrop, Nov. 30, 1957; to Mrs. J. H. Wallace, July 23, 1956; to F. G. Walling, Apr. 24, 1939; to Warden, Rhodes House, Merton College, Oxford Univ., Apr. 4, 1949, Nov. 2, 1953; to Dale Warren, May 12, 1929; to and from Robert Penn Warren, various dates in 1937-39; to Julie Watson, Oct. 16, 1957; to Lewis Watson, Nov. 28, 1945; to A. B. Welch, Sept. 19, 1928; to Bristol Williams, Apr. 25, 1945; to H. P. Willis, Nov. 3, 1953; to Mrs. Sara Wood, July 8, 1902, Aug. 21, 1903, Aug. 23, 1908, Aug. 14, 1910, Jan. 31, Feb. 11, 1911; to Mr. and Mrs. Jack Zaruba, Dec. 15, 1955; to Karl Zeister, July 15, 1957; to Joe ...., July 23, 1927; to and from various other persons in the periods 1928-30, 1941-56.

Letters to Campbell:

Cobb, Irvin S. Oct. 31, 1939.

Cousins, Norman. Feb. 15, 1944.

Crow, Maxine Helen. Series written in the autumn of 1941.

Dixon, A. L. Mar. 16, 1916.

Folsom, Franklin. Mar. 2, 1938.

Gossard, H. G. Undated.

Guggenheim Foundation. Mar. 7, 1930.

Harris, Foster. To L. N. Morgan. Nov. 24, 1938.

Kent, Ira Rich. Nov. 17, 1934; Mar. 19, 1942.

Kunitz, Stanley J., and Howard Haycraft. Apr. 2, 1940.

Kerr, U. S. Sen. Robert S. To Ray Tassin. June 18, 1962. In the possession of the author.

Lawrence, A. June 23, 1927.

Lottinville, Savoie. To Ray Tassin. June 7, 1963. In the possession of the author.

Marquis, A. N., Company. Dec. 2, 1927.

Martin, Gen. To Col. L. S. Ryan. Nov. 24, 1918.

Martinez, Joe A. Various dates from 1937 to 1957.

McCoid, J. D. To Ray Tassin. Apr. 18, 1962. Author's possession.

McCoid, Harvie. To Ray Tassin. Apr. 18, 1962. Author's possession.

Muldrow, Edna. To Ray Tassin. Nov. 12, 1960. Author's possession.

Nordstrom, Ursula. Oct. 23, 1943.

Ray, Miss Grace E. Mar. 23, 1937.

Reynolds, Paul. Oct. 8, 1957.

Rocker, R. Nov. 9, 1942.

Ryan, Col. L. S. To Gen. Martin. Nov. 6, 1918.

Scaife, Roger L. Mar. 22, 1935.

Spradling, G. W. Oct. 15, 1947.

University of Oklahoma (unsigned). Apr. 1, 1930.

White, William Allen. May 21, 1932, and one undated.

Williams, Bristol. Apr. 24, 1945.

Young, Rev. Joseph S. To Ray Tassin. June 22, 1961. Author's possession.

MISCELLANEOUS
(in Campbell Collection)

Linville, R. N. Typewritten copy of a memorial address delivered Dec. 4, 1929, at Southwestern State College, Weatherford, Oklahoma, in honor of James Robert Campbell.

Vestal, Stanley. "Indian Summer." Typewritten manuscript.

Vestal, Stanley. Typewritten manuscripts and notes on various books and autobiographical data, published and unpublished.

——. Application for a Guggenheim Fellowship, typewritten, undated.

——. Biographical sketch of J. R. Campbell.

Graduation program (1908) in the diary of W. S. Campbell.

Index